MW01236087

What the Bible Says About Women in Church Leadership

Fifth edition

By Michael D. Morrison, Sheila Graham,
and Grace Communion International

Copyright © 2019 Grace Communion International
All rights reserved.
Minor edits September 2020

ISBN-13: 9781699236222

In part 1, all Scripture quotations, unless otherwise indicated, are
taken from the Holy Bible, New International Version®, NIV®.
Copyright ©1973, 1978, 1984, 2011 by Biblica, Inc.™ Used by
permission of Zondervan. All rights reserved worldwide.
www.zondervan.com The "NIV" and "New International Version"
are trademarks registered in the United States Patent and Trademark
Office by Biblica, Inc.™

In part 2, unless otherwise indicated, Scripture quotations are from
the ESV® Bible (The Holy Bible, English Standard Version®),
copyright © 2001 by Crossway, a publishing ministry of Good News
Publishers. Used by permission. All rights reserved.

CONTENTS

Part 2: Our Exegetical Study

MIRIAM

"Great queen of Egypt, I believe we can all see that the Hebrew child will not accept nourishment from those not related to him. Why not bring a woman of his own race to feed him?"

In her excitement over finding the beautiful child in the basket among the reeds of the Nile River, the princess had not noticed a young onlooker.

"Please forgive me for my boldness, but I know of a Hebrew woman who has just lost a baby. Your newfound child might allow her to feed him. If her majesty pleases, I would be happy to bring the Hebrew woman to you."

"You speak well for a child of your age," said the princess. "What is your name?"

"Miriam," she said.

"Well, Miriam, bring the woman of whom you speak — and quickly," demanded the princess, now ready to accept whatever help she could get to quiet the hungry baby Moses.

Miriam's forthright courage, her faith and her ability to think and take decisive action, even as a youth, help us to understand why God chose her, along with her brothers, Moses and Aaron, to lead Israel out of Egypt: "I brought you up out of Egypt and redeemed you from the land of slavery. I sent Moses to lead you, also Aaron and Miriam" (Micah 6:4).

The Bible doesn't tell us when God began to use Miriam as a prophetess. The first biblical description of her in this role occurs after God miraculously stopped the pursuing Egyptian army at the Red Sea.

> Miriam the prophetess, Aaron's sister, took a tambourine in her hand, and all the women followed her, with tambourines and dancing. Miriam sang to them:
>
> Sing to the Lord,
> for he is highly exalted.
> The horse and its rider
> he has hurled into the sea. (Exodus 15:20-21)

According to Josephus, Miriam was married to Hur of the tribe of Judah — the same Hur who, along with Aaron, supported Moses' arms in Israel's battle with the Amalekites (Exodus 17:11-13). As part of this powerful family, Miriam was there when Moses, Aaron, Hur and various other family members discussed Israel's problems, and developed strategies to solve them. As a prophetess and the oldest member of the family, her opinion was valued. She was accustomed to being approached for her advice and was revered as the first lady of Israel.

Compared to some other ancient cultures, women in early Israelite history enjoyed many freedoms. A woman, whether married or single, could appear without a veil. She could travel about alone, and meet and talk with men publicly.

Yet, in spite of her prominence, Miriam, and her brother Aaron, both began to fear their influence was waning. Out of jealousy, they began to gossip about Moses' marriage to an Ethiopian woman: "Has the Lord spoken only through Moses?... Hasn't he also spoken through us?" (Numbers 12:2).

The Bible records that God heard what Miriam and Aaron said about Moses, and God was not pleased. God knew that it was not so much Moses' marriage, as Miriam and Aaron's envy of their younger brother's authority over them, that underlay their criticism.

Miriam and Aaron did not fear Moses' reprisal. After all, their brother usually did not defend himself against reproaches. Hadn't he always listened patiently to the endless complaints of Israel? Miriam and Aaron knew that Moses was long-suffering and humble — perhaps in their judgment, a little too much so.

God, however, did not view what had happened in the same way as Miriam and Aaron. He saw clearly their presumptuous attack, at Miriam's instigation, against his chosen leader. If they wanted God's attention, they now fully had it. God commanded: "Come out to the Tent of Meeting, all three of you" (verse 4). Reminding Miriam of his special relationship with Moses, God said:

> When a prophet of the Lord is among you, I reveal myself to him in visions, I speak to him in dreams. But this is not true of my servant Moses.... With him I speak face to face, clearly and not in riddles; he sees the form of the Lord. Why then were you not afraid to speak against my servant Moses?" (verses 6-8)

When the cloud lifted from above the tabernacle, signifying that God had departed, Aaron sheepishly looked over at Miriam. Recoiling in horror at the sight of his sister's pasty-white scaly skin, he must have quickly looked at his own hands and arms as well. No, only Miriam was leprous.

Aaron's tone and approach toward Moses were now remarkably changed: "Please my lord, do not hold against us the sin we have so foolishly committed. Do not let her be like a stillborn infant coming from its mother's womb with its flesh half eaten away" (verses 11-12).

Moses didn't have to be persuaded further. He fervently cried out to God: "O God, please heal her!" (verse 13). God agreed to do so, but not immediately. Miriam was shut out of the camp for seven days before God removed her humiliating punishment.

We read little more about Miriam in the annals of the Bible. According to Josephus, however, Miriam and Hur were the grandparents of Bezalel, whom God commissioned as the chief craftsman and builder of the tabernacle and its furniture in the wilderness (Exodus 31:2-11; 35:30; 38:22). Hur was also father of three sons who founded the towns of Kiriath Jearim, Bethlehem and Beth Gader (1 Chronicles 2:20, 50-51).

Miriam went on to travel with Moses and Aaron and the Israelites for almost 40 years in the desert. She died shortly before Aaron, near the end of Israel's wanderings, at Kadesh (Numbers 20:1). Like her brothers, Miriam did not enter the Promised Land, and was buried in the wilderness. Thus ended the life of this multitalented woman of courage, faith and firm resolve, who, alongside Moses and Aaron, rejoiced in the triumphs and suffered the trials and dangers of God's calling in the wilderness of Sinai.

As with the many other heroes of the Bible, Miriam's strengths and weaknesses were recorded for our education, inspiration and encouragement.

DEBORAH: A LEADER IN ISRAEL

After Joshua died, before Israel had a king, in the time of the judges, the Israelites repeatedly sinned against God. On one occasion, God gave them "into the hands of Jabin, a king of Canaan, who reigned in Hazor" (Judges 4:2). Joshua had defeated an earlier King Jabin, and had burned the city of Hazor to the ground. But the Israelites had failed to expel all the Canaanites from the land, to their later cost. The city of Hazor had been rebuilt by the time of this later Jabin, who oppressed the Israelites for 20 years.

God responded to Israel's cry for help and used Deborah, a faithful prophetess who was judging Israel at that time, and Barak, her military commander, to deliver the nation. This detailed story is told twice: once in skillfully narrated prose (verses 4-24) and once in a magnificent poem known as The Song of Deborah (Judges 5:1-31). This song resembles another victory hymn, The Song of Moses and Miriam, or The Song of the Sea (Exodus 15:1-18).

Deborah told Barak to raise an army and go to Mt. Tabor, for God would give Israel a great victory over the Canaanites. Barak agreed to do so only if Deborah would accompany him. Deborah complied, but told Barak that because of his lack of faith in God's promise of victory, the honor of killing Sisera, who commanded Jabin's army, would fall not to Barak but to a woman (Judges 4:6-9).

Deborah and Barak summoned the Israelites from Kedesh. Not all the tribes responded (Judges 5:13-18). However, Barak was able to assemble some 10,000 soldiers, chiefly from the tribes of Naphtali and Zebulun. Sisera countered by gathering his troops in the Kishon basin, relying on his 900 iron chariots to overwhelm Barak's force.

But God decided the battle in Israel's favor. He demonstrated his superiority over the Canaanite storm god, Baal, by causing an unexpected thunderstorm to transform the Kishon basin into mud, thus immobilizing the Canaanite chariots. Deborah roused Barak to attack, and he routed Sisera's army. The Israelites would later sing, "The river Kishon swept them away, the age-old river, the river Kishon" (verse 21).

Sisera had managed to escape the initial onslaught of Barak's army and fled to the tent of Heber the Kenite, a friend of Jabin. Heber's wife, Jael, welcomed Sisera and gave him some milk to drink. Sisera, believing he was safe, fell sound asleep. Jael then picked up a tent peg in her left hand and a hammer in her right hand, and drove the peg through Sisera's temple. This act fulfilled Deborah's prophecy and immortalized Jael in Hebrew poetry (verses 24-27).

Some have tried to understand God's selection of Deborah by reasoning that he could not find any man suitable for the job, so he was forced to use Deborah. While this reasoning may keep male egos intact, it ignores the testimony of Scripture. God is able to use whoever he wants. He does not appoint leaders by using human criteria.

When Samuel considered Eliab a suitable successor to King Saul, God corrected Samuel's limited perception: "Do not consider his appearance or his height, for I have rejected him. The Lord does not look at the things man looks at. Man looks at the outward appearance, but the Lord looks at the heart" (1 Samuel 16:7).

Some find it surprising that God used a woman as a judge of Israel. But we should not allow preconceived ideas or prejudices to get in the way of respecting those whom God appoints to lead us. Barak, a man of faith, loyally followed the individual God chose.

The account in Judges reveals that Deborah's personality drew people together. She was also a prophetess and led the people to obey God. God used Deborah to influence Israel to remain faithful long after the battle was over. Leaders inspired by God are concerned with the spiritual well-being of those they are called to serve. Deborah certainly was.

RUTH: A STORY OF ROMANCE AND REDEMPTION

What's in a name?

Ruth is the leading character in this book, which is named after her. The name Ruth means "mercy." The story shows that God's grace and mercy extend beyond Israel to include all peoples.

Outline

Ruth can be read as a drama in four acts, with a prologue and epilogue attached. The prologue tells us how Naomi, her husband and two sons went to Moab, where her sons married. Eventually, Naomi's husband and sons died, and she decided to return to Bethlehem in Judea (1:1-7).

In the first act, Naomi tells her Moabite daughters-in-law, Orpah and Ruth, to stay in Moab. Orpah eventually agreed, but Ruth refused to leave Naomi and accompanied her to Bethlehem (1:8-22). The next act sees Ruth gathering barley in the fields of Naomi's relative, Boaz, who showed special concern for Ruth (2:1-23).

The third act takes place at the threshing floor where, at Naomi's

instigation, Ruth hides until Boaz falls asleep and then quietly lies down by his feet. When Boaz awakes, Ruth expresses her desire to marry him according to the custom of the kinsman-redeemer. But Boaz tells her that another man has a prior claim (3:1-18). Finally, at the city gate, the other relative renounces his claim, and Boaz marries Ruth (4:1-12). The epilogue relates Naomi's joy at this turn of events and then lists some of Ruth's descendants, including David (4:13-18).

How to read this book

In stark contrast to Judges, the book of Ruth shows us a community that did what was right in God's eyes. It is

> the story of God's grace in the midst of difficult circumstances. Ruth's story occurred during the time of the judges — a period of disobedience, idolatry, and violence. Even in times of crisis and deepest despair, there are those who follow God and through whom God works. No matter how discouraging or antagonistic the world may seem, there are always people who follow God. He will use anyone who is open to him to achieve his purposes. (*Life Application Bible*, NIV, Introduction to Ruth)

Learning about God

Our fascination with the characters of Ruth, Naomi and Boaz notwithstanding, "God is the primary actor in the drama" (Edward F. Campbell, Jr., *Ruth*, The Anchor Bible, Vol. 7, p. 29). Even though human beings are free moral agents, God's unseen hand directs events to accomplish his purpose, transforming Naomi's sorrow into exultant joy and rewarding Ruth's commitment to Israel's God and community with an enduring place of honor in its heritage.

In Boaz, we see a foreshadowing of the redemptive work of Jesus Christ. "Ruth's inability to do anything to alter her estate typifies absolute human helplessness (Rom. 5:6); and Boaz's willingness to pay the complete price (4:9) foreshadows Christ's full payment for our salvation (1 Cor. 6:20; Gal. 3:13; 1 Pet. 1:18, 19)" (*The Spirit-Filled Life Bible*, NKJV, Introduction to Ruth).

Other topics

- Steadfast love: According to rabbinic tradition, the main theme of Ruth is steadfast love (Hebrew: *chesed*, meaning "faithfulness born out of a sense of caring and commitment"). All the main characters in the book — Ruth, Naomi and Boaz — acted with *chesed*.

- Salvation: The story of Ruth takes place between the seasons of Passover and Pentecost. (Pentecost came at the end of the grain harvest season.) In the Hebrew Bible, Ruth is one of the Megilloth (Festival Scrolls) and is read during Pentecost. In accepting the God of Israel, Ruth foreshadows the gentiles becoming a part of spiritual Israel, the church. This became possible only after the Pentecost that followed Christ's ascension (Acts 2).

What this book means for you

If the most effective teaching is by example, this book can teach us much about how to live:

> The religious truths found in this book relate more to practical life than to abstract theology. Loyalty, love, kindness, the value of persons, and the need to understand one another stand out. In the midst of the chaos then in the land, meaning could be found by returning to the first principles of simple truth. The book of Ruth tells us that no matter how bad things may be, goodness can exist, if we are willing to make the effort. (Walter A. Elwell, ed., *Baker's Bible Handbook,* p. 166)

Naomi and Ruth: Ruth 1

"In the days when the judges ruled, there was a famine in the land, and a man from Bethlehem in Judah, together with his wife and two sons, went to live for a while in the country of Moab. The man's name was Elimelech, his wife's name Naomi, and the names of his two sons were Mahlon and Kilion" (verses 1-2).

Eventually, Elimelech died and Naomi was left with her two sons, who took Moabite wives, one named Orpah and the other Ruth. After about 10 years, Mahlon and Kilion also died, and Naomi had lost both her husband and her sons. When Naomi heard that the famine in Judah had ended, she had no reason to stay in Moab and decided to return home (verses 5-6). She told her daughters-in-law: "Go back, each of you, to your mother's home. May the Lord show kindness to you, as you have shown to your dead and to me. May the Lord grant that each of you will find rest in the home of another husband" (verses 8-9).

Naomi then kissed her daughters-in-law good-bye, but they were reluctant to leave. Naomi wanted Orpah and Ruth to start a new life — to marry again — but she told them she could not provide them husbands, and so again she urged them to return home (verses 11-13). Naomi's comment here refers to the biblical custom of Levirate marriage, by which a dead man's unmarried brother was obligated to care for his widow (Deuteronomy 25:5-10). Naomi could provide no new brothers-in-law for the women to marry.

Orpah was convinced by Naomi's plea, and tearfully kissed her mother-in-law good-bye. But Ruth pleaded with Naomi, "Don't urge me to leave you or turn back from you" (Ruth 1:16). Unlike Orpah, she did not return to her own people and gods, but chose Naomi's people and, significantly, Naomi's God. In one of the most famous passages of the Bible, Ruth pledged to Naomi: "Where you go I will go, and where you stay I will stay. Your people will be my people and your God my God. Where you die I will die, and there I will be buried. May the Lord deal with me, be it ever so severely, if anything but death separates you and me" (verses 16-17).

As God's chosen nation, Israel was to be God's servant as a light to the nations in witness to him. Sadly, the nation often fell short, but God's purpose for his people did not. In the story of Ruth — which was set in the time of the judges, a period of much unfaithfulness to God — we see that Ruth became a member of the community of God largely because of the examples of faithful people in that community.

This is a great lesson for us today. The Israelites were not the only people God loved. God chose the Israelites to be the people through whom the rest of the world would ultimately come to know him. The death and resurrection of Jesus Christ made this possible: "He redeemed us in order that the blessing given to Abraham might come to the Gentiles through Christ Jesus" (Galatians 3:14). Through Christ, the entire world can come to know God.

The book of Ruth, which is the festival scroll read at Pentecost, foreshadows what the Day of Pentecost began to make possible — gentiles becoming part of spiritual Israel, the church. On the Pentecost after Christ's resurrection, the Holy Spirit came upon Jesus' followers, thus beginning the fulfillment of Joel's prophecy: "I will pour out my Spirit on all people" (Joel 2:28; Acts 2:17). Later, during his meeting with the Roman centurion Cornelius, the apostle Peter acknowledged: "I now realize how true it is that God does not show favoritism but accepts people from every nation who fear him and do what is right" (Acts 10:34-35).

None of us should feel disqualified to serve God because of our sex, race, color or national or ethnic origin. The gentile Ruth, for example, became a great-grandmother of King David, through whom Jesus was descended. God can use anyone to do his work and to prepare for his kingdom. The Day of Pentecost also pictures the church, foreshadowed in the book of Ruth by the community of Bethlehem, being a light to the world.

When Naomi eventually returned with Ruth to Bethlehem, she was warmly greeted, but she felt discouraged, saying: "Call me Mara [bitter], because the Almighty has made my life very bitter. I went away full, but the Lord has brought me back empty. Why call me Naomi [pleasant]?" (Ruth 1:20-21).

Naomi was a righteous woman who had suffered the great anguish of losing her husband and two sons. Orpah and Ruth had shared her grief, but Naomi still considered herself to be the most bitterly unfortunate of the three (verse 13). However, she would gradually come to understand that, despite the tragedies she had undergone, God had not abandoned her. Naomi would yet experience great joy in her life and in her God.

The chapter closes, as do the next two chapters, with a succinct summary of the preceding action, which simultaneously sets the stage for what is about to unfold: "So Naomi returned from Moab…arriving in Bethlehem as the barley harvest was beginning" (verse 22).

Levirate marriage

The book of Ruth is permeated with ancient Israelite customs that seem strange to us: the gleaning of grain by the poor (Ruth 2:2), inheritance laws (Ruth 4:9-10), the removal of sandals in business exchanges (Ruth 4:7).

Another custom alluded to in the story is that of levirate marriage (Ruth 1:11-12). If a married man died without any children to carry on his name and inheritance, it was his unmarried brother's responsibility to marry the widow. The purpose: "The first son she bears shall carry on the name of the dead brother so that his name will not be blotted out from Israel" (Deuteronomy 25:6). This is known as a levirate marriage, from the Latin word for brother-in-law, *levir*.

According to *The Anchor Bible Dictionary*, "Levirate marriage existed in Ugarit, in the Middle Assyrian (no. 33) and Hittite law codes (no. 193), and possibly in the Nuzi texts" (vol. 4, p. 567). It was a common middle eastern custom.

The earliest biblical example of a levirate relationship is complex. It concerns Judah's sons: Er, Onan and Shelah (Genesis 38). When Er died, Judah told Onan to have children by his brother Er's widow, Tamar, so that Er's name would carry on. Onan, knowing that any children borne by Tamar would legally be Er's, slept with Tamar but selfishly ensured that she did not have any children. God was displeased and put Onan to death. Judah did not then give Tamar to Shelah as his wife, lest Shelah die also.

When Tamar realized that Judah would not allow Shelah to fulfill the obligations of levirate marriage, she disguised herself as a prostitute and sat where she knew Judah would approach. Judah did not recognize her and purchased her services. In due course, Tamar became pregnant and bore Judah twin sons, Perez and Zerah.

We do not know why Tamar embarked upon this action, but we are told that Judah acknowledged, "She is more righteous than I, since I wouldn't give her to my son Shelah" (verse 26). She had been faithful to her family obligations, whereas Judah had not been. Through her son Perez, Tamar became an ancestor of Jesus Christ (Matthew 1:3, 16).

In the book of Ruth, Naomi told Ruth and Orpah that she had no other sons who could perform the duties of levirate husbands (Ruth 1:11). Boaz was a near relative of Ruth's late husband, Mahlon. Boaz performed the duties of kinsman-redeemer (Hebrew: *go'el*) by marrying Ruth and buying the property that had belonged to Mahlon's father, Elimelech (Ruth 4:9-10).

The son of Boaz and Ruth would thus become the legal inheritor of Elimelech's property, a "son" of Elimelech and Naomi (verse 17). This seems to be an extension of levirate marriage as discussed in Deuteronomy, but many details concerning the transaction remain unknown.

Letting her light shine

Ruth is rightly remembered for her pledge of total devotion and loyalty to Naomi (Ruth 1:16-17). Ruth clung to Naomi even at the cost of renouncing her people and her gods in favor of Naomi's people, the Israelites, and Naomi's God, Yahweh: "Your people will be my people and your God my God" (verse 16). The totality of this commitment is emphasized by its terseness (merely four words in the Hebrew: *'amekh 'ami we'lohaikh 'elohai,* which literally means "your people my people; your God my God"). Yet Ruth extended her commitment still further, beyond death itself: "Where you die I will die, and there I will be buried" (verse 17).

These words may sound anticlimactic compared to accepting Naomi's people and her God. But to understand their significance, we must appreciate the cultural mind-set of the ancient Near Eastern peoples. All the death accounts of the patriarchs mention the burial, often at length (Genesis 23:1-20; 25:8-10; 35:19-20, 28-29; 49:29-33; 50:1-14, 24-26). When a patriarch died, he was "gathered to his people." Jacob and Joseph died in Egypt, but their bones were laid to rest in the Promised Land. The location of burial was important to them.

Ruth concluded her pledge by calling down God's punishment on herself if "even death" (Ruth 1:17, NRSV — a preferred reading to "anything but death") parted her from Naomi. Even after the death of Naomi, Ruth would live, die and be buried in Bethlehem. In so doing, Ruth identified herself with Naomi's community in the most absolute manner possible.

Ruth was willing to forgo everything — her future in Moab, her people, her gods and even her ancestral burial plot — to be joined with Naomi. Yet as we remember Ruth, as we acknowledge and strive to emulate her devotion, her loyalty, her total commitment, let us not forget that other remarkable woman, Naomi. As F.B. Huey, Jr., explains, "Naomi's consistent living must have so impressed her daughter-in-law to cause her to abandon her homeland and her gods" ("Ruth," in *The Expositor's Bible Commentary,* vol. 3, p. 524).

What sort of woman was this Naomi, to inspire such affection in a daughter-in-law? What relationship with God must she have had to cause Ruth to forsake the gods of Moab and worship Naomi's God alone?

The biblical account is sparse, but it witnesses to the powerful effect Naomi had on those around her. Even during her more sorrowful moments, she put the welfare of others first. Naomi's example brought Ruth into the Israelite community of faith, foreshadowing the day when gentiles would be grafted into spiritual Israel, the church.

Naomi is also an example for us all. Jesus Christ, the "light of the world" (John 9:5), told his followers: "You are the light of the world" (Matthew 5:14). William Barclay comments, "It may well be said that this is the greatest compliment that was ever paid to the individual Christian, for in it Jesus commands the Christian to be what he himself claimed to be" (*The Gospel of Matthew,* rev. ed., The Daily Study Bible Series, vol. 1, p. 122). A Christian is not merely a follower of Christ, but a Christlike person.

The Christian is further commanded: "Let your light so shine before men, that they may see your good works and glorify your Father in heaven" (verse 16, NKJV). Naomi's light shone, and Ruth glorified God; we should let our lights shine so that others may glorify God.

Ruth meets Boaz: Ruth 2

In Israel, the barley harvest began in the spring. The community in Bethlehem observed God's law concerning harvesting: "When you reap the harvest of your land, do not reap to the very edges of your field or gather the gleanings of your harvest…. Leave them for the poor and the alien" (Leviticus 19:9-10).

Ruth was both poor and an alien. She had few prospects in Judah, as

Naomi had warned her. However, she was able to provide for Naomi and herself by working hard gleaning the grain left by the harvesters (Ruth 2:2).

There is an almost idyllic quality to the Bethlehem community described in Ruth, which — especially when one considers it existed during the turbulent period of the judges — testifies powerfully to the difference a few people living God's way can make. Bethlehem would later become famous, first as the "town of David" and later as the birthplace of the Messiah (Luke 2:4-7).

"As it turned out, [Ruth] found herself working in a field belonging to Boaz, who was from the clan of Elimelech" (Ruth 2:3). Boaz was a "man of standing [Hebrew: *'ish gibbor chail*, implying Boaz was physically impressive and had noble character]" (verse 1).

Boaz asked his foreman who the stranger gleaning in the field was. The foreman replied that she was the young woman who had accompanied Naomi back from Moab. Boaz then told Ruth to continue gleaning in his field, and helped her far beyond the demands of the law. He even ordered his harvesters to make Ruth especially welcome, enabling her to gather extra barley.

Ruth then asked Boaz, "Why have I found such favor in your eyes that you notice me — a foreigner?" (verse 10). Ruth's expression about finding favor in Boaz's eyes, used by her on three occasions (verses 2, 10, 13), was a culturally appropriate way of showing respect. Ruth thus displayed the type of attitude the apostle Paul later taught Christians to have, when he said, "In humility consider others better than yourselves" (Philippians 2:3).

Boaz, in turn, was impressed by Ruth's reputation: "I've been told all about what you have done for your mother-in-law since the death of your husband — how you left your father and mother and your homeland and came to live with a people you did not know before. May the Lord repay you for what you have done" (Ruth 2:11). A good reputation, founded on God-centered character, is of great value (Proverbs 22:1; Ecclesiastes 7:1).

At the end of the day, Ruth returned home to Naomi with an exceptionally generous amount of grain. Naomi immediately realized someone had taken special care of Ruth, and upon hearing that it was Boaz, she exclaimed, "The Lord bless him!" and "He [the reader is made to ask to whom Naomi is referring — Boaz or Yahweh] has not stopped showing his kindness to the living and the dead" (Ruth 2:20). Naomi's bitterness toward God had begun to lessen. She now gladly encouraged Ruth to continue to glean in Boaz's field.

Naomi's plan for Ruth: Ruth 3

Ruth continued to glean in Boaz's field for about seven weeks, until the end of the barley and wheat harvests, around the time of Pentecost. Naomi had earlier hoped that Ruth would find "rest" (Hebrew: *minuchah*) in the home of another husband in Moab (Ruth 1:9). Now Naomi said to Ruth, "Should I not try to find a home [Hebrew: *manoach,* which, like the related word *minuchah,* means "a condition of rest and security attained by marriage"] for you, where you will be well provided for?" (Ruth 3:1). Naomi's hopes for Ruth now centered upon Boaz, who might act as a "kinsman-redeemer" (verses 1-9).

A kinsman-redeemer was a relative who could redeem a poor person's inheritance (Leviticus 25:25). In certain circumstances, where there was no heir, a near relative could act as kinsman-redeemer by marrying the relative's widow to redeem the inheritance. A relative was not obligated to act as kinsman-redeemer, however. If no relative chose to help, the widow would probably live in poverty.

Naomi therefore suggested to her daughter-in-law a plan of action: "Wash and perfume yourself, and put on your best clothes. Then go down to the threshing floor, but don't let [Boaz] know you are there until he has finished eating and drinking. When he lies down, note the place where he is lying. Then go and uncover his feet and lie down. He will tell you what to do" (Ruth 3:3-4).

Ruth did as Naomi told her. Something startled Boaz in the middle of the night, and he awoke to discover a woman lying at his feet. Boaz asked who she was. Ruth identified herself and then seized the initiative: "Spread the corner of your garment over me, since you are a kinsman-redeemer" (verse 9). Ruth was boldly asking Boaz for a pledge from him to marry her. This same expression is used for God's relationship with Israel: "I spread the corner of my garment over you" (Ezekiel 16:8). Ruth's action was in accord with the law of levirate marriage, which required the initiative of the widow in seeking the marriage (Deuteronomy 25:5, 7-10).

Boaz felt honored by Ruth's request because she was "a woman of noble character [Hebrew: *'esheth chail,* the term applied to the 'Proverbs 31 woman']" (Ruth 3:11). Boaz informed her, however, that Naomi had a closer relative. This man had the first option to marry Ruth and redeem Naomi's inheritance. Boaz assured Ruth that if this other relative was not prepared to act as kinsman-redeemer, then he certainly would be. Ruth would now have to wait until the matter was settled with the other relative.

Ruth, Boaz and Christ

To appreciate how Boaz foreshadowed Christ, we must first understand the significance of an ancient Israelite law concerning the kinsman-redeemer (Hebrew: *go'el*). This law helped ensure that inherited land remained within the family. It stated, "If one of your countrymen becomes poor and sells some of his property, his nearest relative is to come and redeem [Hebrew: *ga'al,* the same root as *go'el*] what his countryman has sold" (Leviticus 25:25).

Both words, *go'el* and *ga'al,* occur frequently in chapters 2 and 3 of Ruth. Since Boaz was a kinsman (*go'el*) of Naomi, he was eventually able to redeem (*ga'al*) her land through marriage to Naomi's daughter-in-law Ruth. (Presumably, Naomi and her husband had previously sold the land before they moved to Moab.)

The concern Boaz displayed as kinsman-redeemer to the widow reflects an aspect of God's own character. "Yahweh is the go'el of the fatherless and widow and pleads their cause" (*Theological Dictionary of the Old Testament,* vol. 2, p. 353; see also Proverbs 23:10-11 and Jeremiah 50:34).

In the New Testament, we see the ultimate kinsman-redeemer in Jesus Christ, who redeemed us from sin by dying for us (1 Peter 1:18-19). In many respects, Boaz typifies Christ. Donald A. Leggett writes, "In the actions of Boaz as goel we see foreshadowed the saving work of Jesus Christ, his later descendant."

Dr. Leggett goes on to explain: "As Boaz had the right of redemption and yet clearly was under no obligation to intervene on Ruth's behalf, so it is with Christ. As Boaz, seeing the plight of the poor widows, came to their rescue because his life was governed by Yahweh and his laws, so also of the Messiah it is prophesied that his life would be governed by the law of God and that he would deal justly and equitably with the poor and with those who were oppressed (Ps. 72:2, 4, 12, 13; Isa. 11:4)" (*The Levirate and Goel Institutions in the Old Testament With Special Attention to the Book of Ruth,* Mack Publishing, 1974, p. 298).

Boaz marries Ruth: Ruth 4

Boaz went to the city gate, the traditional center of business and civic activity. The husband of the idealized "Proverbs 31 woman" is said to be "respected at the city gate, where he takes his seat among the elders of the land" (Proverbs 31:23). Boaz knew he was likely to find the other relative here, and it was also a suitable place to find citizens to witness the business transaction.

Boaz presented the case to the relative. He explained that the relative had the first right to redeem Elimelech's land. The relative agreed to do so, but when Boaz told him that buying the land obligated him to marry Ruth, he promptly backed down — as Boaz hoped he would. Perhaps the relative feared that if he would have a son by Ruth, his investment in the new property would be transferred from his family to the family of Elimelech. Whatever the reason for the man's refusal, the right to marry Ruth now passed to Boaz. This transaction was witnessed by all the people at the gate.

In due course, Boaz married Ruth and she bore him a son, Obed. Obed later became the father of Jesse and the grandfather of David (Ruth 4:17). Through David, Ruth became an ancestor of Jesus Christ (Matthew 1:5, 16).

This was also a reversal of fortune for Naomi. Although the sorrow of her previous loss undoubtedly never left her, Naomi could now rejoice in Ruth's happy family life and share in the joy of raising a new son, Obed (Ruth 4:14-17).

The book of Ruth is unquestionably a delightful story. Edward F. Campbell, Jr., writes,

> The speeches fit the characters who speak them.... Boaz and Naomi talk like older people. Their speeches contain archaic morphology [word forms] and syntax [word order].... Ruth is pleased by every good thing done for her; Naomi moves as though she were gradually realizing that things are not as bitter as she had thought. As for Boaz, he moves through the story like the patriarch he is, warmly greeting his workers in the field, ceremoniously blessing Ruth in the name of Yahweh, recovering his aplomb quickly at the threshing floor so as again to bless Ruth, conducting the hearing at the gate methodically, but with alacrity. (*Ruth,* The Anchor Bible, vol. 7, p. 17)

This story, short and delightful as it is, contains important spiritual lessons. Like Naomi, we should not turn our backs on God when tragedy strikes our lives. We may feel anger at God and express our emotions in honest prayer to him, and still remain righteous — looking beyond the short term toward his eternal plan. God will reward the righteous in due time.

The events recorded in Ruth were part of God's preparations for the births of David and of Jesus, the promised Messiah. Just as Ruth was unaware of this larger purpose in her life, we will not know the full purpose and importance of our lives until we are able to look back from the perspective of eternity. We must make our choices with God's eternal values in mind.... Because of Ruth's faithful obedience, her life and legacy were significant even though she couldn't see all the results. Live in faithfulness to God, knowing that the significance of your life will extend beyond your lifetime. (*Life Application Bible,* NIV, commentary on Ruth 4:16-17)

Hannah's Gift

Hannah, the God-fearing mother of Samuel the prophet, displayed an extraordinary faith and courage during a time of spiritual laxity in Israel. Hannah, one of two wives of Elkanah, was unable to have children. Barrenness in a Hebrew woman disgraced both her family and nation. Elkanah's other wife, Peninnah, had several children, and often scornfully reminded Hannah of her failure to fulfill her duty as a wife and an Israelite.

As the years passed, Hannah's apparently hopeless situation and Peninnah's constant taunting caused Hannah increasing unhappiness and distress. During one of the family's yearly visits to Shiloh (as was the custom), Hannah went to the temple and begged God to give her a child. In fervent prayer, she faithfully pledged her child to God in lifelong service. Nine months later, Samuel was born. Despite having waited so long for this child, Hannah willingly gave her son, when he was three years old, to the service of God at the tabernacle. She provided him with clothing and visited him throughout his childhood.

What importance does the story of Hannah have for us today? We often find it difficult to see beyond our particular problems. Our difficulties can seem insurmountable, and our situation grossly unfair. Doesn't that describe Hannah's situation? Yet Hannah did not give up hope. In faith, she depended on God to change her circumstances. In faith, according to her promise, she gave up her only child to God, and God rewarded her with five more children. Because of Hannah's trust in and commitment to God, she was given a son, who eventually became the last and perhaps the greatest of the judges. When times are difficult and remaining faithful seems too hard, take a moment to think of the story of Hannah, a woman of great faith.

Julie Wilson

BATHSHEBA: MOTHER AND QUEEN

The following story is based on events
in 2 Samuel 11–17 and 1 Kings 1–2.

Dozing beneath the tapestries hung to shade the roof, the teenage girl smiled and opened her eyes at the sound of familiar voices. She peered through the wall hangings to see her grandfather Ahithophel greet King David in the courtyard below. The powerful king of Israel almost ran in his eagerness to greet her grandfather, a close friend and counselor to the king.

Although she had seen David many times, and heard the adventurous stories that her father, Eliam, one of David's 30 mighty warriors, told about the king, it was always a thrill to see the man God had chosen to rule Israel. She noticed how strong and handsome King David was, so like her own father standing tall and militarily straight by the king's side. Then she noticed another warrior stride up — Uriah the Hittite.

Bathsheba felt her face redden as she quickly drew back within the woven coverings. She thought of the arrangements her father was making for her to marry Uriah, and she certainly didn't want Uriah to see her staring down at him.

No doubt the king and his men had come to discuss some military matter with her grandfather, perhaps to use his keen insight to plan a battle against the Ammonites. She hurried on down the steps to see if her grandmother might need help in preparing food for their royal visitor and his men. But not today. After about an hour with David, Ahithophel returned to his house alone. The king, along with Ahithophel's son (Eliam), Uriah and the other soldiers, had to leave Giloh to return to Jerusalem.

Bathsheba handed her grandfather a cool cup of water as he relaxed before his meal. "My beautiful Bathsheba, and as usual, as kind and thoughtful as you are beautiful," Ahithophel said as he accepted the cup with a smile. "Before long, my little girl, you will be a happily married woman. What do you think about that? Will you still come to see your grandfather once you're married to the mighty Uriah?"

"Of course, grandfather. You know I will never love anyone as much as I love you," said Bathsheba, pulling back her long hair as she knelt to kiss him on the top of his head. "A likely story, my girl, with such a man as Uriah as your husband," Ahithophel retorted with a laugh. "Many must be the daughters of Israel who envy you, marrying King David's finest warrior."

Ahithophel's smile faded as he continued: "And, not only is Uriah courageous in battle, he is a disciplined and dedicated man. I have high hopes for him. He will go far in Israel. That is what is most important, child. I would not be pleased to have my granddaughter marrying anyone less."

Bathing for purification

Almost a year later, Bathsheba had time to think of her grandfather's words many times. Adjusting to the life of a soldier's wife wasn't easy. Now she understood her own mother's loneliness and constant worry when her father was gone for months to the battlefield. Daily she prayed to God to bring Uriah home safely.

One spring day, around the community well, she anxiously listened to the talk of the other soldiers' wives. As they discussed the day's rumors from the war, she wished she could feel as calm as they appeared. That evening at her apartment next to the palace, Bathsheba carried water to the roof and prepared to bathe. The time of her purification was over. She undressed and carefully washed herself as instructed by her mother some years before.

High above her, King David paced back and forth on the roof of his palace. Maybe he made a mistake not going with Joab and the army to Rabbah, he thought. As he made yet one more turn walking around the roof, he suddenly spotted Bathsheba. There's a woman down there, he thought, and she's taking a bath! He found when he knelt down he could see her even better through the tapestries.

David was stunned. He had not seen such exquisite beauty. He couldn't take his eyes off her. As soon as Bathsheba had completed her bath and wrapped herself in a robe, David hurried downstairs. Who was this beautiful woman? He must know. "David sent someone to find out about her. The man said, 'Isn't this Bathsheba, the daughter of Eliam and the wife of Uriah the Hittite?' Then David sent messengers to get her" (2 Samuel 11:3-4).

Bathsheba was bewildered. Why was she being hurried by the king's servants through the back alleys from her house to the palace? She hoped this unexpected invitation from the king didn't mean something had happened to Uriah. When the servants reached the king's private rooms, they quickly released Bathsheba, bowing as they left.

"Bathsheba, my dear. Please come in. How gracious of you to accept my invitation on such short notice. Would you like some wine?" "She came to him, and he slept with her" (verse 4). David was the king; Bathsheba was a subject; it could have been difficult, even dangerous, to refuse.

The results of impurity

Several weeks after her sexual relations with King David, feeling queasy and trembling, Bathsheba sat on the edge of the bed she had shared with Uriah and wept. There could be no doubt. She sent her terse message to the king, "I am with child." Under Israel's law, she knew she could receive the death penalty for adultery. She did not know, however, that her message to King David would mean her husband's death, not her own.

Motivated by his guilt and his concern for Bathsheba, after several unsuccessful attempts to have Uriah return to his wife's bed, David tried to cover up the sin by having Uriah killed in battle. Bathsheba's life would never be the same, nor would David's. Though David married Bathsheba and sorrowfully repented of his adultery with her and the murder of Uriah, this couple would see one tragedy after another strike their families.

David and Bathsheba's child would die soon after birth. David's son Amnon, by one of David's other wives, raped his half-sister Tamar. To avenge his sister, another of David's sons, Absalom, killed Amnon.

Perhaps as a result of being embittered by David's treatment of Uriah and Bathsheba, Ahithophel turned on his old friend and helped David's son Absalom as he attempted to forcibly take the throne from his father. It was on Ahithophel's advice that Absalom violated his father's concubines on the roof of the palace in the sight of all Israel (2 Samuel 16:21-22).

Bathsheba saves Solomon

A few years after Absalom's rebellion and death, when it was obvious David was near death himself, David's son Adonijah attempted to have himself crowned king. Seeing the danger, the prophet Nathan, the same man God used to confront David with his sin, knew where to turn —

Bathsheba.

Why did Nathan go to Bathsheba? Because over the years he had gained great respect for this woman. He knew David had confidence in his wife. The prophet had noted the good influence Bathsheba had on her children. Quietly, Bathsheba listened to Nathan's plan. She then went before the ailing king and asked, "Has not the king promised that our son Solomon would be his successor?"

After also hearing from Nathan about Adonijah's premature "coronation" celebration, David realized he must act quickly to save all their lives. At David's command, Solomon was immediately crowned king of all Israel.

Trusting to a fault, Bathsheba was later used by Adonijah to try to get permission from Solomon to take Abishag, who had "waited on" David (1 Kings 1:4), as a wife. This was a presumptuous attempt by Adonijah to strengthen his position as heir to the throne. Solomon used his attempt as reason enough to have him killed.

It is obvious from Solomon's warm greeting of his mother how much he loved and honored her. Looking to her as an important adviser, Solomon had a throne for her placed at his right hand — the first king of Israel to have a queen mother in his administration.

Overcoming the ignoble beginning of their lives together, patiently suffering the consequences of their sin, both Bathsheba and David learned from their mistakes and grew in the knowledge and righteousness of God. Although there is some controversy over whether the writer of Proverbs 31 refers to Solomon, if rabbinical commentators are right, Bathsheba is the imperial mother here advising her kingly son.

PROVERBS 31:
PORTRAIT OF A GODLY WOMAN

For thousands of years, God-fearing women have looked to the noble, or virtuous (KJV), woman of Proverbs 31 as their ideal. Mary, the mother of Jesus Christ, probably had this role model of the virtuous woman in the forefront of her mind from earliest childhood. Most Jewish women did, for this poem was traditionally recited in the Jewish home every week on the eve of the Sabbath.

But what about today's woman? Of what value can this ancient poem be to the diverse, complex life-styles of women today? To the married, to the single, to the young, to the old, to those working outside the home or inside the home, to women with children or without children? It is more relevant than you might at first expect — although it is also too good to be true.

When we examine this ancient biblical ideal of womanhood, we do not find the outmoded stereotyped housewife occupied with dirty dishes and laundry, her daily life dictated by the demands of her husband and her children. Nor do we find a hardened, overly ambitious career woman who leaves her family to fend for itself.

What we find is a strong, dignified, multitalented, caring woman who is an individual in her own right. This woman has money to invest, servants to look after and real estate to manage. She is her husband's partner, and she is completely trusted with the responsibility for their lands, property and goods.

She has the business skills to buy and sell in the market, along with the heartfelt sensitivity and compassion to care for and fulfill the needs of people who are less fortunate. Cheerfully and energetically she tackles the challenges each day brings. Her husband and children love and respect her for her kind, generous and caring nature.

But with all her responsibilities, first and foremost, she looks to God. Her primary concern is God's will in her life. She is a woman after God's own heart. Let's examine the characteristics of this remarkable woman — a role model for Christian women today.

Verse by verse

"A wife of noble character who can find? She is worth far more than rubies." The Hebrew word *chayil,* translated here "noble," means a wife of valor — a strong, capable woman with strong convictions. This description of the ideal wife does not agree with those who associate femininity with weakness and passivity.

"Her husband has full confidence in her and lacks nothing of value." Her husband trusts her management of their resources. Her industriousness adds to the family income.

"She brings him good, not harm, all the days of her life." This woman does not do right only when it is convenient and profitable. Her actions are not based on how she is treated by others or by what others think. Her character is steady. She is reliable and dependable.

"She selects wool and flax and works with eager hands." This woman enjoys working so much that she plans ahead for what she needs in order to accomplish her responsibilities.

"She is like the merchant ships, bringing her food from afar." She does not settle for the mediocre—this trait is portrayed by a woman who goes the extra mile for quality items.

"She gets up while it is still dark; she provides food for her family and portions for her servant girls." Though the woman described here has servants to take care of many of the household duties, she sets the pace. She understands that good managers have a responsibility to take care of those under their authority. That is one of her top priorities.

"She considers a field and buys it; out of her earnings she plants a vineyard." Every woman doesn't have to go into real estate and horticulture — the principle here is that this woman uses her mind. She does not act on a whim, but logically analyzes a situation before making a decision. Her goals are not only short term — she envisions the long-range benefits of her decisions.

"She sets about her work vigorously; her arms are strong for her tasks." We get a picture of a woman who vigorously goes about her duties. She keeps herself healthy and strong by proper health practices — good diet, adequate rest and exercise. Many people depend on her.

"She sees that her trading is profitable, and her lamp does not go out at night." She takes pride in doing a good job and knows that her merchandise is good. Night or day, no one worries that her responsibilities are not taken care of.

"In her hand she holds the distaff and grasps the spindle with her fingers." She sets an example of skill and industriousness. Whether this woman would be a computer programmer, a concert pianist, a mother, or all three, she develops her talents and hones her skills through education and diligent application.

"She opens her arms to the poor and extends her hands to the needy." Although it's good to donate to needy causes, this means far more than writing a check. This woman shows personal concern. She visits the sick, comforts the lonely and depressed, and delivers food to those in need.

"When it snows, she has no fear for her household; for all of them are clothed in scarlet." Providing clothing for the family is one of her responsibilities. She takes this seriously, and plans ahead. She does not practice crisis management.

"She makes coverings for her bed; she is clothed in fine linen and purple." This woman has high standards and dresses properly for the occasion.

"Her husband is respected at the city gate, where he takes his seat among the elders of the land." This man does not have to spend half his time trying to straighten out problems at home, and his success in the social world comes partly from her support, just as her success comes partly from his support. The original woman of Proverbs 31 couldn't phone her husband for his opinion on matters. She made many of the day-to-day decisions about their property and goods. He trusted her to manage the estate efficiently.

"She makes linen garments and sells them, and supplies the merchants with sashes." This woman runs a business from her home. Her efforts and industry add to the family income.

"Strength and honor are her clothing; she shall rejoice in time to come" (NKJV). Not only does this woman benefit each day from her wise and diligent actions, long-term lifetime benefits and rewards lie in store for her.

"She speaks with wisdom, and faithful instruction is on her tongue." This woman is educated and has the facts. She knows what she is talking about. Whether about her job, her personal values or her opinion on world events, she is able to express herself intelligently, tactfully and diplomatically. People come to her for good advice.

"She watches over the affairs of her household and does not eat the bread of idleness." She is an organized, energetic person who carries out her responsibilities.

"Her children arise and call her blessed; her husband also, and he praises her." This woman is not a doormat, slavishly trying to appease and please her family, no matter how unreasonable their demands. She is honored in her home. Here we gain an insight into the character of her husband as well. He teaches their children to respect her and the virtues she personifies.

"Many women do noble things, but you surpass them all." High praise for this extraordinary woman — a role model for women of all time.

"Charm is deceptive and beauty is fleeting; but a woman who fears the Lord is to be praised." Here is the key to this woman's effectiveness. Her priorities are determined by God's will, not her own. She is concerned about what God thinks, rather than with what other people think. Physical beauty and clever conversation are admirable qualities. But if a woman's beauty and charm are the extent of her virtues, what happens when time and the trials of life take their toll? This woman does not depend on beauty and charm for her success. She recognizes her need for God.

"Give her the reward she has earned, and let her works bring her praise at the city gate." This woman is actively doing, not merely talking. She does not boast about her plans for the future or her successes of the past. They are obvious.

Too good to be true

Does this woman sound too good to be true? She is. The woman described here is *an idealized woman,* a composite of many capable women. After all, not all people have the same skills. Some women's strengths are in music or art. Others may be in mathematics, teaching or business. Some are better managers and organizers than others. While some women may excel at coming up with ideas, others may be more skilled at creating or producing what has been invented by someone else. No one excels at everything.

Some women work for several years after high school or college before marrying. Others, for one reason or another, do not marry at all. Does this mean that unmarried women cannot be Proverbs 31 women? No. Although this chapter describes a married woman, marriage and motherhood are not prerequisites for successful Christian life. The essential characteristics of the Proverbs 31 woman can be applied to single women, too.

The model woman described in Proverbs is a portrait of *ideal* womanhood. The focus of this portrait is a woman's relationship with God, not her specific abilities or marital status. The Proverbs 31 woman realizes that regardless of her natural talents or acquired skills, or all her accomplishments, her strength comes from God.

Who is a virtuous woman today? Proverbs 31 tells you that it is the woman who puts God first. The ideal woman of Proverbs 31 should encourage all women everywhere. Cultures change, but this woman's God-inspired character still shines brightly across the centuries.

ESTHER: A QUEEN RISKS HER LIFE

God's unseen hand guides, directs and preserves his people by working out circumstances, often in unexpected ways. God gave Esther, a beautiful Jewish girl, special favor in the eyes of Ahasuerus, king of Persia, and the king chose Esther to become his queen in place of his previous wife, Vashti. You can read the story in the book of Esther.

Esther's cousin and guardian, Mordecai, had a powerful enemy in the court—King Ahasuerus' favorite prince, Haman. Mordecai wouldn't bow to Haman each day at the city gate, and it made the prince furious. When Haman discovered that Mordecai was Jewish, he determined not only to destroy Mordecai but also his entire race along with him.

As soon as Mordecai heard about Haman's plans, he told Esther it was time to plead for the life of her people. She had not yet revealed to the king that she was Jewish. Esther said to her uncle, "I haven't been to the king for 30 days and those who approach the king without being called are executed unless he extends the golden scepter to them" (Esther 4:11.)

Mordecai said to Esther: "Do not think that you will escape in the king's palace any more than all the other Jews.... Who knows whether you have come to the kingdom for such a time as this?" (verses 13-14). Mordecai was beginning to realize that God had been working this out all along.

Esther made a brave decision: "Tell the people to fast three days and three nights and I shall go in to the king. If I live, I live and if I perish, I perish" (verse 16). Esther put on her royal apparel and bravely went to the king's throne room. As she entered the room, a hush fell over the royal court. They knew the king favored this woman above all others, but they also knew the king had not called for her. What mood would the king be in? As Esther began to walk toward him, the king stretched out his scepter. It was a signal that her life was granted her. At that moment Esther doubtlessly said a silent thank-you prayer to God.

To summarize the rest of the story, the king commanded that Haman be hanged for being presumptuous. The king promoted Mordecai, and the Jews (including Queen Esther) were spared. God is always working behind the scenes. There are times when most of us have questioned events in our lives and wondered where God was. The story of Esther tells us he's here for us. God's hand is not only guiding his church, but also working out circumstances in our individual lives. When you get a little discouraged or you can't understand why certain things happen to you, remember Esther.

JESUS AND WOMEN

In first-century Palestine, the way Jesus
treated women was considered revolutionary.

When she became a teenager, her father made the arrangements. This was the custom of the first century. Miriam would be married to a carpenter, Joseph, the son of Heli. From birth, Miriam's role in life was set, for she was born female to a Jewish family. Yet her role in history was to be extraordinary. God chose her to be the mother of Jesus. We know her by the English name Mary.

Woman of courage

When the angel Gabriel came to Mary, she was initially troubled by what the angel's appearance might mean. The angel reassured her, explaining that she was the one chosen to be the mother of Jesus.

"How will this be," Mary asked the angel, "since I am a virgin?"

The angel answered, "The Holy Spirit will come upon you, and the power of the Most High will overshadow you. So the holy one to be born will be called the Son of God. Even Elizabeth your relative is going to have a child in her old age, and she who was said to be barren is in her sixth month. For nothing is impossible with God."

"I am the Lord's servant," Mary answered. "May it be to me as you have said." Then the angel left her. (Luke 1:34-38)

Though she knew she was facing shame and humiliation, Mary, in faith, willingly submitted herself to God's will. She understood that it was possible that Joseph would not marry her. She would be considered damaged goods. Mary acted in great courage and faith.

God protected her by showing Joseph in a dream that he should accept her in marriage in spite of her being pregnant. Nevertheless, the story of her pregnancy was out. Following the instructions given to him in his dream, Joseph married an already pregnant Mary. A legacy of raised-eyebrow, finger-pointing gossip would follow them and Jesus throughout their lives. [For more on this, see "Jesus' Birth: A Story of Shame," at https://archive.gci.org/articles/the-birth-of-jesus-a-story-of-shame/.]

Jesus Christ honored his mother throughout his life and at his crucifixion. Mary was at the foot of the cross. When Jesus saw her there, no doubt in shock at what she was witnessing, he compassionately let her and John know how she would be cared for after his death and after his resurrection:

> When Jesus saw his mother there, and the disciple whom he loved standing nearby, he said to his mother. "Dear woman, here is 'your son,' and to the disciple, 'Here is your mother.' From that time on, this disciple took her into his home. (John 19:26-27)

Jesus' honor and respect was not reserved simply for his mother. It was extended to all women—an attitude largely unexpected and unknown in his culture and time. Jesus, unlike the men of his generation and culture, taught that women were equal to men in the sight of God. Women could receive God's forgiveness and grace. Women, as well as men, could be among Christ's personal followers. Women could be full participants in the kingdom of God. Jesus offered full discipleship to women.

These were revolutionary ideas. Many of his contemporaries, including his disciples, were shocked. Women were overjoyed and grateful, of course, and many dedicated their lives to his service. Let's take a look, from the historical narratives in Scripture, at a few of these women of faith and how Jesus dealt with them.

Mary of Magdala

In the early days of Jesus' ministry, one of the most unusual examples is the devoted following of Mary Magdalene. Among the group of women who traveled with Jesus and his 12 disciples was Mary of Magdala (Luke 8:2). Mary is almost always mentioned first in a list of the female disciples of Jesus Christ. She may have been one of the leaders of that group of women who followed Jesus from the outset of his ministry in Galilee to his death and afterward.

The risen Jesus appeared to her first. It's ironic that in a time when women could not be legal witnesses, Jesus Christ chose women as the first witnesses of his resurrection. As British writer Dorothy L. Sayers said:

> Perhaps it is no wonder that the women were first at the Cradle and last at the Cross. They had never known a man like this Man— there never has been such another. A prophet and teacher who never

nagged at them, never flattered or coaxed or patronised: who never made arch jokes about them...who rebuked without querulousness and praised without condescension: who took their questions and arguments seriously. *(Are Women Human?,* page 47)

Mary and Martha

Jesus Christ taught that women were just as responsible for growing in grace and knowledge as men when it came to being one of his followers. This is clearly expressed in Luke's account of Christ's visit to the home of Martha and Mary, who lived in Bethany, a village about 2 miles from Jerusalem. Martha had invited Jesus and his disciples to her home for a meal. But while Martha was busily preparing to serve her guests, her sister, Mary, was listening to Jesus along with the rest of his disciples.

> As Jesus and his disciples were on their way, he came to a village where a woman named Martha opened her home to him. She had a sister called Mary, who sat at the Lord's feet listening to what he said. But Martha was distracted by all the preparations that had to be made. She came to him and asked, "Lord, don't you care that my sister has left me to do the work by myself? Tell her to help me!" (Luke 10:38-40)

Martha seems to have been the older sister and head of her own house. Jesus didn't chastise Martha for being busy serving, but he told her that her sister, Mary, was the one who actually had her priorities straight. "Martha, Martha," the Lord answered, "you are worried and upset about many things, but only one thing is needed. Mary has chosen what is better, and it will not be taken away from her" (verses 41-42).

Jesus expected women as well as men to learn from him. Jesus did not feel that women's work— or men's work, for that matter— wasn't important. He was not saying it is wrong to be diligent and careful about our responsibilities. Christ was saying we should get our priorities straight. Women were called to be disciples of Jesus, just as men were, and women were expected to fulfill their spiritual responsibilities, just as men were.

A daughter of Abraham

Another fascinating account is Luke's story of the healing of a disabled woman—on the Sabbath day, in the synagogue, right in front of the synagogue ruler. The healing not only shows Christ personally contrasting his new way of life with the old legalistic, pharisaical restrictions, but it also shows his deep regard for women.

> On a Sabbath Jesus was teaching in one of the synagogues, and a woman was there who had been crippled by a spirit for eighteen years. She was bent over and could not straighten up at all. When Jesus saw her, he called her forward and said to her, "Woman, you are set free from your infirmity." Then he put his hands on her, and immediately she straightened up and praised God. (Luke 13:10-13)

The ruler of the synagogue immediately protested. He indignantly told the people there were six other days they could be healed. This was his means of chastising Christ for what the religious ruler considered as breaking the Sabbath. Was Christ intimidated by these words? Not in the least.

> You hypocrites! Doesn't each of you on the Sabbath untie his ox or donkey from the stall and lead it out to give it water? Then should not this woman, a daughter of Abraham, whom Satan has kept bound for eighteen long years, be set free on the Sabbath day from what bound her? (verses 15-16)

Jesus not only faced the wrath of the Jewish leaders by healing this woman on the Sabbath, he showed his regard for her by calling her a "daughter of Abraham." "The idea of being a *son* of Abraham was common enough. Jesus used that term in reference to Zacchaeus a few chapters later in Luke. But Jesus with this one modification of the phrase— from 'son' to 'daughter'—raises this formerly pitiful woman to a new status," say authors Ruth A. Tucker and Walter Liefeld (*Daughters of the Church,* page 31).

Before his most venomous critics, Jesus publicly showed his concern and high regard for this woman, someone whom others had probably seen for years as she struggled in her affliction to come to the synagogue to worship God. Someone whom they may well have shunned because she was a woman and because she was disabled.

Female followers

The Bible doesn't specify just how many women traveled with Jesus and his male disciples, but Luke records the names of a prominent few, and mentions there were "many others."

> After this, Jesus traveled about from one town and village to another, proclaiming the good news of the kingdom of God. The Twelve were with him, and also some women who had been cured of evil spirits and diseases: Mary (called Magdalene) from whom seven demons had come out; Joanna the wife of Cuza, the manager of Herod's household: Susanna: and many others. These women were helping to support them out of their own means. (Luke 8:1-3)

Think about these remarkable words. Here were women not only associating with Jesus Christ and his male disciples, but traveling along with them. Also, notice that at least some of these women—possibly widows—had control of their own finances. It was out of their generosity that Jesus and his disciples were at least partially supported.

Although Christ worked with the cultural traditions of the first century, he ignored the limitations that had been placed on women by their culture. Women were free to follow him and to take part in his ministry to the world.

All are one in Christ

In Christ we are all children of God. As the apostle Paul wrote: "You are all [children] of God through faith in Christ Jesus, for all of you who were baptized into Christ have clothed yourselves with Christ. There is neither Jew nor Greek, slave nor free, male nor female, for you are all one in Christ Jesus" (Galatians 3:26-28).

Paul's significant words, especially where they concern women, are bold even now, and certainly were astonishing in the time he wrote them. This was another of Paul's transitional statements showing that a new covenant relationship through Christ had begun.

Now we have a new life in Christ. All Christians have a new relationship with God. Through Christ, we—both male and female—have become God's own children and one in Jesus Christ. Christ is calling all—men and women—to repentance and a new way of life. Jesus showed through personal example that it's time to put aside the old biases, the feelings of superiority over others, the feelings of resentment and anger, and to walk in newness of life with him and through him.

Many of you are striving to be women of faith. Many of you, like the bent-over woman healed by Christ in the synagogue, have to overlook some discrimination as you faithfully worship God and serve him. Don't get discouraged and give up. Jesus Christ calls you equal in every way in his sight, and heirs to his promises. And, as you humbly follow him, Christ will use you in his service.

And, for those of you who haven't taken that step, just as he freed that poor woman from Satan's debilitating physical affliction on her, Christ promises to free you, and all his "daughters of Abraham" who repent and follow him. Jesus Christ wants you in his kingdom.

Sheila Graham

The Prominence of Women in the Gospel of Luke
Women were prominent in Luke's portrayal of Jesus' life.

Elizabeth, mother of John the Baptist:
Elizabeth was the mother of John the Baptist, whose work paved the way for Jesus (Luke 1:5-7).

After Elizabeth conceived (verse 25), her unborn baby jumped when Mary visited (verses 41-44).

Elizabeth said that her son's name was John (verses 57-60).

Mary, mother of Jesus:
An angel told Mary she would be the mother of Jesus Christ (verses 26-38).

Mary offered a poem of praise, the Magnificat (verses 46-55).

Mary gave birth (2:5-7) and thought about the wonderful things said about Jesus (verse 19).

Mary was blessed by Elizabeth and Simeon (1:42; 2:34-35).

Mary did not understand, but treasured Jesus' sayings (2:50-51).

Mary kept in contact with Jesus during his ministry (8:19).

Women healed by Jesus:
Jesus healed Simon Peter's mother-in-law (4:38-39).

He healed a 12-year-old girl (8:41-42, 49-56).

He healed a woman with a 12-year infirmity (verses 43-48).

He healed a woman who had been crippled 18 years (13:10-17).

Women as good examples:

A sinful woman anointed Jesus and was forgiven (7:37-50).

Mary listened while Martha worked (10:38-42).

A woman in a parable found a lost coin (15:8-10).

In another parable, a widow kept going to a judge to obtain justice (18:1-5).

A poor widow gave two small coins to the temple (21:1-4).

Other roles of women:

Anna, a prophetess, blessed the child Jesus (2:36-38).

Women, part of Jesus' traveling party, helped pay his way (8:1-3).

An anonymous woman blessed Mary (11:27-28).

Witnesses to the resurrection:

Women were among those who observed the crucifixion (23:27, 49).

Women prepared spices to anoint Jesus' body (verses 55-56).

Women were the first to find Jesus' tomb empty (24:1-3).

Angels told the women that Jesus had risen (verses 4-8).

Women were the first to tell the other disciples (verses 9-11).

Although first-century culture usually minimized the importance of women, Luke portrayed women as good examples in the early church.

Michael Morrison

"A HERITAGE OF REACHING OUT": AN INTERVIEW WITH RUTH TUCKER

At the time of this interview, Historian Ruth A. Tucker was a visiting professor at Trinity Evangelical Divinity School. Dr. Tucker has also taught at Calvin College and Fuller Theological Seminary. She holds a doctorate in history from Northern Illinois University and speaks at seminars and Christian conferences. Her books include *Daughters of the Church* (with Walter Liefeld) and *Guardians of the Great Commission.*

Question: You have said in several of your books that the Bible shows that Jesus Christ had an unusual sensitivity toward women.

Ruth Tucker: Jesus certainly did have a remarkable perspective and attitude toward women. He was the Messiah, and he had come to bring the kingdom of God. He had come to live and to die and send a message to the whole world. He needed to mobilize all of those who would believe, all of his followers, including women as well as men.

We read about the 12 men who followed Jesus, but there were women in his company as well. Mary Magdalene and the other Marys followed him and carried the message of who Jesus was. What these women did goes along well with Jesus Christ's great commission that he gave before he died.

The men and women who followed Jesus had that great commission. It was not a commission that should cause people to rival each other in leadership or prestige or position and power, but rather a commission that calls for servitude.

The great commission is radical. It demands sacrifices and self-denial and calls for servanthood. Unfortunately in the church today, often following the management model in the world, we look for prestige and power, even as followers of Jesus. We may not intend that, but often that happens.

Q. Can any woman today— whether she is a young mother with several children, or perhaps a mother whose children have grown up and left home—serve Christ?

A. Absolutely. Any woman, and any man, should reach out to follow

Jesus. We have such an incredible heritage of women reaching out in their communities. Often, when they have little children, they will involve the little children in their ministry. They will get their adolescents, teenagers, all involved in the ministry as well. This can be done in the family setting. It can be done in groups.

We have women reaching out, often in social service ministries, helping others, meeting the needs of others in the community, but bringing the message of the risen Savior at the same time.

Q. As you know, Paul refers to the older women teaching the younger women. How do you feel older women can serve the younger women in the church?

A. Older, more mature women in the faith certainly can teach younger women and less spiritually mature women in the church. This ministry should also include women who may not be closely associated with the church, but in the community, who may have an interest in knowing more of the gospel of Jesus Christ.

Women working together to serve in the community have been a major factor in church growth through the generations. When women reach out to other women, to other families, they help and encourage them and also bring the gospel message at the same time.

Women, young and old, ought to see themselves as they read the pages of the New Testament, that they are there, and that they have been there through the generations, following the command of the great commission.

Often, women are the ones who carry on the faith. That may be partly because men have been secularized more than women. Men are out in the marketplace, out in the workplace and in the world. They are often challenged in their faith more than women. Women have traditionally been in the home. They are the ones rearing the children. They are the ones passing along the faith.

Women have to see themselves from New Testament times on through history in this role. God has especially used women, given them a gift of faith from the very women at the cross, for proclaiming the resurrection down through the centuries. We must continue that in our neighborhoods, not just in our homes, but in our communities.

Today, women are going out in the workplace; more and more. I am concerned that passing on the faith in the family and in the neighborhood may be getting left behind. As women are getting more secularized and involved in their own jobs and positions, they find their time more and more .limited.

As women, we need to hang on to our heritage, and encourage men also to be involved in bringing the gospel into the home and into the community, carrying on that great commission, to preach, teach, disciple and baptize.

Q. Yes, women are busy, but economic realities here and around the world have forced many women out of the home into the labor force. How can these women find time to serve?

A. I think they need to serve the Lord wherever they are. I would challenge working women that the workplace is a wonderful place to carry out the great commission. When Jesus said to go out to all the world, certainly the workplace is one of those places to reach out and simply share the faith, even as Mary Magdalene did, telling others about the risen Savior whom she had encountered.

WOMEN OF FAITH

Yesterday, Now and Forever

"God is not ashamed to be called their God." This profound statement is found in Hebrews 11, the faith chapter of the Bible. Can you imagine your name being listed along with Noah, Abraham, Isaac, Joseph and Moses in God's list of the faithful?

But, wait, before we go any further, let's look at that list a little more closely. Faith is not only a masculine virtue, we see. Sarah and Rahab and the women who received their dead raised to life again are also listed. And they were among those courageous nameless people who "were tortured, not accepting deliverance."

Let us take a new look at faith—from the point of view of women. Let us see how women of the Bible also used faith in their walk with God.

God's choice

Deborah, the only recorded female judge of ancient Israel, is described in Judges 4 and 5 as the deliverer of Israel for 40 years from Canaanite oppression. Before we analyze how this extraordinary woman did this, think about what it might take for a female to become the spiritual, judicial and military leader of Israel. It was a time of anarchy. The Hebrew tribes had settled among the Canaanites and began to worship their gods. Israel failed to stand apart from its pagan neighbors, as God commanded them. Instead of being righteous examples to the surrounding cultures, they took part in customs repulsive to God.

Though God made it plain that both mothers and fathers—women and men—are to be treated with equal respect (Exodus 20:12), in this degenerate disunited society, the rights of women were often overlooked. Women today complain about rights, but what do you think it took for a woman of that era to achieve what Deborah did? It took one major ingredient—a strong belief and faith in God.

God chose a faithful woman as Israel's judge and prophetess. It was a woman who encouraged Barak, the son of Abinoam, to heed God's call to duty and lead Israel's army against Sisera's 900 iron chariots. It was a woman who accompanied the troops to the battleground at Mount Tabor to fortify Barak's wavering courage (Judges 4:8-9).

To be fair to Barak, when he looked at the odds against him, he clearly

43

saw that unless God was on Israel's side, he and his troops would be massacred. Being a practical man, he made sure God's prophetess would be at the battle scene to provide divine insight. Barak is also on God's list of the faithful (Hebrews 11:32).

Deborah knew, in spite of the circumstances of her time and culture, that in God's sight, women were not second-class citizens, that God was not a respecter of persons. Her strong faith gave this woman the conviction and courage to allow God to use her in a most unusual way.

How satisfying it must have been for Deborah to look down on the Plain of Megiddo, 20 miles of battleground, and see God miraculously deliver Israel's army. "So let all your enemies perish, O Lord," was Deborah's battle cry. You can read in Judges 5 a stirring description of ancient Israel's deliverance from Sisera's oppression.

Rahab saves her family

Even before the time of Deborah and Barak, let's look at another remarkable Old Testament example of feminine faith — that of the innkeeper Rabab. Some scholars believe she (like most female innkeepers) was a prostitute, others deny the possibility. But one thing we do know: she is the only woman other than Sarah who is listed by name in God's account of his faithful in Hebrews.

Rahab lived in the ancient city of Jericho during the time that Joshua was leading the Israelites out of the desert into the promised land. According to archaeologists, a double wall of brick protected the city. Rahab's house was probably built over the 12-to-15-foot space that separated Jericho's 12-foot-thick inner wall from its 6-foot-thick outer wall.

The city of Jericho was the most important city in the Jordan Valley. The Canaanites of Rahab's time excelled in the arts and sciences. Morally, however, they were perverse. Their pagan religions were lewd and base, their civilization was decadent. Even though Jericho was heavily fortified, the Canaanite inhabitants of Jericho were understandably nervous about the Israelite hordes camped close by on the plains of Moab.

As they walked toward Jericho, two Hebrew spies sent by Joshua, Israel's military leader, may have noticed Rahab's house, with its window on the side of the massive outer wall of the city. When they entered the city, they were pleased to learn that this house on the wall was a place where two strangers would be accepted.

Rahab had heard about the miracles God had performed to rescue Israel from the Egyptians. She knew that the Amorites across the Jordan had been conquered. When the Israelite spies came to her house, she seized on the chance to save her family from what she saw as certain destruction.

Her neighbors had heard the stories, too. But, unlike her, they trusted in the thick walls of Jericho. Somehow, out of all these people, Rahab could see beyond the brick and stone of her familiar world and trust in the Hebrews' God. It must have been difficult to decide to forsake all that she knew and was comfortable with.

Following the spies' instruction, she acted on her faith and marked her home with a sign—a red rope. God respected her trust in him, and she and her family were spared when Jericho's walls fell. One woman of faith out of a whole city. You can read the account of Rahab's deliverance in Joshua 2-6.

Jesus and women

Jesus Christ constantly surprised his followers by the way he treated women. Women were real people to Jesus. Ignoring local custom, Jesus expected women as well as men to listen to and follow his teachings. Remember the account of Jesus' gentle rebuke of Martha for criticizing her sister Mary because she chose to listen to Jesus rather than help serve the male guests?

> Jesus answered and said unto her, Martha, Martha, you are careful and troubled about many things: But one thing is needful, and Mary has chosen that good part, which shall not be taken away from her. (Luke 10:41-42)

Jesus revealed the marvelous truth of his messiahship to, of all people, a Samaritan woman (John 4:21-26). The Jews despised the Samaritans and their religion. For a Jewish man to speak to a woman in public, especially a Samaritan woman, was unheard of at the time. Jesus' disciples were astonished when they saw him so at ease with women, talking to them, teaching them and admonishing them, as he did men. Women were amazed as well—and appreciated his concern for them, expressed so openly.

Unrecorded heroes

The multiple hundreds of thousands of women of faith over the centuries go unrecorded for the most part. Whatever our backgrounds, wherever we live, we all, no doubt, have our personal Joan of Arcs to add to the list.

About 100 years ago, women weren't satisfied with the world they saw around them and began to complain. Women campaigned against war, alcoholism, long work hours, low wages, child labor, high infant death rate, and filthy living conditions. In the United States in 1909, Nannie Helen Burroughs gave her National Training School for Women and Girls in Washington, D.C., the motto "We Specialize in the Wholly Impossible." The National Training School, a model for many others,

> offered young African American women a liberal-arts education and more.... Mary Breckenridge of the Frontier Nursing Service sent nurse midwives riding on horseback through the woods of Kentucky in the 1920s. Jane Addams founded Chicago's Hull House, one of the first and most important of the establishments of the settlement house movement, and won the Nobel Peace Prize in 1931. ("Smithsonian News Service," Mary Combs)

Edie Mayo, curator in the Division of Political History at the Smithsonian's National Museum of American History in Washington, D.C., adds, "What is truly astonishing is the fact that they accomplished most of it without the power to vote."

These few and far between examples from the past are fine, you may think, but what about now? Can today's women expect God to answer their prayers? Can they have faith? Does God discriminate against women today?

God is no respecter of persons (Acts 10:34-35). He expects women, as well as men, to faithfully believe in him. "There is neither Jew nor Greek, there is neither slave nor free, there is neither male nor female; for you are all one in Christ Jesus" (Galatians 3:28, New King James). God expects both men and women to actively express that faith by following him.

Why is active faith in God so important? To answer that question, we must first understand what faith is— and what it isn't.

Faith is...

Here's one definition of faith: "Faith is the substance of things hoped for, the evidence of things not seen" (Hebrews 11:1). Faith is confidence in God's will, God's purpose, and belief that God through his Son Jesus Christ will answer your prayers — *before* you see any physical proof.

Deborah knew, before she called for Barak, that God would grant Israel the victory. But how? Everything she could see and hear seemed to point toward Israel's defeat. Sisera had 900 chariots; he had thousands of well-trained and well-armed troops. Barak had neither. From what could be physically detected, it was not logical (in human terms) for Deborah to expect to win. But Deborah had faith in God, and knew that he would help Israel overpower the mighty Canaanites.

Deborah's faith was not an emotion. It wasn't some kind of feeling she had worked up over several hours or days. Her faith was not just hope, either. Wishful thinking does not win battles against iron-tipped spears and battle-hardened troops.

Deborah's faith was the unwavering belief in the face of overwhelming odds that God exists and that he will do what he promises he will. This faith is based on experience of what God has done, knowing he will not change his great purpose for humans. It is the kind of faith that wins wars and, in Rahab's case, saves lives.

The kind of faith that leads us to believe in and obey God is the only kind that pleases him. "But without faith it is impossible to please Him, for he who comes to God must believe that He is, and that He is a rewarder of those who diligently seek Him" (Hebrews 11:6, New King James).

Those who believe don't let circumstances cause them to doubt God. And God answers their prayers. "But let him ask in faith, nothing wavering. For he that wavers is like a wave of the sea driven with the wind and tossed. For let not that man think that he shall receive any thing of the Lord" (James 1:6-7).

Is faith out-of-date?

How strong is your faith? Can God look down at you as one he could add to his list of faithful servants? Or does faith seem to be an old-fashioned virtue, not as necessary in our modern technological world? Jesus wondered whether in the latter days of our civilization faith would be a scarce commodity: "When the Son of man comes, shall he find faith on the earth?" (Luke 18:8).

Does having faith still matter? Yes, it does. The gift of faith—true godly faith—is needed for our salvation. "For by grace you have been saved through faith, and that not of yourselves; it is the gift of God" (Ephesians 2:8, NKJV).

God does not discriminate. Whether Abraham or Sarah, Barak or Deborah, Hebrews says that the world was not worthy of those faithful people. Male or female, let's be sure we have the faith as well.

Sheila Graham

Faith, Hope and BBQ Sauce

In 1991, if you took Route 98 west through Columbus, Mississippi, crossed the Pearl River, continued to the second bridge over the railroad tracks, drove up the dirt road until you passed the Highway Department's garage, and asked someone where Leatha's is, then you could have found one of the best restaurants in the United States.

There were no signs; it was nothing fancy. A ramshackle house, rickety tables and chairs, and an assortment of old plates, cups and flatware. But the steaks were thick, the chicken tender and cooked just right. And the barbecue sauce was prepared from a formula that only Leatha knew. You'd never forget it, nor Leatha herself. (The restaurant later moved to Hattiesburg, and as of 2003, 80-year-old Leatha still works there).

Leatha Jackson is a grandmother with a simple formula for success— her secret recipe for BBQ sauce and an ironclad faith that God helps those who help themselves. She was raised in poverty. From age 5 to 25 she picked cotton. But her dream was to own and operate a restaurant. "In those days, a poor black girl in rural Mississippi with a third-grade education didn't have too much chance," she said. "But my father taught me to trust in God. When I got my first job in a restaurant, I didn't even know how to split a hot dog bun and put a wienie on it," she remembered.

She learned cooking and food management by watching others. Then she took the plunge and opened a small restaurant in her home far off the beaten track. There was no money for advertising. "We couldn't even afford a sign," she said. "So I asked God for customers, and they began coming." When her husband became ill, Leatha, who had always refused welfare and never owed anything, was forced to mortgage the property to meet the unexpected medical expenses. "We were $100,000 in debt. But I knew God would not put on us more than we could bear." And she paid the debt off.

Leatha has personal interest in each of her customers. She provided a service that few other restaurants could match. "When I have done all I can to serve them, I sometimes go to my room and pray for them. I thank God for each one. I ask him to help me give them good food, and to treat them right. Then I pray for their spiritual and financial welfare. I want them to be happy."

Leatha's is a family business. There are jobs for her children and their families— "if they are willing to work," she adds. She sees the business as a way to keep the family together. "It's like a bundle of sticks," she explains. "Separate us and we are easily broken. Together, we're strong." In a world of ruthless greed and cutthroat competition, Leatha's decent, hard-working little enterprise is a reminder that "old-fashioned" values still work. Be fair, treat people right, give good value for a fair price, work hard, share with others and don't be greedy. And above all, trust God to look after you.

John Halford

THE ALABASTER GOSPEL— WHAT ONE WOMAN'S DEVOTION TELLS US ABOUT JESUS

Matthew 26 records an interesting episode in the life of Jesus, just two days before he was killed. This was an action-packed week, filled with highly significant events — and this event is no exception. In Matthew 26, we find a description of Jesus being anointed with perfume. The story begins in verses 1-2:

"When Jesus had finished saying all these things, he said to his disciples, 'As you know, the Passover is two days away — and the Son of Man will be handed over to be crucified.'"

Jesus knows that his time is short – he has only two days to live – but his disciples seem to be unaware of it. Jesus will soon be given another opportunity to tell his disciples about his impending death. Then there is an abrupt change of scene, in which Matthew tells us what is happening in another place at about the same time.

"The chief priests and the elders of the people assembled in the palace of the high priest, whose name was Caiaphas, and they plotted to arrest Jesus in some sly way and kill him. 'But not during the Feast,' they said, 'or there may be a riot among the people'" (verses 3-5).

Jesus anointed with perfume

Matthew then takes us back to Jesus. "While Jesus was in Bethany [two miles from Jerusalem] in the home of a man known as Simon the Leper, a woman came to him with an alabaster jar of very expensive perfume, which she poured on his head as he was reclining at the table" (verses 6-7). A whole jar of perfume! The smell would have filled the entire room.

"When the disciples saw this, they were indignant. 'Why this waste?' they asked. 'This perfume could have been sold at a high price and the money given to the poor.'"

"Aware of this, Jesus said to them, 'Why are you bothering this woman? She has done a beautiful thing to me. The poor you will always have with you, but you will not always have me. When she poured this perfume on my body, she did it to prepare me for burial.'"

Then Jesus, with special emphasis, then said, "I tell you the truth, wherever this gospel is preached throughout the world, what she has done will also be told, in memory of her" (verses 8-13).

Why is this so important?

I would like to ask a follow-up question: Why is this story so important that it will be told wherever the gospel message goes?

The woman had done a nice favor for Jesus, and it was appropriate for Jesus to thank her in a nice way. But surely this does not mean that the disciples, no matter where they went in the world, would have to tell this story everywhere they told the gospel? If the disciples were running short of time, couldn't they just preach the gospel and skip this particular story? No, said Jesus. Wherever the gospel is preached, this story must be told, too. It is practically as important as the gospel itself!

When the disciples were inspired to write the stories of what Jesus did, they also wrote the story of what this woman did. In the Gospel accounts, it is on an equal level with the teachings and miracles of Jesus. What this woman did is an essential part of the story of Jesus.

That is not just long ago and far away. It also applies right now, and right here. Wherever the gospel goes, this story must be told, too. Why is that?

The context: Jesus' death

This section of Matthew is about Jesus' death. It begins in verse 2 with Jesus mentioning his death. It moves in verse 3 to the conspiracy to kill Jesus. And in verse 12, Jesus connects the anointing with his burial.

And right after Jesus says that this story will be told around the world, Matthew tells us in verse 14 that Judas went out and conspired with the chief priests to betray Jesus. This was the event that was the last straw for Judas. He was so upset about this waste of money that he went out to betray his master for 30 pieces of silver – ironically, money that he himself would waste.

The story is set in the context of Jesus' death. It is part of the introduction to what is called the passion – Jesus' suffering and death. That helps make the story significant. There are several points of resemblance between what this woman did and what Jesus did on the cross. Her action was in some ways a parable, a drama that portrayed spiritual truth about

Jesus.

Many of Jesus' own actions were object lessons for spiritual truths. He did many more miracles than could be recorded in the Bible, but some are reported to us because they have special significance.

The miracle of feeding 5,000 people, for example, helps show that Jesus is the bread of life. Just as he gives food for physical life, so also he gives what we need for eternal life. The fact that he could do something we can see, gives us assurance that he can do something we cannot see. Just as he heals diseases, so also forgives sins. The physical action pictures a spiritual truth.

This is also true of what this woman did for Jesus. What she did illustrates for us some lessons about the sacrifice of Jesus Christ. It also pictures the way that we should respond to Jesus. What this woman did is a miniature picture of the gospel itself. That is why it is so important that this story has become part of the gospel message. It can help us explain the nature of the gospel.

A powerful devotion

"Mary took about a pint of pure nard, an expensive perfume; she poured it on Jesus' feet and wiped his feet with her hair" (John 12:3).

Let's look at three ways in which this anointing resembles the sacrifice of Jesus himself.

First, let's give this woman a name. John 12 tells us that she was Mary, sister of Lazarus, and that this was shortly after Jesus had raised Lazarus from the dead. (Not everyone agrees that this is the same anointing as Matthew 26, but we can still call her Mary.) The story can be told without a specific name — the action is more important than who did it — but it does help us understand a little more of what went on behind the scenes.

First, we can see that Mary was motivated to do this out of love. Nobody told her to do it. It was not commanded. It was just something Mary took upon herself to do, and she did it out of love.

Jesus also made his sacrifice out of love. He had no obligation to die for us, but he chose to do it, willingly, motivated by love. Even while we were sinners, he loved us with incredible intensity.

Mary may have known that Jesus was soon to die, but perhaps not. The disciples didn't understand that Jesus was going to die, and Mary probably didn't, either. Otherwise, she would have saved the perfume for the actual burial. She seems to have poured the perfume on Jesus simply because she had an incredibly intense devotion to Jesus. She was overwhelmed with love. Maybe it was a response to the resurrection of Lazarus.

Mary may have bought that perfume to anoint the dead body of her brother. Now that Lazarus was alive, Mary did not need the perfume for him — thanks to what Jesus had done. How could Mary thank Jesus for his wonderful gift of life? Why, she could use that same perfume to lavish it on Jesus, as a token of her thanks and love. Mary was praising Jesus, honoring Jesus, in effect, worshipping Jesus, sacrificing to Jesus.

Many people today are concerned with right beliefs. Right beliefs are good. We need them. Many people today are concerned with right behavior. Right behavior is good. We need it — but we need something else, too, and that is something that Mary demonstrates for us. Mary shows us right emotion, right feeling. The heart we need for God is an intensely personal devotion, a powerful dedication of ourselves to his service.

This intensity of emotion is unusual, and like most unusual things, this was criticized. This kind of devotion was not within the ordinary range of acceptable behavior. People would call Mary eccentric, maybe even out of her right mind. Society says, Don't get carried away with your emotions. Mary did. Her society criticized her, but Jesus praised her. Society says, Moderation in all things. Mary was not moderate. Her society criticized her, but Jesus praised her. The jury of 12 men said this is wrong, but Jesus said, she is better than you all.

Mary had an intense affection and devotion for Jesus. We can see it when she sat at Jesus' feet listening to him teach. She was a contemplative person who liked to think. Here, she is an expressive person — expressive not in words but in actions. Her quiet nature did not prevent her from making a powerful statement — more powerful than words could have possibly done.

An enormous sacrifice

The second way in which Mary's action was like the sacrifice of Jesus is that was a sacrifice. This was some incredibly expensive perfume. Mary could have sold it for a large amount. Mark tells us it was worth about one year's wages — the amount of money that a working person would earn in an entire year. In today's economy, it might be worth several thousand dollars.

Can you imagine one jar of perfume that costs several thousand dollars? Now, can you imagine taking that and just pouring it out? Thousands of dollars evaporating into thin air — gone forever. A year's worth of manual labor, gone, just like that.

This shows us something of the intensity of Mary's love for Jesus. She must have known what she was doing, and how much it had cost her. But she did not care. Her love for Jesus was so great that she was not concerned about the cost. She was probably happy about it — she was getting a chance to demonstrate her devotion to Jesus. If she had sorrow, it was not about how much she was giving up, but that she had so little to give. Love often expresses itself in self-sacrifice, with little thought for self.

If an offering is to be meaningful, it should cost us something, and it should be done out of our own free will. We should give up something that is of value to us. Worship always involves sacrifice — sacrifice of money, time or pride, or all three. Maybe it requires everything we have, and everything we are.

The disciples were concerned with self. They wanted to be great in the kingdom of God. But Mary was achieving greatness already, through her devotion to Jesus. She was not concerned for self and what she would get out of it. She was concerned for nothing but Jesus, and in that, she was already great.

Concern about the money

The disciples suggested that the money could be given to the poor. It wasn't just Judas who objected to this "waste" of money. All the disciples were indignant. It is good to give money to the poor. The traditional Jewish understanding of righteousness included giving money to the poor, and apparently the disciples sometimes did it. (When Judas went out from the last supper, the disciples thought that he might be going to give something to the poor. If Jesus had never given any money to the poor in three years, the disciples probably would not guess that he would start right then. Charity seems to have been part of what they normally did.)

When someone has lots of money, it is appropriate to share some of it with those who need it. That is a good use of money. But in this case, Mary had picked an even better use of the money. She used it in an act of tremendous devotion, an act of worship. That is a legitimate use of money, too.

Some Christians make a religion out of social work, and they do it very well. Social work is part of the Christian faith. But some unfortunately see that as the only form of religion, and they have forgotten about devotion to Jesus. Social work is good, but it is not supreme. Jesus is supreme — and our devotion to him will cause us to help those who need help. It's a question of priorities, and Jesus must always be first. For Christian service to really count, it must be done for Christ. We are serving him.

What Mary did, from an observer's perspective, was a big sacrifice. But because she was willing, it was for her a small price to pay, a token of her love. Jesus' crucifixion, from all perspectives, was a tremendous sacrifice, but he was willing to make it. For the joy set before him he endured the cross. He knew that glory was waiting not just for him, but for all who would be saved by what he did. He was willing to pay the price.

As we grasp the enormity of his sacrifice, we cannot help but respond in love and devotion — and there is no sacrifice too great. Nothing we do could ever compare to what he has done for us. Our love for him causes us to live for him, to give all that we are.

Extravagant sacrifice

The third way in which Mary's action was similar to Jesus' crucifixion is that it was extravagant. It was far more than what was necessary. It was outrageous! Mary was not a calculating person who thought, what is the least I can do? How much do I have to spend to be enough? What is my duty? Nor was she tied down to tradition.

Mary did not think, How do other women show respect for a rabbi? She was not afraid of public opinion. Her love freed her from that fear. She was not afraid to do something out of the ordinary. Mary did not ask the disciples if it was OK. No, Mary broke traditions. She broke the limits of what is public propriety. Mary didn't even ask Jesus if it was OK. She just seized the opportunity, and did it. She did what she could, because only that expressed her devotion to Jesus. Her love was so great that it called for an exceptional act of creative devotion.

The disciples didn't object to the anointing in itself. They didn't object to perfume. What they objected to was the extravagance. This was just too much of a good thing — way too much. This was ridiculous, wasteful, even sinful. No so, said Jesus. What she has done is a beautiful thing, Jesus said. It had an aesthetic value, like a beautiful work of art, a beautiful piece of music. It was a beautiful action — a beauty that defies cost analysis. It is impossible to put a price on such personal devotion.

Sometimes we are too concerned about the usefulness of something. I often think that way. But that may mean that I do only the ordinary things, never the unusual, never the beautiful, never anything heroic, never anything requiring faith.

The disciples wanted the money to be put to good use, for something practical, like food for the hungry. And that is a very good use for money. It was the ordinary thing to do, the normal thing to do, even a respectable thing to do. But usefulness is not the most important thing in the universe. Usefulness is not our god. Efficiency is not our god. Public opinion is not our god. Traditional boundaries of politeness are not our god.

Jesus is our God, and it is useful to expend our material resources to honor and glorify him. Maybe there aren't any tangible results, but a sacrifice of love and devotion has a usefulness of its own. An act of great beauty has a usefulness of its own when it is done for Jesus Christ. Mary's act of extravagant waste was actually a picture of spiritual beauty — a heavenly fragrance. It pictured the sacrifice of Jesus Christ in a way that words could not. It was extravagant, and that is part of its beauty. God himself is extravagant.

Of course, when something is done out of the ordinary, someone is going to complain about it. Someone is not going to understand the motive, or understand the beauty, or they are going to say, "That's not right. We don't do things that way." To them, it seems that mediocrity is better than intense emotion. But Jesus praises extravagance, not mediocrity.

God gave us an extravagant gift in the person of Jesus Christ. It was an outrageous gift, worth far more than what we deserve. Grace is extravagant. Jesus gave everything he had for us. He gave his very life. And he gave even more than necessary — he died for the whole world, and yet the whole world does not accept him. He died even for the people who reject him.

What a waste!, some people might think, but it was really an act of love, of sacrifice, of extravagance. Some people said, "That can't be right. That's not the way God normally acts with us." But God does things out of the ordinary. Jesus shows us total commitment, total sacrifice, so that we might respond to him with all that we have.

An extravagant response

We need to respond to him the same way that Mary did — with a supreme focus on him, a single-minded love that counts everything else loss for Jesus Christ, a love that does not ask how little we can do to get by, a love that is not worried about public opinion, a love that is no longer concerned about what is within the boundaries of normal devotion — a love that is willing to be extravagant.

When Mary poured perfume on Jesus, she was not only picturing some aspects of what Jesus did on the cross, she also pictured the way that we should respond to Jesus, with such complete devotion, such willingness to sacrifice, such willingness to go beyond the boundaries of normal and to have an extraordinary love for Jesus.

Have you ever done anything extravagant for Jesus Christ? Have you ever done anything so outrageous for him that other people thought you were foolish? Have you ever been so bold with love that other people have criticized what you did? Some of us have. Maybe it was a long time ago. Whenever it was, it was sweet-smelling aroma offered to God.

The example of Mary tells me that I am too reserved. I am too often concerned with what others think. I am not loving Jesus as much as I ought. I am too concerned with myself. I need to think more about actions of extraordinary beauty. God has been extravagant with me. He has lavished on me the riches of his grace. He has repeatedly given me things I did not deserve and things I did not appreciate the way I ought. His grace toward me abounds and abounds and abounds. How do I respond to him who gave his life for me?

WOMEN WHO SPOKE THE WORD OF GOD

Women have an increasing role in the work of the church. Women not only lead women in "women's ministries," but also lead men and women in music, prayer, teaching and speaking. Some people wonder why women should be allowed to do anything in church; others wonder why women can't do everything in church.

To give biblical perspective on this issue, let's look at evidence that God has used women to speak to his people. Women have spoken the word of God, and they have done so with divine approval and divine authority.

Hagar

The Lord gave Hagar a promise similar to the promise given to Abraham (Genesis 16:7-10). Hagar then "gave this name to the Lord who spoke to her: 'You are the God who sees me,' for she said, 'I have now seen the One who sees me' " (verse 11).

What Hagar said is now in the word of God. She told us one of the names that tell us who God is. He is the God who sees us, and Hagar is the person who spoke that truth.

Miriam

After God brought the Israelites through the Red Sea, Miriam sang praises that are now part of the word of God: "Miriam the prophetess, Aaron's sister, took a tambourine in her hand, and all the women followed her, with tambourines and dancing.

"Miriam sang to them: 'Sing to the Lord, for he is highly exalted. The horse and its rider he has hurled into the sea' " (Exodus 15:20-21). In public worship, Miriam sang what is now the word of God.

Miriam was a prophetess, which means that she spoke the word of the Lord. A prophet is someone who speaks on behalf of God to the people; a prophetess had the same role. Miriam had a role of spiritual leadership.

Deborah

The next prophetess in the Bible is Deborah. "Deborah, a prophetess, the wife of Lappidoth, was leading Israel at that time. She held court under the Palm of Deborah between Ramah and Bethel in the hill country of Ephraim, and the Israelites came to her to have their disputes decided"

(Judges 4:4-5).

Deborah was a prophetess and a judge, and in both roles she spoke the word of God. Her role was not just a one-time event, but an ongoing responsibility. The people came to her for leadership on a regular basis—and there is nothing in the Bible to suggest that anyone thought it was unusual for a woman to perform this role. She was simply the most qualified person, and people accepted that.

God can raise up stones to do his work, and if he needed a man to do his work, he could raise up a man. But in this case he chose to work through a woman, showing that there is no theological reason that God can't use a woman to speak on his behalf, or to have a woman lead his people.

There were many men in Israel at that time, but God wasn't searching for one to be the judge, and apparently the Israelites weren't, either. They were quite willing to go to Deborah to have their disputes decided. She had wisdom, and her wisdom was more important than her gender.

Deborah was a prophetess, someone speaking the words of God.

> She sent for Barak son of Abinoam from Kedesh in Naphtali and said to him, "The Lord, the God of Israel, commands you: 'Go, take with you ten thousand men of Naphtali and Zebulun and lead the way to Mount Tabor. I will lure Sisera, the commander of Jabin's army, with his chariots and his troops to the Kishon River and give him into your hands.'" (verses 6-7)

Here the Bible describes a woman speaking the words of God, giving commands to a man who was apparently enough of a leader that he could raise an army of ten thousand men. God is quite willing for a woman to give his commands to men. There is nothing in the nature of God or the nature of men and women that makes such a thing inappropriate. God can use women, and we need to be alert for the possibility that he is, and we need to be willing to respond.

Deborah went with Barak, and in verse 14 she again gives the word of the Lord to Barak: "Go! This is the day the Lord has given Sisera into your hands. Has not the Lord gone ahead of you?" So they went, and they won. It was a great victory, and Deborah and Barak commemorated their victory with a song of praise that is now part of the word of God.

"On that day Deborah and Barak son of Abinoam sang this song:

'When the princes in Israel take the lead, when the people willingly offer themselves—praise the Lord! Hear this, you kings! Listen, you rulers! I will sing to the Lord, I will sing; I will make music to the Lord, the God of Israel'" (Judges 5:1-2)

Who is this "I" who is singing? In verse 7 we see that it is Deborah: "Village life in Israel ceased," the song says, "ceased until I, Deborah, arose, arose a mother in Israel." Deborah is the primary author of this part of Scripture. Like Miriam, she was singing praise to God in public worship. She is expressing spiritual leadership, speaking the word of God. This is a legitimate thing for women to do.

When the best person for the job is a woman, then God is quite willing to use a woman to do the work that needs to be done. Even in a patriarchal society, God can use women to speak his words.

A similar thing happened with Hannah, the mother of Samuel. "Hannah prayed and said: 'My heart rejoices in the Lord; in the Lord my horn is lifted high. My mouth boasts over my enemies, for I delight in your deliverance. There is no one holy like the Lord; there is no one besides you; there is no Rock like our God'" (1 Samuel 2:1-2).

Again, a woman's words are now inspired Scripture. She spoke the word of God with words of worship that have inspired synagogues and churches for thousands of years, and that is a notable achievement for anyone. God inspired her to sing a song of praise.

Most of God's spokesmen were men. In this patriarchal society, all the priests were men, the kings were men, the military leaders were men. But even in that male-dominated society, God could use women to do his work.

Huldah

In 2 Kings 22, we catch another glimpse of what God was doing with women. In the 18th year of Josiah's reign, workers found a scroll of the law in the temple. Josiah told the high priest what he should do: "Go and inquire of the Lord for me and for the people and for all Judah about what is written in this book that has been found" (verse 13).

The high priest wanted to ask the Lord about the scroll, so he "went to speak to the prophetess Huldah, who was the wife of Shallum son of Tikvah" (verse 14). They could have looked for Jeremiah, but there was no reason to. Huldah spoke the word of the Lord just as much as Jeremiah did. A prophet speaks the words of God, and a prophetess speaks the words of God, and God inspires one just as much as the other.

So they asked Huldah, and in verses 15-16 we read her reply: "She said to them, 'This is what the Lord, the God of Israel, says: Tell the man who sent you to me, "This is what the Lord says: I am going to bring disaster on this place and its people, according to everything written in the book the king of Judah has read."'"

Huldah was commenting on the meaning of the Scriptures and predicting the future, giving an authoritative message from God. Again, there is no indication that anything unusual was happening. No one said it was strange to go to a woman instead of a man. Huldah was known as a prophetess, which means that she was known to speak the word of the Lord. She was doing the same thing she had on many other occasions: She spoke on behalf of God to the people. That is what prophetesses did.

New Testament

In the New Testament we learn of other women who spoke the word of God. Mary sang praises that are now in Scripture (Luke 1:46-55). Anna was a prophetess (Luke 2:36-38). After Jesus was resurrected, he appeared to some women and gave them a message: "The women hurried away from the tomb, afraid yet filled with joy, and ran to tell his disciples.

"Suddenly Jesus met them. 'Greetings,' he said. They came to him, clasped his feet and worshiped him. Then Jesus said to them, 'Do not be afraid. Go and tell my brothers to go to Galilee; there they will see me'" (Matthew 28:8-10).

Jesus has no problem with women delivering commands to men. There is nothing inherently wrong with that. He gave them that authority by giving them the message, and in doing so, these women were speaking the words of the Lord. Jesus expected the men to listen to the women and obey the command they delivered.

There were prophetesses in the early church, too. When the disciples were speaking in tongues, Peter told the crowd what was going on. It was a fulfillment of Joel's prophecy: "In the last days, God says, I will pour out my Spirit on all people. Your sons and daughters will prophesy, your young men will see visions, your old men will dream dreams. Even on my servants, both men and women, I will pour out my Spirit in those days, and they will prophesy" (Acts 2:17-18).

God inspires both men and women to speak. That was not unheard of in Old Testament times, and this is the way it should be in the new covenant age, too. God will cause both men and women to speak. Luke does not tell us what the women were inspired to say. All the preaching done in the book of Acts is done by men. That was probably a practical necessity in that culture. But there is nothing theoretically or theologically wrong with women being inspired to speak.

Luke mentions in Acts 21:9 that Philip had four daughters who prophesied. As prophetesses, they would speak the word of God, as they were inspired by God. They may have composed songs of praise, like Miriam and Deborah did, or they could have commented on the meaning of the Scriptures, as Huldah did. All of those are within the range of what is biblically possible.

For a discussion of the passages that Paul wrote, see the next chapter.

Peter gives us a fitting conclusion when he says, "Each one should use whatever gift he [or she] has received to serve others, faithfully administering God's grace in its various forms. If anyone speaks [whether man or woman] he should do it as one speaking the very words of God" (1 Peter 4:10-11). Anyone who speaks in church should strive to speak the words of God, and women are included in those who may speak the words of God in church.

WOMEN IN LEADERSHIP

The New Testament teaches that all Christians should minister to one another, each person serving as his or her gifts allow. Elders are appointed in the church to shepherd, direct and teach. Elders lead and serve by equipping others. May women serve as elders and pastors? Are they permitted to shepherd, lead, direct and teach? Should the church recognize and train women as pastors and teachers?

Let's begin our examination of this question by making a historical review of how God has used women to help his people. We will then examine the question in greater detail to see what the evidence says and does not say.

In the beginning

When Jesus answered a question about divorce, he used the Genesis story to show God's original intent for marriage (Matthew 19:4-5). In the beginning, "God said, 'Let us make man[1] in our image, in our likeness, and let them rule over the fish of the sea and the birds of the air, over the livestock, over all the earth, and over all the creatures that move along the ground.' So God created man1 in his own image, in the image of God he created him; male and female he created them" (Genesis 1:26-27).

This passage tells us that, despite differences in appearance, both men and women are created in the image of God. Both men and women were given dominion over creation. "Let *them* rule," God said. Verse 28 tells us: "God blessed them and said to them, 'Be fruitful and increase in number; fill the earth and subdue it. Rule over the fish of the sea and the birds of the air and over every living creature that moves on the ground.' " These commands were given to both male and female. Genesis 1 treats men and women equally.

In Genesis 2, however, we see gender distinctions in the story: The male was created before the female. Genesis 2 also tells us that God gave a certain job and certain commands to the man before Eve was created (Genesis 2:15-17, 19). But it was not good for the man to be alone. God therefore made a woman for him. Paul notes this, but observes that "woman is not independent of man, nor is man independent of woman" (1 Corinthians 11:8-11). Adam recognized that the woman was the same kind of being that he was, made out of the same stuff: "bone of my bones and flesh of my flesh" (Genesis 2:23). This text emphasizes similarity, not difference. Verse 24 then says that husband and wife become a unity.

Then sin entered the picture. Both Eve and Adam sinned, and both were ashamed. God spoke to Adam first, and then to Eve. Then God explained to Eve and Adam the negative consequences of their sin. When he explained the consequences, he made some distinctions based on sex. To the woman, he said that childbirth would become painful. To the man, he said that agricultural work would become difficult (Genesis 3:16-17).

Genesis does not directly answer the question we want to answer, but it does give us some clues. First, men and women are equally made in the image of God (Genesis 1). Since the story tells us that God did not deal with the man and woman in identical ways, we conclude that some sex distinctions can be legitimate.

Old Testament women who were leaders

The Old Testament reflects a male-dominated society. Many of the laws are written from a male perspective, and give preferential treatment to men. There are few Old Testament examples of female leaders. Nevertheless, at various times in history, God has used women as leaders for his people. They led in various ways. Just as with male leaders, some of the female leaders were good and some were not.

Women had important roles in the Exodus and in the formation of the Israelite nation. Miriam the prophetess sang praises to God, leading other women in public praises to God (Exodus 15:20-21). Later, when she exercised leadership in a wrong way, she was criticized for rebellion, but not for being a woman in leadership (Numbers 12:1-15). Miriam continued to be credited as one of the nation's original leaders (Micah 6:4).

Deborah led the Israelites for several years (Judges 4:4-5). The text says nothing about this leadership role being inappropriate; it says nothing to suggest that none of the Israelite men were qualified. It just says that she was a prophetess and served the Israelites by judging their disputes, just as other judges had done. God spoke to her, apparently on a regular basis, and she gave the Lord's commands to Barak (verses 6, 14). She had civil, military and religious roles. Deborah and Barak sang a song of praise (Judges 5:1-31). Verse 7 attributes the song primarily to Deborah.

Huldah the prophetess gave an authoritative message to the high priest and several men (2 Kings 22:14-20).

Although ancient Israel was a male-dominated society, and female leadership was unusual, it is not incompatible with the way God works. God sometimes called women to positions of leadership, including civil, military and religious roles, and the people accepted that leadership.

Female leaders in the New Testament

Women were important in Jesus' ministry, too. Unlike most rabbis, Jesus taught women (Luke 10:38-42). Women were among his traveling disciples (Luke 8:1-3). Martha was given the spiritual insight to recognize Jesus as the Messiah, the Son of God (John 11:27).

Jesus told the Samaritan woman that he was the Messiah (John 4:7-26). The lesson he gave her about living water was just as profound as the lesson he had taught Nicodemus — and the woman had a better response. She went and told her townspeople about the Messiah, and she was effective in testifying about Jesus. Many of the people believed in Jesus because of what she reported (verses 28-29, 39).

After Jesus was resurrected, he could have chosen to appear to men first, but he did not. He revealed himself to women first, and told the women to relay his orders to the men (Matthew 28:8-10). He apparently expected the men to follow the women's instructions.

Women continued to be an important part of the early church. They were included among the 120 disciples (Acts 1:13-15). Peter said that the Holy Spirit caused women as well as men to speak (Acts 2:17). The story of Ananias and Sapphira shows that women were held equally accountable (Acts 5:1-11). The church grew in men and women alike (Acts 5:14; 8:12).

When Paul persecuted the church, trying to stop its growth, he felt it necessary to imprison not only men but also women (Acts 8:3). Apparently women were also spreading the gospel. (Although men did all the public preaching that we know about (which is to be expected in that society), women were apparently effective evangelizers in other settings.)

Women were prominent in the start-up of the church in Philippi. Lydia, apparently the head of her household, was the first to believe (Acts 16:12-15). The church met at her house (verse 40). In Colosse, the church met at Nympha's house (Colossians 4:15). In Thessalonica and Berea, prominent women became Christians (Acts 17:1-4, 12). These women were probably influential leaders in their cities and in their congregations.

Priscilla was another prominent woman. She and Aquila gave Apollos an important lesson in Christianity (Acts 17:26). Paul called Priscilla and Aquila "fellow workers" (Romans 16:3), a term Paul also used for Timothy, Titus, Epaphroditus and other men.

Paul mentioned a number of other women who were important to his ministry, although their specific roles are not given in detail. He commended Phoebe, a *diakonos* servant of the church in Cenchrea (Romans 16:1). Paul asked the Romans to receive Phoebe and help her in any way she wanted, which indicates she was a person of importance (verse 2).

Paul greeted Mary, Tryphena, Tryphosa and Persis, "women who work hard in the Lord" (verses 6, 12). Similarly, Paul said that Euodia and Syntyche "contended at my side in the cause of the gospel, along with Clement and the rest of my fellow workers" (Philippians 4:2-3). It is clear that these women had important roles in Paul's evangelistic work, but it is not clear exactly what their roles were. They may have been key support staff, or they may have taught women, or they may have worked with men to teach men, like Priscilla did. *All* believers should be servants of the church, working hard for the Lord, contending for the cause of the gospel.

Paul had a much higher view of women than most Jewish rabbis did. For example, he gave women just as much control over conjugal rights as he gave men (1 Corinthians 7:3-5). He considered all believers equal in Christ (Galatians 3:26-28). Of course, this does not imply a complete elimination of sex differences. Paul himself gave certain commands specifically to males and other commands specifically to females (1 Corinthians 11:10; 14:34; Ephesians 5:22, 25; 6:4; Colossians 3:18-21; Titus 2:2-6).

Women also influenced the church through the gift of prophecy. Anna was a prophetess (Luke 2:36). Philip's daughters had the gift of prophecy (Acts 21:8-9). Since they spoke the word of God, they spoke with authority.

In Corinth, both men and women prayed and prophesied (1 Corinthians 11:4-16). Paul's concern about head coverings shows that this praying and prophesying was done in public. He was concerned about their appearance when they met or came together "as a church" (verses 17-18). Women were praying and speaking in the Corinthian church, and Paul praised that.

Prophecy is inspired speaking that strengthens, encourages, comforts and edifies (1 Corinthians 14:3-4). In church meetings, prophecy may convict people of sin and bring them to faith (verses 23-25). In Corinth, the Holy Spirit was inspiring both men and women to speak edifying messages during church services. Paul encouraged all the Corinthians to seek the gift of prophesying, and he did not forbid women from using that gift if they had it.

1 Corinthians 14:34-35

However, Paul also wrote: "Women should remain silent in the churches. They are not allowed to speak, but must be in submission, as the Law says. If they want to inquire about something, they should ask their own husbands at home; for it is disgraceful for a woman to speak in the church."

Earlier in this letter, Paul gave guidelines about how women should appear when they pray and prophesy in public (1 Corinthians 11:4-15). Does he now forbid them to pray and prophesy at all? How are we to understand 1 Corinthians 14:34-35 without making it contradict what Paul wrote earlier in his letter? The context indicates that Paul's command in 14:34-35 is limited to certain situations.

First, we understand that Paul does not forbid all speaking. He does not mean that women cannot say *amen* after a prayer; he does not mean that they cannot whisper to their children. Although the verse says that women are not allowed to speak, it should not be interpreted in a literal extreme. It does not contradict what Paul wrote in chapter 11, and it does not contradict what he wrote in 14:1 and 14:39, telling all the Corinthian Christians to seek the gift of prophesying.

Second, we should note that women are not the only people Paul told to be silent. In verse 28, he told tongues-speakers to be quiet (same Greek word) if interpreters were not present. In verse 30, he told prophets to stop (same Greek word) if a revelation came to someone else. For these groups, the silence Paul commands is for some church situations but not for others. This appears to be true for his comments about women, as well.

Paul's concern throughout this chapter is peace and order in the church meetings. The Corinthian meetings apparently had been rather chaotic, and Paul was giving some basic rules of order. Everybody wanted to speak at once — some with tongues, some with interpretations, some with prophecies, some with teaching, some with hymns (verse 26). So Paul told them to speak one at a time (verses 27-31). He was putting some order on the chaos.

We see why Paul told tongues-speakers to be silent: to reduce the confusing babble. We see why he told prophets to be quiet: to reduce the confusion. Why did he tell women to be quiet? He does not tell us why he specifically mentions women but not men, but his concern is probably the same as it was earlier in the chapter. Instead of everyone talking at once, Paul wanted one person to talk at a time. When someone else was talking, the women were to be quiet.

Quiet, please!

What were the women talking about? Paul does not directly tell us, but verses 34 and 35 give us some evidence. Verse 34 indicates that women were speaking in a nonsubmissive way. Verse 35 indicates that women were asking questions, presumably in such a way as to add to the confusion. We do not know exactly what the situation was, but we might speculate that women were speaking at the same time as the men, perhaps acting disrespectfully toward the men. Whatever it was, Paul told them to stop talking.

Why did Paul tell women not to ask questions in church? Obviously, he did not intend to forbid absolutely all questions. For a modern example, if a woman is taking notes on a sermon and misses a point, she is allowed to quietly ask her husband (or someone else) what the speaker said. Questions are permissible if they are not disruptive. When we read verse 35, we should consider the context. Paul is concerned about reducing chaos in the church; he is not forbidding all questions.

Presumably the Corinthian Christians would know what kind of questions were causing problems. In the chaotic meetings at Corinth, questions would have to be asked in a loud voice. The problem seems to have been wives asking questions of their husbands. Paul's command for women to ask their husbands at home obviously would not apply to women who had no husbands, or women whose husbands were not Christians.

Paul's main concern was order.[2] After Paul wrote about how women should appear when prophesying in public, and after exhorting everyone to seek the gift of prophecy, he is not now forbidding women to speak at all. Rather, his command for quiet is not a demand for absolutely no talking. Rather, it is a directive for order, just as his command for the tongues-speakers and prophets to be quiet was also a directive for order.

We should understand verses 34-35 in their context: the need for peace in a disorderly situation. Verse 34 is not a complete prohibition of all speaking, and verse 35 is not a complete prohibition of all questions. We prohibit inappropriate speaking, disruptive questions, argumentative interruptions, and more than one speaker at a time. But we do not forbid women from praying in church. Likewise, we do not forbid prophesying — we do not forbid women from giving messages that comfort, encourage and edify.

Cultural details and timeless principles

Paul dealt with a similar subject when he wrote to Timothy. He urged that prayers be made for everyone (1 Timothy 2:1). He gave instructions for how men should pray (verse 8 uses the Greek word *anēr,* meaning males, rather than the generic word *anthrōpos,* meaning humans). "I want men everywhere to lift up holy hands in prayer, without anger or disputing."

This command contains a temporary, cultural aspect, and a timeless aspect. Christians generally conclude that the physical details (lifting hands) are not universally required today, but the attitudinal principles (without anger) are timeless and appropriate today. This distinction between physical details on one hand and attitudes on the other illustrates the way the modern church sometimes needs to analyze the instructions Paul gave the first-century church.

Starting in verse 9, Paul gave some instructions for women — first, that they "dress modestly, with decency and propriety, not with braided hair or gold or pearls or expensive clothes." Again, the principle that Paul uses — modesty and the avoidance of excess — is timeless, but the physical details he mentions are shaped by culture and are temporary.

There is nothing inherently wrong with braided hair; the Bible does not forbid braids. Likewise, the Bible does not forbid women from wearing gold on their fingers or in their hair. It does not forbid pearls. And many of the dresses that American women wear to church would be judged "expensive" in many other cultures. The concept of "expensive" is culturally determined.

Paul's instruction is essential, but the details of form he gives are based on a specific culture. The principle of modesty is valid across cultures and centuries, but the prohibition of braids, gold and pearls is not. In first-century Ephesus, these things indicated immodesty, perhaps a lack of humility. In modern America, they do not necessarily indicate immodesty.

1 Timothy 2:11-12

Paul then says, "A woman should learn in quietness and full submission. I do not permit a woman to teach or to have authority over a man; she must be silent" (verses 11-12). Why did Paul need to say this? Probably because some women in Ephesus were not learning in quietness and not learning in submissiveness. They were attempting to teach and exercise authority over men. So Paul told them to be silent when they were being taught.

Just as in the previous verses, some of what Paul wrote concerns attitudes, and some of it concerns the details of how attitudes are expressed in behavior. Paul's primary concern here seems to be the attitude of submission. Different cultures express submission in different ways. Judging by what Paul wrote here, apparently women who taught men in public were not considered submissive in first-century Ephesus — just as it was considered inappropriate for them to wear braided hair and gold.

In most nations today, however, customs are different. For example, a professor may say near the end of a lecture, "If there is any part of the lecture you do not understand, I want you to ask your questions now." A submissive student, whether male or female, would obey by asking questions in class rather than later in private. In other situations, men might recognize that a woman has more knowledge about a specific subject and ask her to teach them about it. In such a case, a submissive woman would teach the men.

Modern cultures do not expect women to be completely silent. Expectations are different today. In Bible-study discussion sessions, for example, women may ask questions, comment and interact with the leader. If a woman has access to facts that the others do not know, she may supply that information. In most cultures, this is not seen as rebellious or immodest.

In church services, too, women are not required to maintain strict silence. We do not forbid them from singing hymns and/or solos. They can be completely submissive, willing to learn, yet without being completely silent. For our services today, most men and women are expected to act in almost identical ways: singing when everyone sings, speaking when everyone speaks (saying *amen*), and listening when everyone listens.

Whatever the Ephesian situation was, we do not believe that women must be completely silent in church today. Likewise, we do not forbid women from all forms of teaching. Women teach at home; they teach children during children's church; they teach other women and they conduct training sessions that include men and women.

Women can teach men

Can women teach men? We have already seen some biblical examples of women teaching men, both in private and in public. It was not wrong for Deborah to tell men the word of the Lord. It was not wrong for Huldah to give authoritative information to the high priest. It was not wrong for Anna to publicly speak about Jesus "to all who were looking forward to the redemption of Jerusalem" (Luke 2:38). These are all forms of teaching, of conveying information.

It was not wrong for Rhoda to inform everyone that Peter was at the door (Acts 12:14). It was not wrong for women to relay commands to men (Matthew 28:10). It was not wrong for women to tell the apostles that the Lord had risen (verse 7). They were relaying spiritually significant information to the men, and Jesus wanted the men to learn from the women. It was not wrong for the Samaritan woman to tell people what Jesus had done (John 4:29). It was not wrong for Priscilla and Aquila to work together to teach Apollos (Acts 18:26). It was not wrong for Philip's daughters (Acts 21:8-9) to tell their inspired messages to men.

It is not wrong for a woman to teach her husband through her example (1 Peter 3:1-2). We also see in Scripture that is sometimes appropriate for a woman to teach with words, as well. It is not wrong for a woman to give an answer if a man asks a reason for the hope within her (verse 15). It is not wrong for a woman to prophesy edifying words during church services (1 Corinthians 11:4-16). When Paul told the Colossians to teach each other (Colossians 3:16), he did not mention any sex restrictions.

Paul is not saying that it is wrong for a woman to say anything that a man might learn something from. Nevertheless, 1 Timothy 2:12 says that he did not allow a woman to teach a man. The context is the church, and yet we have already seen that Paul allowed women to pray and prophesy in the Corinthian church. To avoid interpreting Paul in such a way as to make him contradict himself, we conclude that Paul allowed women to teach in some situations, but not others. What he wrote here was not a universal prohibition that applies to all situations and all ages.

In fact, there is no verse or biblical principle that makes any permanent restriction on what women may do in the church, and we do not make any restriction, either. A woman may serve as an elder or pastor when she is the best person for the job.

What may women do?

Every member is important part to any fully functioning church. All members are spiritually gifted and should be equipped for works of ministry. No matter what one thinks about the ordination of women, everyone can agree that there are numerous activities that women can participate in — some traditional, and some not. Traditional roles include singing and teaching children. Our tradition also includes the service roles that go with the office of deaconess: organizing socials, serving the ill, helping new mothers, etc.

An important, but underutilized, role includes the teaching of other women to help new members mature in the faith. Spiritually mature women may serve as ministers to other women. They may train other women for works of ministry. (This can be done in women's ministry, women's classes or through one-on-one mentoring.) Women may also share the gospel, either in a public forum or in a private home, for either men or women. They may answer questions from both men and women.

Women may also pray publicly in church. Many songs are actually prayers, and there is no reason to say that a woman may sing a prayer but not say one. Paul allowed women to pray and to prophesy (1 Corinthians 11:4-16). Prayer is not a function restricted to men. It is not a teaching function nor an authoritative function. A woman may also lead the congregation in songs of praise and worship as well as lead choirs.

A woman may serve as treasurer of the local church account. Women may supervise the organization of socials, telling men where to put tables and food, etc. They may supervise children's church or teen church teachers, even if some of the teachers are men. Women may also chair committee meetings, facilitating discussion and decisions. Women may facilitate small groups. A woman may serve as an usher, to help people find seats. She may count attendance. She may help collect offerings and may help distribute bread and wine at the Lord's Supper.

Just as first-century women could pray and prophesy in public, women today may speak to the church. They may give reports, read announcements, give personal testimonies, read and explain the Scriptures, officiate at communion, perform baptisms and all other pastoral tasks.

Conclusion

Women and men are of equal value to God. Jesus Christ came and died to serve and save women as well as men. But equality does not require identical roles. The same verse that says that women are equal heirs of salvation also tells men to treat women differently than they do men (1 Pet. 3:7). Just as God values women highly, the church should also value women highly.

God gives spiritual gifts for the common good, and it is through the exercise of those gifts that the church grows. Individual members also grow as they use their gifts to serve others. To help women grow spiritually, the church needs to help them use their Spirit-given gifts, to encourage them to participate in works of ministry in the church.

Let us return to one of our introductory questions: "As pastors equip the members for works of ministry, should they be training and equipping women to pastor and to teach?" The answer is yes. Many women have pastoral or shepherding skills. This does not automatically make them ordained pastors or elders, but it does mean that they have pastoral responsibilities in the church: toward other women, toward children and teens, and sometimes toward men. If a woman's gifts are in this area, she should be encouraged to pastor and teach.

A wise pastor will find a way to equip and enable women and men to use their spiritual gifts for the common good. They may be given training and allowed to minister as God gives them the ability and as Scripture allows. Pastors should strive to maximize the ministry potential of all members, each according to his or her gifts.

For more on this topic, see part 2 of this book.

Endnotes

[1] The Hebrew word *ha'adam,* which the NIV translates as "man," refers to all humanity, both men and women.

[2] Paul does not tell us why he mentions women but not men. If we want to discuss his purpose, it is necessary to speculate as to what the situation was. We are trying to use hints in the text to sketch the historical situation in which Paul would tell women to be silent, just a few chapters after indicating that they could prophesy in public. What is appropriate in

GRACE COMMUNION INTERNATIONAL

Western culture may or may not be appropriate in some other cultures.

1 Timothy 5:16 is another example of an instruction given specifically to women when the same instruction would apply to men as well: "If any believing *woman* has relatives who are widows, let her care for them. Let the church not be burdened, so that it may care for those who are truly widows." Paul mentions women here presumably because the immediate situation involved women.

DOES THE BIBLE
ALLOW WOMEN TO BE PASTORS?

Many Christians think that the Bible does not allow women to be pastors. For many people, the key verse is 1 Timothy 2:12: "I do not permit a woman to teach or to exercise authority over a man; rather, she is to remain quiet" (ESV throughout). Let's start by looking at this verse in more detail.

If we look at only this one verse, we might see that it would forbid much more than being a pastor:

- "A woman cannot teach a man." This means that women cannot be doctors, professors, or high-school teachers. The verse does not say that it is restricted to the church.
- "A woman cannot have authority over a man." This means that a woman cannot be elected to political office, or to be a manager in a store that has male employees, or to be a principal of a school that has male teachers. The verse makes no exceptions.
- "Women are to remain quiet." They cannot be entertainers, news reporters or have any role in mass media.

However, almost no one understands the verse in this way. Conservative Bible scholars, theologians and church leaders all say that the verse should not be understood in such a literal way. We need to understand why. This will involve a lesson about how we should read and apply the Bible.

Two lines of reasoning tell us that the verse does not prohibit women from all forms of teaching, authority, or speaking. The first is an examination of the context of the verse, and the situation in which it was written. The second is to see that God sometimes inspired women to speak, teach, and have authority over men.

The context of the verse

1 Timothy is an open letter from the apostle Paul to Timothy, giving him some public instructions about what Timothy should do in Ephesus (1 Timothy 1:3). Timothy would not be able to implement these instructions anywhere except in the church, so that is the focus of the letter and its instructions.

Paul is concerned about what people were teaching in Ephesus (1:3-4), and he urged that believers should pray for everyone, specifically the civil authorities (2:1-2). Paul then gives instructions about how the men should pray: "I desire then that in every place the men should pray, lifting holy hands without anger or quarreling" (2:8). What does Paul mean by "in every place"? Taken literally, it would mean that believers should travel throughout the city, to every building and open area, to pray. But we do not take those words literally.

Additionally, very few Christians believe that men must lift their hands when they pray. Paul may have *meant* for men to lift their hands, and that is what he said, but we do not take it literally. It was appropriate in his culture, but it is not necessary in ours.

Similarly, in the next verse, Paul says that "women should adorn themselves in respectable apparel, with modesty and self-control, not with braided hair and gold or pearls or costly attire" (2:9). Taken literally, the verse says that women should not wear their hair in braids, and should not wear gold. But few churches today think that women have to follow these rules. No one gets upset when these details are ignored. Although "costly" is hard to define, some of the clothing worn to churches today would probably violate what Paul writes.

Then Paul says that women should learn quietly, not teaching the men (2:11-12). But as we have just seen, we do not always take what Paul wrote literally. Therefore, when we come to verse 12, we have to choose: do we take it literally, or do we make allowance for cultural changes? How can we decide?

Some scholars say that we should continue Paul's policy because he supports his policy by referring to the biblical story of sin in the Garden of Eden: "Adam was not deceived, but the woman was deceived and became a transgressor" (2:14). It is hard to follow the logic of this. If Adam was not deceived, then he sinned deliberately, out of rebellion rather than ignorance. It is difficult to argue that men should be in charge because the first man was a deliberate rebel. It seems that some people are trying to explain verse 12 by appealing to a verse that is even more difficult to understand.

Verse 15 is also puzzling, since it says that women can "be saved through childbearing," which contradicts verses that say that salvation comes only through Christ. These puzzling verses tell us that we don't understand the passage as well as we'd like to. Something was happening in the church in first-century Ephesus, and we presume that Paul's

instructions made sense to people in that historical context, but readers today are puzzled because we are missing part of the picture.

Paul's policy is clear: he did not allow women to teach in the first-century church in Ephesus. However, it is not clear that we should have the same policy today. We make allowances for changes in culture when it comes to prayer posture and women's clothing. Should we also make allowances for changes in culture when it comes to women teaching and having authority in the church?

How God has used women

One way to answer our question is to see how God has used women in the past, and we will see that God has not required women to be silent, even in a religious setting, and that he has sometimes allowed – even appointed – women to have authority over men.

An illustration of that is Deborah. "Deborah, a prophetess, the wife of Lappidoth, was judging Israel at that time. She used to sit under the palm of Deborah between Ramah and Bethel in the hill country of Ephraim, and the people of Israel came up to her for judgment" (Judges 4:4-5). She had political authority, and the people respected her decisions.

Deborah had religious authority, too – in verses 6-9 she gave the Israelite general an authoritative message from God. Chapter 5 is her victory song; her words have become part of the Bible, and men have been learning from Deborah ever since (see Judges 5:7 for evidence that the song was written by Deborah).

Some have suggested that God used Deborah because all the men were incompetent or unwilling. The Bible does not say that – it just says that God was working through Deborah as a civil judge, as a spokesperson for God, and as a worship leader for his people.

When Paul says, I do not permit a woman to have authority over a man, was he giving a permanent and timeless principle from God? Apparently not, for it seems that God does not have that policy. Paul's policy may have been appropriate for first-century Ephesus, but we have evidence in the Bible that it is *not* a statement about the way that God wants his people to work together at all times and in all places.

Most leaders of Israel were men, but it takes only one example to show that it is not a universal principle. The Bible never says that Deborah is an exception to what would otherwise be a rule – it just says that God worked through her. He is willing to put women in positions of authority.

Huldah is another example of a woman God used. In the time of King

Josiah, as workers were cleaning the Temple, they found a scroll. "Hilkiah the high priest said to Shaphan the secretary, 'I have found the Book of the Law in the house of the Lord'" (2 Kings 22:8). They took the scroll to the king, and he told them, "Go, inquire of the Lord for me, and for the people, and for all Judah, concerning the words of this book that has been found" (v. 13).

Where did they go to ask the Lord? They "went to Huldah the prophetess…and they talked with her" (v. 14). The text says nothing about this being unusual – it was apparently normal to go to a prophetess for a word from the Lord. God used a woman to give his words to the men of Israel (vv. 15-20).

If God saw anything improper or irregular about using a woman to teach men, he could have raised up a man to do his work. But he was apparently willing for a woman to serve in this way, and he was happy for this woman's words to be in Scripture, and for this example to be there for our instruction. So again we see that God does not have a permanent policy against women speaking authoritative words to men.

New Testament women

In the New Testament, we again see that most of the leaders were men, but God occasionally used women to teach men, and these again indicate that God does not require all women to be silent. This does not mean that Paul was wrong in having his policy for first-century Ephesus, but it means that Paul's policy should not be taken as a permanent rule for all churches in all places.

When Jesus was raised from the dead, he appeared first to women. "Jesus said to them, 'Do not be afraid; go and tell my brothers to go to Galilee, and there they will see me'" (Matthew 28:10). The women were not merely transferring information – they were delivering a *command* from Jesus, given to his "brothers" (apparently the apostles; see the angels' message in v. 7) – and Jesus expected these men to obey the message delivered by the women. Jesus gave the women authority to relay his instructions to the men.

Women were an important part of Paul's missionary work, too. Paul mentions two women, named Tryphaena and Tryphosa, and says they are "workers in the Lord" (Romans 12:12). In his letter to the church in Philippi, Paul says that another two women, Euodia and Syntyche, "labored side by side with me in the gospel together with Clement and the rest of my fellow workers" (Philippians 4:3). In both passages, Paul says that women were working *in the gospel,* apparently teaching. Women are able to teach Christian doctrine accurately and effectively.

The verses do not specifically say that the women were teaching men and women in public. Some modern commentators therefore say that it is permissible for women to be teachers, but not teach the church *when it is gathered as a church.*

However, this distinction between public and private teaching leads to an odd application: The commentators admit that women can be effective teachers, and that they can be spokespersons for God, but they say that it would be wrong for these women to deliver the message in church. However, we have already seen examples that show that God sometimes gives his message to a woman and wants men to learn from what she says. So, if men want to hear the message that God has given these women, then men have to go *outside* of the church to hear the word of God. The church is not allowed to have the whole counsel of God!

Women can write books, and men might learn from what women write, and men can quote from the female-written books (just as they can quote from the female-written parts of Scripture), but women are not allowed to deliver the message themselves. This is a distinction that is foreign to what Paul wrote.

When Paul listed various gifts of the Spirit, he did not designate any as restricted to men (1 Corinthians 12:4-11). The gifts of teaching, administration and leadership can be given to women as well as to men. When the Holy Spirit filled the disciples on the day of Pentecost, men and women were given the gift of prophecy, or inspired speaking (Acts 2:17).

Paul gave instructions to the church at Corinth for how men and women were to dress when they prayed and prophesied (1 Corinthians 11:4-10). Although Paul does not explicitly say that this was "in church," that is the most likely place for men and women to pray and prophesy, and the most likely place for clothing styles to be important. Paul's next instructions in this chapter are about the church participating in the Lord's Supper (vv. 17-34), with no hint that he is talking about a different location. God was apparently inspiring women to speak in public, and if their words were from God (as Paul presumes that they were), then they were words of authority.

In Corinth, Paul allowed women to pray and prophesy. In Ephesus, he had a different policy. This change in policy was most likely due to a change in the circumstances. Paul was inspired to write this prohibition as his own policy, not as a command from God, and it is a mistake for us to take it as a command for us today. God sometimes gives authority and words to women, and he expects men to listen, learn and heed.

Considering the nature of Paul's letter to Timothy, it is not surprising that Paul described a policy that was of temporary validity. It was written to help Timothy refute some heresies that were causing problems in Ephesus; its directives include cultural matters such as the posture of prayer and the way in which women might adorn themselves. Paul's instructions about widows (1 Timothy 5:3-16) is not required for the church today. The letter was written for a specific situation, and we should not assume in advance that its instructions are timeless truths.

Should women be silent?

We can now discuss one more New Testament verse that is sometimes used to restrict what women can do in church. This is also in Paul's letter to Corinth: "As in all the churches of the saints, the women should keep silent in the churches. For they are not permitted to speak, but should be in submission, as the Law also says. If there is anything they desire to learn, let them ask their husbands at home. For it is shameful for a woman to speak in church" (1 Corinthians 14:33-35).

Paul's instructions are good only for married women, because widows are unable to "ask their husbands at home." And what about women who had unbelieving husbands? We do not have the complete picture here.

In chapter 14, Paul is dealing with the somewhat chaotic Corinthian church services, and women are not the only people he tells to be silent (vv. 26-33). People were interrupting each other, and more than one person was trying to talk at a time. Paul's instructions here would be needed if (this is the most likely situation) women were being unruly and asking their husbands questions during the church service. So Paul tells them to stop talking, and ask their questions later.

Paul does not say to what (or whom) they should be submissive. The Law of Moses does not tell women to be submissive to their husbands (although that was probably assumed in their patriarchal society). However, the Law does say that people are to be submissive to the word of God. The word of God was being preached in Corinth, but the women were talking and not being submissive. (The Greek word for "speak" in these verses does not refer to public speaking in particular – it is the general word for talk, and it is in the present tense, which often denotes an ongoing activity.)

In chapter 11, Paul allowed women to pray and prophesy, presumably at a public meeting, but in chapter 14 he tells women to stop talking. Was Paul contradicting himself in the same letter? No matter what kind of literature we are reading, we normally want to read in such a way that the author is not contradicting himself. If there are other ways to understand what the person wrote, then we should prefer an interpretation that is not contradictory.

If this case, interpreters have a choice: either chapter 11 is about a limited situation, or chapter 14:33-35 is about a limited situation, or both passages are limited. Some interpreters choose the first, saying that the first part of chapter 11 is not about church, even though the last part of chapter 11 is.

We believe that the passage in chapter 14 is limited, because (at the minimum) it is applicable only to women who have husbands who believe in Jesus. Almost no one takes this passage literally – no one expects women to be *silent* during all parts of the worship service. Those who allow women to sing (for example) but not speak are allowing their own traditions to filter what Paul has written. We are being submissive to Scripture when we understand Paul to be writing about a limited situation – that of noisy, chaotic meetings – and he did not intend to make universal prohibitions on what women can do in church. If the Spirit leads a woman to prophesy, then she may do so, even if it's in church.

Conclusion

Two passages in the New Testament have traditionally been used to say that women cannot speak in the church or have authority over men, and therefore cannot be pastors. But this interpretation contradicts other scriptures that show that God sometimes places women in positions of authority over men, and gives them authoritative words. Some modern scholars try to maintain the traditional interpretation by suggesting a distinction between what women can do in church and what women can do outside of church, but this leads to the improbable idea that the church cannot include all of God's gifts.

We believe that the verses of restriction were written for specific situations, and should not be used as mandatory for all churches in all times and places. Rather, if God gives a woman abilities in speaking and leadership, then those gifts may be used in the church and if the most spiritually gifted woman in the church is a woman, then she may be a pastor, and speak and teach with authority.

PART 2
OUR EXEGETICAL STUDY

PREFACE

When we announced that our denomination would be formally considering the role of women in the church, we invited members and pastors to send us their research. As we expected on this controversial issue, we received a variety of responses. Some responses were well thought out; others gave opinions without any particular support.

Members of our doctrinal team read these papers, consulted numerous books and journal articles, and discussed this issue for almost two years, eventually distilling their thoughts in this series of studies. These studies are a committee product, and since not every member of the doctrinal team sees this issue in exactly the same light, it has been necessary for us to take a cautious approach with the evidence.

The question is sometimes phrased as "women in ministry," but we should note that we have always had women in ministry. That is, we have always had women who served in the church, in a variety of roles, and we've had women who were leaders of groups within the church (although their role as leader was not always acknowledged with a specific title). The question before us is whether women can be ordained as elders. A related question would be whether women can serve in leadership offices that are generally reserved for elders, such as senior pastor, superintendent, etc.

This is not simply an academic question. In some of our smaller congregations, even before this study began, women were already serving in roles of spiritual leadership. As we learned more about spiritual gifts and lay ministries, we also observed that gifts in areas of spiritual service, such as worship, biblical studies, public speaking, and pastoral care, are not limited to men. In some cases, women were serving on congregational leadership teams, not because of any push for feminine representation, but because the congregation believed, and the district superintendent agreed, that these particular women had spiritual maturity and belonged on the pastoral leadership team.

Before we entered this study, some members of our doctrinal team felt that these women could be ordained as elders; other members believed that the Scriptures forbid the ordination of women as elders, and some were undecided. Our goal was to understand what the *Bible* says to us about this subject.

Each chapter of this book originated as a distinct study. One member of the doctrinal team wrote a draft, and it was then circulated to all members of the doctrinal team. After their edits were incorporated, the draft was sent to all our national leaders and district superintendents. After their input and edits, the revised paper was sent to all of our pastors by email. It was then revised again, based on their input, and published for all our members to read. We published approximately one study every two months, as we worked through the questions in a systematic way. Most of this work was done in 2005-2006.

We believe it is just as important for members to see *how* we reach our conclusion, as it is to read the final decision. It is my prayer that we will all learn from the process, and be filled "with the knowledge of his will through all the wisdom and understanding that the Spirit gives, so that [we] may live a life worthy of the Lord and please him in every way: bearing fruit in every good work, growing in the knowledge of God" (Colossians 1:9-10).

Joseph Tkach

Editor's note: Joseph Tkach was the president of Grace Communion International; he retired from that role in 2018 and is now the chairman of the board. The default translation for our study was originally the 1984 version of the New International Version. We have updated the quotes to be from the 2016 version of the English Standard Version, which is a fairly literal translation.

WOMEN IN CHURCH LEADERSHIP:
AN INTRODUCTION TO THE QUESTION

Our denominational *Statement of Beliefs* does not say anything about women in church leadership. However, it does say that the Bible is "infallible in all matters of faith and salvation." It is the basis for Christian life and church life. Our question, then, is what the Bible says about women's role in the church. Our starting point, and the final authority, is Scripture.

Our *Statement of Beliefs* also says that we are willing to grow in knowledge, willing to respond to God's guidance. We recognize that we do not always understand Scripture perfectly. Some parts of Scripture are difficult to understand. Others parts are easy to understand but difficult to apply.

Scripture often calls on us to resist trends within society; at other times it encourages us follow cultural customs. For example, Scripture includes the following command: "Greet one another with a holy kiss" (Romans 16:16; 1 Peter 5:14). Although Christians in some cultures have no problems with this command, people in America generally do, and we have long considered this command to be based in culture and not a timeless truth. We encourage members to implement the *principle* of the command, without obeying it literally, even though Paul probably never thought the day would come when a kiss would be objectionable rather than friendly.

When Peter and Paul wrote their commands for a holy kiss, they were influenced by their culture. When Paul told slaves to obey their masters (Ephesians 6:1), he was accommodating himself to culture. He was not advocating slavery itself. There is no question that *some* of his commands apply only to his culture. Others just as clearly are timeless, and there are a few in the middle that are debatable.

So, the question is, how do we tell when a biblical command is based on culture and in need of modification for the different cultures we live in today? How do we tell when a command is timeless? When Paul writes that he does not permit a woman to teach or have authority over men (1 Timothy 2:12), is he just expressing his own opinion (after all, he states it as what *he* does, and not as a command), or should we treat his policy as a permanent rule for the church?

How do we decide what God's will is? It is a question not just of what Scripture says, but *what it means for us today*. Should we apply it literally? Or should we (as with Romans 16:16) analyze what principle lay behind Paul's words, and follow that? Let us look at an example of a conflict between Scripture and culture. Although this example is *not* an exact prototype for the issue of women in the church, it does help illustrate the question.

Comparison with slavery

In 1 Timothy 6:1-2, Paul tells Christian slaves to respect their Christian masters, and he never commands the masters to free their slaves. Is Paul therefore supporting slavery, as many 19th-century Americans argued? Or was he simply going along with culture, so the gospel would not be seen as an enemy of society—"so that the name of God and the teaching may not be reviled"?

Slavery had a few positive functions in ancient society, but Paul could have challenged slavery itself as demeaning, as contrary to the love that should characterize God's people, and as a violation of the created order. But he did not; neither did he challenge the political system of Rome, the frequent brutality of the army, or unfair methods by which taxes were collected.

Nevertheless, the gospel challenges culture. It challenges us to treat poor people with respect, not to favor the rich (James 2:1-7). The gospel challenged Jews to treat Gentiles as equals; it challenged Philemon to treat his slave Onesimus "as a beloved brother" (Philemon 16). If masters treated their slaves as family members, then slavery would soon disappear—and in this way the gospel challenged the attitudes that allowed slavery to exist. The gospel sowed the seeds that undermined the injustice of slavery—but the Bible does not attack slavery directly.

Some people today say that the gospel sows the seeds that undermine gender restrictions, too. Galatians 3:28 says, "There is neither Jew nor Greek, there is neither slave nor free, there is no male and female, for you are all one in Christ Jesus." This verse is about equality in salvation, but does it sow the seeds for leadership equality within the church, too? Is it possible for people to have equal importance within the church without having the same roles? The church no longer treats Jews and Gentiles differently; we denounce as unjust the existence of slavery; so should we also stop differentiating between men and women when it comes to leadership in the church?

In other words, when Paul said that women should be silent in the churches, was he simply going along with his culture, just as he went along with slavery, knowing that the gospel would eventually correct the problem? Did he expect his comments in Gal. 3:28 to eventually counteract his comments in 1 Tim. 2:12? Or was he so close to his culture that he never really thought about it, just as he probably assumed that a holy kiss would always be fitting and appropriate? Or was Paul giving a policy that provides permanent guidance for the church?

History

The church has not always been on the right side of cultural questions. When it came to slavery, some Christian churches were in the forefront of the move for emancipation. But in the 20th century, many American churches resisted the cultural move for social equality for the descendants of those slaves. Sometimes culture is right, sometimes it is not.

Culture sometimes *asks* ethical questions, but for Christians, culture cannot answer them. Rather, we look to Scripture as the foundation for what we do. Even if some cultures in the 1930s said that we should treat Jews as subhuman, the gospel says that Christians should have resisted the cultural trend, even though some church bodies went along with it. But when it comes to the authority of women in the church, it seems that the church is *responding* to culture rather than being an initiating force.

We believe that the scriptural record as it pertains to women in roles of leadership requires careful study and a detailed response to the question of the ordination of women as elders.

Dealing with differences

The issue *does* require careful study. When it comes to a holy kiss, we can't just say, "The Bible says it, I believe it, that settles it." That approach may sound humble, but it is simplistic and arrogant, because it assumes that "I" have the only accurate understanding of what Scripture teaches.

We all come to Scripture with some assumptions from our own culture. Some of us come from a culture where women are expected to submit to men in particularly restrictive ways; others of us come from a culture that encourages women to think for themselves and to take leadership roles. Some cultures today are similar to ancient cultures in their attitudes about women; others are quite different. Some people are afraid that any change in gender roles will cause more social chaos; others feel that changes are necessary. Each of us needs to be aware of the bias we bring to the Bible and, through discussion with one another, see how our particular bias might be influencing our understanding. In that way we let the Bible speak to our biases.

Prayer is an indispensable part of the process—we want to discern God's will, rather than assuming that we have already got it right. We want to understand why some sincere Christians come to different conclusions on this issue, and then we want to decide which explanation seems more likely to be what God intended when he inspired the Scriptures. We want the Holy Spirit to guide us into all truth (John 16:13)—and that means that we don't have it all yet. No one does.

Since no one group has a perfect understanding of all the issues, there are some differences of opinion on biblical interpretation, even when there is agreement on the most basic doctrines of the faith. Some Christians think that the Bible instructs women to be completely silent in church; others do not, even when those holding each view have an equal belief in the authority and accuracy of the Bible. Some Bible-believing Christians believe that women must wear a covering on their head when in church; others do not. The question we have is not whether to believe the Bible; it is how to understand what the Bible is teaching. Are the biblical restrictions on women cultural, like the holy kiss, or are they permanent, like the prohibition on adultery?

Since conservative Christians are divided on this issue, we would be naïve to think that we will achieve unanimous agreement. No matter what conclusion we come to, *some* members will think we have not weighed the evidence fairly. What should they do then? Is this issue important enough for them to leave the church? We don't think so. Our unity depends on Christ, not on complete agreement on every point of doctrine.

There are many doctrines that are essential to Christian faith—for example, the church must teach that there is only one God, and that we are saved by grace through faith in Jesus Christ. Yet there are many other doctrines that are not essential to our faith, but are practical guidelines or policies for our physical life, and these may differ from culture to culture, or from one time in history to another. We *want* to get them right, but we must also understand they are not essential to what it means to be a Christian. We believe that eldership of women is one of those doctrines. It is a policy matter. People do not need to leave the church if they think we are wrong about the millennium, nor do they need to leave if they think we are wrong about women's role in the church.

No matter who our congregational elders are, they are not perfect, and we all have to respect them anyway. We have to weigh what they say, accept the true and overlook minor mistakes. That will be the case whether an elder *is or is not* a woman. We might like to be part of a church with all the guaranteed correct answers, but such a church does not exist. Spiritual growth does not depend on being in a perfect church. Rather, we must learn to do the best we can in the circumstances we are in, trusting in Christ to cover us with his righteousness.

Some people will be disappointed if we permit women to be elders; others will be equally disappointed if we do not. We do not know how many hold one opinion, or how many the other—for our task, it does not matter. Our job is to discern what God wants us to do, and we will therefore concentrate on prayerful study. We ask you to study the issue along with us, not just react to the conclusion. We will all learn, and as we share the strengths and weaknesses of various arguments, we hope the great majority of us will agree on the results.

THE NATURE OF LEADERSHIP
IN THE CHURCH

As we examine what the Bible says about whether women may serve as elders, we need to clarify what the office of elder entails. One of the key scriptures under discussion is 1 Tim. 2:12: "I do not permit a woman to teach or to exercise authority over a man; rather, she is to remain quiet." One of the key words in this verse is "authority." What authority is involved in the office of elder? Is this the sort of authority that Paul did not allow women to have? We will address the meaning of this verse in more detail in a future study, but first we want to explore what the Bible says about church leadership and authority in general. This study discusses valid principles of Christian leadership no matter who the leaders may be.

Not like the Gentiles

Jesus told his disciples, "The kings of the Gentiles exercise lordship over them, and those in authority over them are called benefactors. But not so with you. Rather, let the greatest among you become as the youngest, and the leader as one who serves" (Luke 22:25-26).

In the church, authority must be viewed in a different way than it is in the world of government and business. Jesus did not say that it was wrong to lead, but that leaders should *serve others* rather than expecting others to serve them. They are to be motivated by love, not selfishness. They are to be humble, rather than giving themselves important-sounding titles. There is nothing wrong with *being* a benefactor, but it is wrong to call attention to how "good" you are.

Those who seek authority more than they seek to serve, no matter whether they are men or women, are not viewing church leadership in the right way. Church leadership is not a place to assert the importance of a particular person, ethnic group, personality type, or gender. Leadership roles are a means of service, not a means of venerating the leaders or the groups to which they belong.

Leaders in the church do have authority, and Christians are told to obey them, but that authority does not rest in themselves—they are servants "who will have to give an account" to God (Heb. 13:17). Their authority is authentic only as it reflects God as he has revealed himself in Jesus

89

Christ as described in Scripture. God wants leaders to use their authority to serve. Paul twice wrote that the Lord gave him authority for building people up (2 Cor. 10:8; 13:10). That is the purpose of authority in the church. Leaders are to build up the church, edify the believers, and help them grow spiritually.

Responsibility to teach

Not every leader is a pastor, but for the purposes of this study, let us look at how Ephesians describes the role of a pastor (ESV: "shepherds"; footnote "pastors.") God gave pastors to the church "to equip the saints for the work of ministry, for building up the body of Christ" (Eph. 4:12). Pastors serve by preparing believers for service and helping them work together, so that the church grows (verse 16). This involves doctrinal instruction (verses 13-14). Teaching is one of the main responsibilities of leaders who are pastors and teachers. This is suggested not just in Ephesians 4, but also by the following points:

- Ephesians is the only book in the Bible to use the word "pastor" to describe church leaders; in other places the primary leaders of congregations are called elders and overseers—apparently two terms for the same role. The ability to teach is part of the description of an elder or overseer (1 Tim. 3:2; 2 Tim. 2:24; Titus 1:9), but it is not part of the description of a deacon, suggesting that the primary responsibility for teaching falls to elders and overseers.
- The apostles decided that it was more important for the apostles to attend to "the ministry of the word" than to supervise the distribution of food (Acts 6:4). They viewed teaching and preaching as their primary role, and this focus on "the word" is apparently appropriate for elders as well.
- Paul told Timothy to devote himself to teaching Scripture (1 Tim. 4:13).

Elders should not teach on their own authority—they should "preach the Word" (2 Tim. 4:2)—teaching truth in agreement with the gospel of Jesus Christ and the Scriptures. Rhetorical skill or volume cannot tell us if a message is inspired. Rather, it is evaluated by whether it is true to the Bible, and by whether it leads people to faith in Christ. An elder "must hold firm to the trustworthy word as taught, so that he may be able to give instruction in sound doctrine and also to rebuke those who contradict it" (Titus 1:9). "You must teach what is in accord with sound doctrine" (Titus

2:1). Members are to weigh carefully what is said, deciding whether it is true to the gospel (1 Cor. 14:29; 1 John 4:1).

The authority of an elder is a derivative authority, as authorized by God. Leadership therefore begins with submission to God's authority. When elders teach false doctrines or attempt to promote themselves, they are misusing the authority of their role. Their authority lies largely in the truth and their ability to teach it. That is the way in which members will be built up, being helped to become more like Christ.

Administrative authority

Sometimes, however, administrative authority is necessary. Since elders are to "care for God's church" (1 Tim. 3:5), the elders usually have a supervisory role in the administrative matters of the church. Paul was involved in administrative matters when he oversaw the collection of resources to aid another part of the body of Christ (1 Cor. 16:1-4). Paul told the Corinthians that if he could not correct them through his letter, then he would have to come in person and "be severe in my use of the authority" (2 Cor. 13:10). He had authority, and he had already judged and instructed the Corinthians to expel one particularly blatant sinner (1 Cor. 5:3-5). In another use of authority, he warned them not to associate with people who claimed to believe but persisted in certain sins (verse 11). He gave similar instructions in Rom. 16:17 and 2 Thess. 3:6, 14-15.

Paul told Titus to "exhort and rebuke with all authority" (Titus 2:15). If people do not listen to sound doctrine, they must be rebuked (Titus 1:13). False teachers "must be silenced" (Titus 1:11). For practical purposes, this must be done by *elders*—we do not invite heretics to present their case before the entire congregation (see 2 John 10) to see whether they should be expelled, just as we do not invite wolves into the flock to see whether they might devour anyone.

When false ideas are circulating, leaders need to teach the truth and refute what is false, and do what they can to prevent heresy from being taught. Although biblical truth informs the judgment, elders must use their own judgment to decide whether the sins or heresies are sufficiently grievous to warrant this type of discipline, when repentance is genuine and reinstatement is appropriate, what level of confidentiality or announcement is necessary, etc. This administrative authority is generally given to elders, although it is often appropriate for elders to consult with peers and superiors on such decisions.

Summary

Elders are to…

1) train members for works of service, coordinate their work, and promote unity,
2) devote themselves to prayer and Scripture,
3) preach the gospel of grace,
4) defend the church against heretics, false believers, and divisive people, and
5) supervises administrative functions of the congregation.
6) anoint the sick (James 5:14).

Elders also perform baptisms, officiate at weddings and funerals, and lead communion services, although the Bible does not restrict these functions to elders. The Bible does not mandate, although practical considerations usually do, that the elders be formally appointed. This is the function of ordination.

Peter gave this instruction to elders: "Shepherd the flock of God that is among you, exercising oversight, not under compulsion, but willingly, as God would have you; not for shameful gain, but eagerly; not domineering over those in your charge, but being examples to the flock" (1 Pet 5:2-3). Elders are not to use their position for their own benefit, but to help others.

God will judge church elders on how well they serve in these areas of responsibility (Heb. 13:17), and he gives them authority to serve in these ways. He also gives spiritual gifts that help them lead.

Pastoral gifts

There are many types of spiritual gifts, Paul told the Corinthians, but they are all given "for the common good" (1 Cor. 12:7). Although the gifts are different, they "empowered by one and the same Spirit, who apportions to each one individually as he wills" (verse 11). God distributes these abilities so that we might grow by helping one another.

Paul explained,

Having gifts that differ according to the grace given to us, let us use them: if prophecy, in proportion to our faith; if service, in our serving; the one who teaches, in his teaching; the one who exhorts, in his exhortation; the one who contributes, in generosity; the one who leads, with zeal; the one who does acts of mercy, with cheerfulness. (Rom. 12:6-8)

Elders would find any of these gifts useful, but not all elders are equally gifted in each area. Some are gifted speakers, some are helpful with physical needs, some are good at explaining doctrine; some are very motivating; some are very generous with their time and other resources; some are great personnel coordinators; and some are good at hospital visitation. Elders generally start with some of these skills, and grow in the others as they gain experience. No matter what gifts they have, they are to use them to help others (1 Peter 4:10-11).

When applied to elders these gifts can be deemed as "pastoral" gifts, but the presence of these "pastoral" gifts does not automatically qualify a person to be an elder—particularly when others in the congregation are even more gifted. Pastoral gifts may be used in a variety of roles, such as in children's ministry, lay counseling, or in leading a small group. An elder should be gifted by the Spirit, and responsive to the Spirit in using those gifts. As a practical matter, for spiritual leadership to be effective, the congregation should agree 1) that the person is gifted for pastoral service, and 2) that the person is submissive to the Spirit.

Qualifications

What skills do elders need? Paul gave some guidelines about the people to be appointed:

> An overseer must be above reproach, the husband of one wife, sober-minded, self-controlled, respectable, hospitable, able to teach, not a drunkard, not violent but gentle, not quarrelsome, not a lover of money. He must manage his own household well, with all dignity keeping his children submissive, for if someone does not know how to manage his own household, how will he care for God's church? He must not be a recent convert, or he may become puffed up with conceit and fall into the condemnation of the devil. Moreover, he must be well thought of by outsiders, so that he may not fall into disgrace, into a snare of the devil. (1 Tim. 3:2-7).

This is an idealized portrait, as we can see by a comparison with the similar list in Titus 1:6-9. Since Timothy was working in an older church, Paul said that an elder must not be a recent convert; but he did not specify this for Titus, since the churches Titus was working with were new. Paul himself had appointed elders in new churches (Acts 14:23), which means that he appointed new converts, because those were the only people who were available. Therefore, when Paul told Timothy that an elder must not be a new Christian, he was not creating a rigid requirement for all future churches. This shows that the items in his list should be seen as important guidelines, but not as absolute requirements. For example, elders who have already served well would not be automatically disqualified by a disobedient college-age child. All the factors should be taken into consideration.

We should also comment on what it means to be "the husband of one wife." This is not talking about polygamy (which was rare). Nor does it disqualify single men and remarried widowers, although a literal reading would disqualify both. The Greek term (literally, "a one-woman man") means a man who is faithful to his wife rather than having a mistress on the side (which was common in Greco-Roman society). There was no stigma attached to a widower who remarried, nor to a man who was legally divorced and remarried. What was important for Paul is that the elder, if married, would be faithful to the woman he was married to.[1]

Practical considerations

Ordination as practiced by most churches today serves biblical goals, for it involves a formal ceremony in which people are appointed as congregational leaders, and the congregation asks God to help those leaders as they serve the congregation in the work of God. A formal ordination acknowledges that 1) leaders are not self-appointed, and 2) other Christians agree that these people are gifted and called by God to a leadership/service role. Formal appointment helps a person not only lead within the congregation but also represent the congregation in the community.

If a person claims to be gifted and called to the role of elder, but the congregation does not look to that person for leadership, it is likely that the person has misunderstood the call. Since the *fact* of service is more important than the title that is given, such a person should serve in other

---

[1] Further information on this is in Craig Keener, *And Marries Another: Divorce and Remarriage in the Teaching of the New Testament* (Hendrickson, 1991), chapter 7: "Can Ministers Be Remarried?—1 Timothy 3:2"; see also the discussion in William Mounce, *Pastoral Epistles* (Word Biblical Commentary 46; Nelson: 2000), pp. 170-173.

ways, and perhaps in time the person or the congregation will come to see the situation differently. Not everyone who *claims* to have pastoral gifts is really called to be a pastor.

The selection of elders is a practical matter as well as a spiritual one, and it is affected by social expectations, since leadership itself is a social phenomenon dealing with the functioning of a group of people. Paul wrote that an elder should have a good reputation even among unbelievers. Consequently, cultural matters *must* be considered, and it would be a mistake to appoint someone who was not respected in the particular culture, and it would be a mistake to appoint anyone who was unable to win the respect of the congregation.

Conclusion

This study is not a complete "theology of church leadership." It is designed to survey some of the more important points so that we know what is being discussed when we discuss whether the Bible teaches that women may serve in the office of elder within the church. This overview does bring out certain points for our study:

- We should not ordain anyone on the basis of gender alone. The person has to have the appropriate spiritual gifts, and the congregation must accept the person's leadership.
- Since a church leader must be under the authority of Scripture, we cannot ordain women as elders if Scripture does not allow women to serve in that role. At the same time, we cannot exclude women from serving as elders if Scripture does not prohibit it.
- Since teaching is vital to the role of an elder, we should not ordain people who cannot effectively communicate spiritual principles in a way that edifies the listeners.
- We should not ordain people who are spiritually immature, self-seeking, theologically unbalanced, notoriously disobedient, or abusive with authority.
- We should not ordain people who have a poor reputation in the community.

In subsequent chapters, we will look more closely at what Scripture says about the role of women in church leadership. Our next study will examine Genesis 1-3.

MEN AND WOMEN IN GENESIS 1-3

Does the Bible require men and women to have different roles in the church? Although the Old Testament does not provide the final answer for the question, proponents and opponents of females as elders often look to the Old Testament for evidence.

When Jesus analyzed the question of divorce for his first-century Jewish audience, he cited the creation account in Genesis to show how it was "from the beginning" (Matt. 19:4-5). Since Genesis tells us about the creation of male and female, the account may tell us something about God's original design for male and female roles. We might see what the ideal was before sin distorted the relationship between the sexes. However, Genesis does not say as much as we might like, and perhaps both opponents and proponents of women's ordination have claimed too much for what it says.

Genesis 1

In the beginning, God made humanity male and female, said Jesus (Matt. 19:4). This creation set a pattern for marriage, and it may also set a pattern for relationships between male and female.[1]

We will examine what Genesis says verse by verse. The initial pattern is given in Genesis 1:26-27:

> Then God said, "Let us make man[2] in our image, after our likeness. And let them have dominion over the fish of the sea and

---

[1] The relationship between male and female in marriage is not automatically determinative for roles within the church. These spheres are related, but not identical. Although the focus of our study is roles within the church, we will look at the Old Testament passages to provide a background for New Testament passages, with the understanding that Old Testament society and worship is not necessarily a model for what the church should do today. Further, our conclusions about male-female relations within the church may or may not apply to relationships within marriages.

[2] The ESV footnote says, "The Hebrew word for man (*adam*) is the generic term for mankind and becomes the proper name *Adam*."

over the birds of the heavens and over the livestock and over all the earth and over every creeping thing that creeps on the earth." So God created man in his own image, in the image of God he created him; male and female he created them.

There is a plural use of the word "man." The Hebrew moves without comment from the singular word "man" ('adam) to the plural pronoun *them*, and explains that "man" means both male and female. "Humanity" is a better translation, for in this verse the word 'adam includes all humans, male and female alike. Genesis 5:2 also shows that the word 'adam includes male and female.

Some scholars think it is significant that God names the human race by one sex, "man."[3] In response, we note that 'adam does not mean "male"; as noted above, it can also be used for females. Perhaps the best translation is "human," and it is reasonable for God to name the first person "Human" without implying that all subsequent *males* represent the human race any more than females do. The fact that the same Hebrew word was used for the first male as for all humanity could be *consistent* with male authority, but if male authority is God's design, that should be demonstrated by more than a mere implication from the choice of terms.

Male and female alike are made in God's image. Genesis 9:6 says, "Whoever sheds the blood of man ['adam], by man shall his blood be shed; for in the image of God has God made man ['adam]." The meaning is not man as *male*, but "man" as male and female. The NRSV accurately renders the verse in this way: "Whoever sheds the blood of a human, by a human shall that person's blood be shed; for in his own image God made humankind." Although people might argue about what "the image of God" means, it is generally agreed among conservative and liberal scholars alike that men and women alike are made in the image of God. Most conservatives agree with Ortland when he says, "Both male and female

---

[3] Raymond C. Ortland, "Male-Female Equality and Male Headship: Genesis 1-3," pages 95-112 in *Recovering Biblical Manhood and Womanhood: A Response to Evangelical Feminism* (edited by John Piper and Wayne Grudem; Wheaton: Crossway, 1991), pages 97, 480. This book is the most thorough defense of the conservative position.

display the glory of God's image with equal brilliance."[4]

Although men and women are made in the image of God, Paul writes, "A man [*anēr*, meaning a male] ought not to cover his head, since he is the image and glory of God; but the woman is the glory of man" (1 Cor. 11:7). We will discuss this passage in more detail in a later study, but let us note for now the way that Paul reasons. He says that a woman should cover her head when she is prophesying (verse 6), but a man should not, for *the man* is the image and glory of God. The logic *might* imply that women are not the image and glory of God—but almost all scholars *reject* the conclusion that women are not made in the image of God.

Thomas Schreiner, a conservative, says, "Paul is not denying that women are created in God's image, for he is referring to the creation accounts here and was well aware that Genesis teaches that both men and women are created in God's image."[5] Schreiner focuses on the word *glory,* but he does not discuss why Paul also includes the word *image.* Gordon D. Fee similarly concludes that "Paul's own interest, however, is finally not in man as being God's image, but in his being God's glory. That is Paul's own reflection on the creation of man, and it is the word that finally serves as the means of contrast between man and woman."[6] C.K. Barrett says, "Paul values the term image only as leading to the term glory."[7]

The broad consensus is that Genesis teaches that women are made in the image of God, and it is a mistake to interpret Paul as contradicting that conclusion. This verse shows that it is a mistake to use Paul's arguments (designed for a different situation) to interpret Genesis. When Paul uses Genesis as a supporting rationale, he may be giving only a narrow slice of the situation, only as it applies to his immediate concern, rather than giving

---

[4] Ortland, 97. On page 98, Ortland speaks for the conservative consensus when he writes, "Who…is teaching that men only bear God's image? No contributor to this volume will be found saying that."

[5] Thomas R. Schreiner, "Head Coverings, Prophecies and the Trinity: 1 Corinthians 11:2-16," pages 124-39 in Piper and Grudem; here, pages 132-133.

[6] Gordon D. Fee, *The First Epistle to the Corinthians* (New International Commentary on the New Testament; Grand Rapids: Eerdmans, 1987), 515.

[7] C.K. Barrett, *The First Epistle to the Corinthians* (Black's New Testament Commentary; London: A&C Black, 1971), 252.

a complete statement on what Genesis teaches. Paul uses Genesis to support his argument, but it is hazardous for us to make inferences from his argument to interpret Genesis. When we read between the lines, we may be reading more into it than Paul intended. We will see this illustrated again later in this study.

As our last comment on Genesis 1:26, we note that male and female alike were assigned to rule over the earth and its animals; although God made male and female distinct and different from one another, this chapter says nothing about male and female having different roles. Verses 28-29 say:

> God blessed them. And God said to them, "Be fruitful and multiply and fill the earth and subdue it, and have dominion over the fish of the sea and over the birds of the heavens and over every living thing that moves on the earth." And God said, "Behold, I have given you every plant yielding seed that is on the face of all the earth, and every tree with seed in its fruit. You shall have them for food.

The instructions are given equally to male and female—both were given the command to reproduce and rule. Both were allowed to eat from every fruit-bearing tree.

Genesis 2

The second chapter focuses on the creation of human beings—it begins with a barren land, without rain, plants or humans (verse 5). So God "formed the man [*ha'adam,* the human one] of dust from the ground [*ha'adamah,* a feminine word]" (verse 6). God planted a garden, made trees grow in it, and put the man there to take care of the garden (verses 8-9, 15). Then God warned him not to eat from one particular tree (verse 16).

The LORD God said, "It is not good that the man should be alone; I will make him a helper fit for him" (verse 18). In contrast to all other creation being "good," Scripture highlights that it was *not* good for the man to be by himself. God wants humans to be social and sexual.

Does "suitable helper" imply that the woman was made as a *servant* to the man? No, the Hebrew word "helper" is more commonly used for *God* as a helper of humans (e.g., Ex. 18:4)—the word does not presume lesser authority. The woman could "help" the man by working as his equal just as much as by working subordinately to him. The point being made in

Genesis is simply that the woman is "suitable" for the man—that is, she is the same kind of being. Gordon J. Wenham writes, "The compound prepositional phrase 'matching him,' [*kenegdo*] literally, 'like opposite him,' is found only here. It seems to express the notion of complementarity rather than identity. As Delitsch (1:140) observes, if identity were meant, the more natural phrase would be 'like him.'"[8]

Is it significant that Eve was made "for" the man? The Hebrew preposition does not presume lesser authority—the point being made in Genesis is that the man was incomplete without the woman. This verse says nothing about authority. Paul likewise notes that the woman was made *for* the man (1 Cor. 11:9), but then concludes that men and women are mutually dependent (verse 11)—the word "for" does not imply inferiority or hierarchy.

Genesis explains that God had created animals, and he "brought them to the man to see what he would call them" (verse 19). So the first human named the animals (verse 20). But no "suitable helper" was found for the solitary human. None of the animals was an appropriate partner. God had known this ahead of time, but the exercise of naming the animals helped the first human be aware 1) that he was not like any other animal, and 2) that he (unlike the animals previously created) did not have a partner.

Once the man was aware of his need, God put him to sleep, took one of his ribs, and from it fashioned a woman (verses 21-22).[9] Although the first human was made from the ground (just like the animals were—v. 19), the woman had a *human* origin, apparently to emphasize her organic unity with the man. God brought the woman to the man, and the man said, "This at last is bone of my bones and flesh of my flesh; she shall be called Woman [*'ishshah*], because she was taken out of Man [*'iysh*]" (verse 23). This poetic expression—the first recorded words of any human—are an

---

[8] Gordon J. Wenham, *Genesis 1-15* (Word Biblical Commentary 1; Waco: Word, 1987), 68.

[9] Many interpreters have offered suggestions about the symbolism implied in the rib. For example, Matthew Henry wrote, "Woman is not made of a man's head to climb over him, she is not made of his feet to be trampled on, but from his rib to be by his side as an equal, under his arm to be protected and close to his heart to be loved." No matter how appealing this symbolism is, it cannot be proven that this was the original intent.

100

expression of joy at discovering the suitable partner that the man needed. The two people, although different, were the same flesh.

The words are an expression of similarity, not of hierarchy. However, it is often noted that the man *named* the woman, just as he had earlier named the animals, and the simple act of giving a name is supposedly an indicator of authority.[10] But this is not necessarily so.[11] Hagar gave God a name: "She called the name of the Lord who spoke to her, 'You are a God of seeing'"—a name that God apparently accepted, for it is in Scripture (Gen. 16:13). Naming does not always indicate authority.[12] In the story about naming the animals, the literary context has nothing to do with authority over the animals — it is about the creation of woman and Adam's appreciation of her. When Adam named the woman, the point being emphasized in the text is how *similar* to Adam she was.

The Bible then concludes from the essential similarity of man and woman: "Therefore a man shall leave his father and his mother and hold fast to his wife, and they shall become one flesh" (Gen. 2:24). Curiously, it is the man who is said to leave—this is not said (though it is probably assumed[13]) for the woman. The couple become a new family, not under the authority of the man's father and mother. This indicates that, no matter where they live, the man's primary responsibility is to his wife, not his parents, and similarly, the woman's primary responsibility is to her husband, not her parents. But the verse presumes nothing about the authority of one person over another.

---

[10] "Though they are equal in nature, that man names woman (cf. 3:20) indicates that she is expected to be subordinate to him, an important presupposition in the ensuing narrative" (Wenham, 70). See also Schreiner, 207.

[11] Linda Belleville writes, "Naming in antiquity was a way of memorializing an event or capturing a distinctive attribute. It was not an act of control or power" (chapter 2 in *Two Views on Women in Ministry* (ed. James R. Beck and Craig L. Blomberg [Counterpoints; Grand Rapids: Zondervan], p. 143).

[12] Leah and Rachel named the sons of Jacob; only Benjamin was named by Jacob (Gen. 29-30; 35:18). Moses and Samuel were also named by women (Ex. 2:10; 1 Sam. 1:20).

[13] "Israelite marriage was usually patrilocal, that is, the man continued to live in or near his parents' home" (Wenham, 70). Psalm 45:10 advises the woman to leave her parents.

Genesis 2 (unlike Genesis 1) makes distinctions between male and female. The male was made first, given a job in the garden, warned about the forbidden fruit, told to name the animals, and he responds with joy to his God-given companion. The woman does not do anything in this chapter, nor is anything said about why one was made before the other. Richard Davidson writes, "The movement in Genesis 2…is not from superior to inferior, but from incompleteness to completeness."[14]

However, the next chapter shows that the woman was aware of the forbidden fruit—the silence of chapter 2 does not mean that she was not told. Genesis does not tell us who told her about it, whether it was God or Adam. *Who* told her apparently did not matter. Likewise, we cannot put much significance on the silence of chapter 2 on other issues.

The man was created first, and it is often concluded from this that God thereby gave him authority over the woman.[15] However, this should not be assumed. For example, plants do not have authority over animals, and animals do not rule humans. Throughout Genesis, we see that the firstborn does not always rule over the younger siblings. Beck and Blomberg write, "One wonders if a hypothetical 'first-time' reader of Genesis 1-3, even in the ancient Jewish world, would have picked up any of the six indications of female subordination [such as priority of the male] that Schreiner discusses."[16] This comment suggests that a definitive answer must come from the New Testament; this discussion of Genesis is only a preliminary study. For a conclusion, we need other biblical evidence, and the writings of Paul are relevant for this point.

Paul's comments on creation

In 1 Corinthians 11, Paul says that a woman should cover her head when prophesying, but a man should not, for "woman is the glory of man. For man [*anēr*] was not made from woman, but woman from man. Neither

---

[14] Richard M. Davidson, "Headship, Submission, and Equality in Scripture," pp. 259-95 in *Women in Ministry: Biblical and Historical Perspectives* (edited by Nancy Vyhmeister; Berrien Springs, MI: Andrews University Press), 261.

[15] Schreiner argues that Hebrew readers would assume the laws of primogeniture (chapter 4 in Beck and Blomberg, 203).

[16] Beck and Blomberg, "Reflections on Complementarian Essays," in *Two Views on Women in Ministry*, 312.

was man created for woman, but woman for man" (verses 7-9). There are numerous questions about the way that Paul reasons in this chapter, and a later study will discuss them in more detail. But here we can note that Paul uses the creation priority of the man in support of the *cultural* custom of women covering their heads. Paul can use the creation account to argue for a temporary custom.

Paul is saying that men and women in Corinthian society of his day may prophesy, but they must do it in slightly different ways. He is not addressing the relative authority of men and women.[17] Nor is Paul addressing the authority of what they say, but only the appearance of the person saying it. He also weakens the significance of the priority of the first man by observing that male-female relationships are transformed in the Lord: "Nevertheless, in the Lord woman is not independent of man nor man of woman; for as woman was made from man, so man is now born of woman" (verses 11-12).[18] These verses strike a note of equality in the Lord, and they remind us that although the first woman came from the first man, all subsequent men have come from women, and the argument from priority is inconclusive.

So what does this passage tell us about the meaning of Genesis 2? It means that Genesis 2 can be used to argue for a cultural custom, but it also shows us that an argument for authority based on priority has a logical weakness. The passage does not prove that men are given authority over women, for that is not Paul's purpose in this passage. Rather, he allows women to do the *same* as men, advising appropriate conformity with cultural norms.

To illustrate, we might paraphrase the logic of 1 Corinthians 11 in this

---

[17] When Paul says that "the head of woman is man" (verse 3), Paul may be referring to authority (that is a question for a later chapter), but the rest of the passage argues on the basis of honor and dishonor, not of authority. Men and women have an equal right to prophesy, and their prophecies are of equal authority; the only question in this passage is the manner in which they prophesy. That is why we say above that Paul is not addressing the authority of men and women. That is a tangential comment, not the main subject.

[18] Beck and Blomberg note that "verses 11-12 may suggest that the new creation in Christ goes beyond God's original creation. Clearly it will in the world to come" (312).

way: Women should cover their heads when prophesying because men were created first. Genesis itself does not say that, and it is not self-evident as to how Paul went from premise to conclusion; this may indicate that he was reasoning based on a practice found in his own culture.

The argument of creation priority also appears in 1 Timothy 2:13, and again, a full discussion will have to wait for another study. Verse 12 says, "I do not permit a woman to teach or to exercise authority over a man; rather, she is to remain quiet." Then verse 13 gives this rationale: "For Adam was formed first, then Eve." But as we have already seen, the priority of Adam could be used to argue for a *cultural* custom, and therefore the fact that this passage appears to argue for women's subordination does not in itself tell us whether that role was a cultural one, or a timeless, normative one.

Similarly, 1 Timothy 2 says that women should not teach or have authority over men because men were created first. Again, Genesis 1-3 does not say that, and it is possible that Paul went from premise to conclusion by an assumption of culture. Both passages *use* the creation account, but neither is an attempt to tell us what Genesis means. Both New Testament passages can be read with the understanding that the creation priority of man gives men some sort of authority over women. However, they may also be read with an assumption of equality; we will address them in more detail in later studies.

The evidence of Genesis 1 leans toward equal roles, and the evidence of Genesis 2 would *allow* for different roles. However, neither chapter directly addresses the question of authority that we might bring to them, so we must be cautious about conclusions that we draw. The evidence of Genesis 2 is tempered by the following observations:

1. Our goal in the church is not always to imitate the original, pre-Fall creation. We do not suggest that people remove their clothes, for example!
2. New Testament scriptures may override the conclusions that we draw from Genesis. Genesis 1-2 are not addressing the question of authority and we must not try to infer something from these chapters beyond what they directly say.
3. Scriptural finding relevant to gender authority may not provide a full parallel to questions about church leadership. For example, gender authority in the family structure would not necessarily carry over into the church structure.

4. The New Testament may give us additional insights, since some New Testament verses address the question of church leadership more directly.

Genesis 3

Sin enters the story in chapter 3, beginning with the crafty serpent. The serpent spoke to the woman—even though the man was with her (verse 6). Why did the serpent speak to the woman rather than the man? The text does not say. What the text does say is that both ate it. Eve was deceived by the serpent and Adam went along with her.

The serpent flatly contradicted what God had said, and the woman wanted what the serpent offered, so she ate. She apparently wanted the man to be wise, too, so she gave him some fruit, and he ate. For some unexplained reason, they became ashamed of their nakedness and hid from God even though they had made something to cover their nakedness (verses 7-8). They responded equally to the sin: "the eyes of *both* were opened, and *they* knew that they were naked. And they sewed fig leaves together and made themselves loincloths..... The man and his wife hid themselves from the presence of the Lord God." Genesis does not assign significance to which person sinned first – the important theological point is that they both sinned.

God called out to the man (verse 9). Why the man rather than the woman? The text does not say. Adam said he hid because he was naked, and God asked him whether he had eaten from the forbidden tree.[19] The man blamed the woman, and the woman blamed the serpent. So God cursed the serpent (verses 14-15). The word "curse" is not used for the humans, but God described some unpleasant consequences for them. He told the woman, "I will surely multiply your pain [*'itstsabon*] in childbearing; in pain you shall bring forth children. Your desire shall be contrary[20] to your husband, but he shall rule over you" (v. 16)

Why did God pronounce the punishment on the woman first? The text does not say—it may be for literary style. The sequence goes back and

---

[19] When God pronounced a punishment on Adam, he did not hold Adam accountable for what Eve had done—Eve had to give account for herself (Mary Seltzer, "Women Elders...Sinners or Saints?," 59; unpublished paper).

[20] ESV footnote: "Or shall be toward (see 4:7)."

forth: 1) serpent, woman, man; 2) man, woman, serpent; 3) serpent, woman, man. The most significant curse – death – seems to be reserved for last, in the punishment pronounced for the man. To the serpent, God predicted conflict with the female and conflict with a male offspring; to the woman, God predicted conflict with her husband; and to the man, God predicted conflict with the soil—and the soil would triumph.

Sin affected the relationships between the sexes. God told the woman that "your desire shall be for your husband, and he shall rule over you." The precise meaning of "desire" is debated, but is not essential for our study.[21] In Genesis 3, God made gender distinctions, and he said that husbands would rule their wives. At this point in the story, Adam represents subsequent men, and Eve represents subsequent women.

When God explained the consequences of sin, some things remained the same, and others changed. When God said that the woman's sorrow would increase in childbearing, he was not creating a new role for the woman, but predicting a change in the role he had already designed for her. When God said that the husband would rule over the woman, was he predicting a change? The word "rule" in Gen. 3:16 is from the Hebrew word *mashal,* which *can* be used for oppressive rule, but rule itself does not imply oppression.[22]

Since *mashal* is not necessarily a negative form of rule, it seems that either 1) the fact of male rule is not new, but now that sin has entered the picture male rule will be tainted with sin, or 2) the fact of male rule is new; it is one of the consequences of sin. However, since Genesis has said

---

[21] The Hebrew word is also used in Gen. 4:7 and Song of Solomon 7:10. Susan Foh, a conservative, argues that God is predicting that even though women will desire to master their husbands, the men will continue to rule over the women. (*Women and the Word of God: A Response to Biblical Feminism* [Philadelphia: Presbyterian & Reformed, 1979], 68-69). Ortland also accepts this view (108-9). The more traditional interpretation is that women will want the companionship and protection of men despite the sorrow involved in childbirth.

[22] *Mashal* is used for the sun and moon ruling over the day and night (Gen. 1:18), for Joseph ruling over Egypt (45:8), and for Israel to rule over other nations (Deut. 15:6). The Israelites requested Gideon to *mashal* over them, and he replied that God would *mashal* over them. "The precise nature of the rule is as various as the real situations in which the action or state so designated occur" (*Theological Wordbook of the Old Testament,* 1:534).

nothing before this about one sex ruling the other, a change seems to be implied.[23]

To the man, God said,

> Because you have listened to the voice of your wife and have eaten of the tree of which I commanded you, "You shall not eat of it," cursed is the ground because of you; in pain [*'itstsabon*] you shall eat of it all the days of your life; thorns and thistles it shall bring forth for you; and you shall eat the plants of the field. By the sweat of your face you shall eat bread, till you return to the ground, for out of it you were taken; for you are dust, and to dust you shall return.

The man would suffer because he had "listened" to his wife. Did this mean that he was not supposed to listen to her? The problem is not that he listened, but that he listened (in the sense of obeying) *when she suggested a sin.* There would be nothing wrong with a man listening to his wife if she suggested that he sample a strawberry. Listening is a problem only if sin is being suggested; this verse does not imply anything about God's original design for male-female roles.

Because of sin, the earth is cursed, and the man's work would be greatly increased. Food would become hard to get, and the man would eventually die and return to the ground.[24] At least the latter part of the prediction applies to women as well as men, and in many cultures, women have to toil for food as much as men do, or even more. The negative consequences on family life—although given to the woman—would also

---

[23] William Webb points out that biblical curses often include a change of status vis-à-vis other people, creating a hierarchy where none existed before (*Slaves, Women and Homosexuals: Exploring the Hermeneutics of Cultural Analysis* [Downers Grove: InterVarsity], 117-19). The word "curse" is not always used in these, just as it is not for Eve and Adam.

[24] The death sentence applied to both men and women, so why was it given to the man only? Linda Belleville suggests a plausible literary reason: "The impact on the man is related to the ground from which he was taken.... The impact on the woman is related to the man from whose rib she was formed" (*Women Leaders and the Church: Three Crucial Questions* [Baker, 1999], 104; several Hebrew words have been deleted from the quote without indicating the omissions by ellipses.)

affect the man. Both Adam's curse and Eve's curse contained elements applicable to the other.

When God told the woman about the marital consequences of sin, it was not because she represented family life more than the man did; similarly, when God told the man about death, it was not because he represented humanity more than the woman did. Genesis makes the point that the man and woman both sinned, and both suffered the consequences. Genesis does not say that there is any significance to which sex sinned first.

Paul's comments on the first sin

Romans 5:12-19 teaches that all humanity was sentenced to death because of Adam's sin; it is sometimes said that this shows that Adam represented humanity, not only because he was first, but because he was *male,* implying male authority over females. However, this makes the mistake mentioned earlier: When Paul uses Genesis to support his point, it is hazardous for us to try to use his point to interpret what else Genesis means, because Paul is not intending to explain Genesis. Rather, he is using small portions of Genesis to make his specific point, and we are misusing his words if we try to turn them into something Paul did not intend, i.e., an explanation of Genesis.

In verse 12, Paul says that sin entered the world through one *anthrōpos,* which means a human, either male or female. Paul could have easily used *anēr,* which means a male, but he did not, showing that he is not concerned about the sex of the first sinner. For Paul's purpose, gender is irrelevant. In the last part of verse 12, Paul uses the plural of *anthrōpos* to make his point: death spread to all humans, because all [humans] sinned, including Adam and Eve, who sinned *essentially at the same time.*[25]

Paul then says that death reigned from Adam until Moses (verse 14). He is not saying that Adam was the first person to die. He may be alluding to the fact that Adam was the person to whom humanity's death sentence was given, but more likely, he is referring to Adam as the first *human.* He is designating a time period, from creation to Moses, and he does so by

---

[25] Some have said that Adam sinned first because he was not protecting his wife. Genesis includes the account primarily because both men and women sin, without regard to who did it first.

naming the first person, Adam. Paul focuses on Adam because he is using him as an antetype, or analogy for Christ. The first human, Adam, fore-shadowed the first of God's *new* humanity, Christ. The analogy would be unnecessarily complicated if Paul had used both Adam and Eve.

In verses 15-18, Paul says that the many (i.e., all humanity) died because of one trespass, apparently referring to the transgression of Adam mentioned in verse 14. In Genesis 3, humanity's death sentence was given *to Adam,* even though it applied to Eve as well, and Eve was subject to the death penalty from the instant she sinned.

Throughout this discussion, Paul says nothing to indicate that Adam represented humanity because he was *male.* His theological point is different: Adam is contrasted with Christ, his sin is contrasted with Christ's righteousness, and the death sentence given to humanity through Adam contrasts with the free gift of righteousness given through Christ. Adam is the point of contrast that Paul uses to preach Christ as the solution to the death sentence that applies to all humanity, without respect to sex.

Summary

What does Genesis 3 tell us about male-female relations? Very little, directly—its focus is on how sin entered the human race. Here is what it tells us:

1) The woman was deceived and sinned by eating the forbidden fruit. The man, instead of resisting the sin, ignored God's warning, ate the fruit and blamed his wife.

2) The text also shows that God makes some gender distinctions, although their significance is not made clear in Genesis.

3) Sin affected the roles of male and female, and verse 16 tells us that the man would rule the woman.

Genesis 1 gives both male and female rule over creation. Genesis 2 describes what Adam did before Eve was created, and then describes the woman as similar to the man; it says nothing directly about one person having authority over another. Genesis 3, however, tells us that the man would rule the woman. The chapter concludes by saying that Adam named his wife Eve, and God gave them animal skins for clothing and expelled them from the garden. In our next study, we will examine what the rest of the Pentateuch says about male and female roles.

MEN AND WOMEN
IN THE BOOKS OF MOSES

In our previous study, we surveyed the teaching of Genesis 1-3. Here, we will survey the rest of the books of Moses. Because of the large volume of material involved, we will be brief at many points.

Interpretive difficulties

Many of the practices, events and laws contained in the Old Testament might seem strange to us. However, the Old Testament is part of the Bible, and in our survey of what the Bible says about the relationship between men and women and God, we need to examine what this part of Scripture says. We do not want to sugar-coat what it says, nor to dismiss it. We will see many things that we would not want to imitate, but we will also see positive examples. And we will see that some biblical laws are purposely set in specific cultures to address specific cultural issues, and as such, may not be intended to be followed blindly.

There are numerous interpretive difficulties in this material. Much of it is narrative – it tells the story of what happened without commenting on whether it was good or bad. Other parts give laws about men and women – but even these (such as laws about divorce) may be an accommodation to culture rather than a timeless principle.

Moreover, many of the Old Testament laws are obsolete. Why then should we even examine these passages about an ancient society, when we are asking about a different situation—roles in the church? Many scholars believe that roles in the church are assigned by God in a way that is consistent with God-assigned roles in society. We therefore want to see what the Bible says about male and female roles in general—even if some of that instruction is now obsolete. We will learn, for one thing, that biblical commands are often set in their particular cultural situation. This survey will also provide background for verses in the New Testament, some of which refer to Old Testament passages.

Throughout this survey, we cannot conclude that just because something happened, it therefore presents an example we should follow today. We do not assume, for example, that Abraham is the ideal husband, nor Rebekah the ideal wife. We evaluate behavior based on New

Testament principles, rooted in Jesus' command to love your neighbor as yourself. That command also existed in the Old Testament, yet certain laws of Moses required that men *not* treat women the way they treated one another.

Genesis

The early chapters of Genesis tell us little about women: We are told that Adam and Eve had sons (4:1-2, 25). Cain's wife gave birth to Enoch (4:17). Lamech married two women, Adah and Zillah (verse 19). In one of the most debated verses of the Bible, we are told that the "sons of God" had children by "the daughters of man" (6:4). Noah's wife and his daughters-in-law were saved in the ark (7:13). Genealogies rarely name women, though it is noted that various men had "sons and daughters" (11:11 etc.).

Abram married his half-sister Sarai, and Abram's brother Nahor married their niece, Milcah (11:29). Abram, Sarai, and Lot moved to Canaan, and then to Egypt (12:5, 10). In Egypt, Abram and Sarai assumed that Pharaoh would take Sarai because of her beauty; the only question was whether Abram would survive. So Abram said that Sarai was his sister, and Pharaoh indeed took her into his harem (verses 15, 19). After God punished Pharaoh for this, Pharaoh gave Sarai back and sent them all away.

Later, Abraham did a similar thing with Abimelech, king of Gerar, saying that Sarah was his sister, and Sarah said that Abraham was her brother (20:2, 5). God warned Abimelech, so he stayed away from Sarah (verses 3-4), and Abraham explained that Sarah was his half-sister (verse 12). Abimelech acknowledged that he had offended Sarah, but gave money to Abraham to cover the offense (verse 16). Abraham had told a "half-truth," and Pharaoh and Abimelech were right to protest Abraham's attempts to deceive them.

Sarah told Abraham to have sex with Hagar, her maidservant (16:1-2). According to ancient custom, any resulting children would then be treated as if borne by the wife. Sarah said, "It may be that I shall obtain children by her." (Later, Rachel did a similar thing and said, "go in to her, so that she may give birth *on my behalf,* that even I may have children through her" (30:3).

"Abram listened to [in the sense of obeying] the voice of Sarai," and Hagar became pregnant (16:2-4). Then there was tension between Sarai and Hagar, and Sarai unjustly blamed Abram for the problem (verse 5). Abram let Sarai do whatever she wanted with Hagar, and Sarai mistreated Hagar so much that she fled (verse 6). An angel told Hagar to go back and name her son Ishmael. And Hagar gave a name to God: "So she called the name of the Lord who spoke to her, 'You are a God of seeing'" (verse 13).[1]

When God told Abraham that Sarah would have a son, Abraham laughed and (apparently lacking faith in the promise) suggested that Ishmael might be blessed instead (17:17-18). But God's promise was for Sarah just as much as it was for Abraham (verses 16, 19). Later, God again said that Sarah would have a son, and Sarah laughed (18:12). "But Sarah denied it, saying, 'I did not laugh,' for she was afraid. [The LORD] said, 'No, but you did laugh'" (verse 15).

In chapter 19, Lot set a horrifying example. When the men of Sodom wanted to have relations with Lot's visitors, Lot offered the men his virgin daughters (even though they were pledged to someone else) to "do to them as you please." Lot felt more obligated to protect his visitors than his own daughters! But the angels rescued Lot and his daughters. Lot reached safety in the village of Zoar, and God destroyed Sodom. Lot's wife looked back and died. Lot and his daughters moved to the mountains, and there his daughters got him drunk and became pregnant by him. It is a tragic story.

*Sarah gave birth to Isaac, and when he was weaned, she told Abraham to get rid of Hagar and Ishmael (21:10). Abraham was concerned about Ishmael, but God told him to do whatever Sarah said (verse 12). So Hagar and Ishmael were sent into the desert, where they would have died, except for God's intervention. Sarah died at age 127 and was buried near Hebron. Abraham also had sons (no daughters are mentioned) by Keturah and some

---

[1] "Nowhere else in ancient Near Eastern literature is it recorded that deity called a woman by name, yet the angel of the Lord does just that twice in the case of Hagar (Gen 16:8; 21:17). The conversation between the angel of the Lord and Hagar is just as startling in its cultural milieu as the conversation of Jesus with the Samaritan woman in his day. In both instances God invests a woman with full dignity by solicitously caring for her and by giving her revelations even though both of them come from outside the pure race and are sinners" (Bruce Waltke, "The Relationship of the Sexes in the Bible," *Crux,* Sept. 1983, pp. 11-12).

concubines (25:1-6).

Isaac married Rebekah, the daughter of his cousin Bethuel. She was a girl willing to talk to strangers, industrious enough to volunteer to water ten camels, willing to extend hospitality on behalf of her family, adventurous enough to go on a one-way journey to Canaan, and willing to speak for herself (24:15-61). Abraham said from the start that she had to be willing (verse 8).

Rebekah was barren at first (lack of children was generally assumed to be the woman's fault), but Isaac prayed for her, and she became pregnant (25:21). After the babies fought within her, she inquired of the Lord, who told her that the older son would serve the younger one. (Apparently she did not have to go through her husband to inquire of the Lord, or to receive an answer.) Rebekah knew that the Lord would bless Jacob, and she favored Jacob, but Isaac favored Esau (25:28). When Rebekah learned that Isaac wanted to bless Esau (contrary to God's intent), she conspired with Jacob to deceive Isaac (27:5-10). She prepared the meat, and Jacob pretended to be Esau and obtained the blessing. When Esau wanted to kill Jacob, Rebekah told Jacob to go to Haran. She managed to get Isaac to bless him yet again and send him to northern Mesopotamia to find a wife (27:42-28:5).

Esau married two Hittite women, Judith and Basemath (26:34). His parents did not like his Hittite wives, so he married a cousin, Mahalath, daughter of Ishmael, and others (28:9; 36:2-3).

Isaac moved to Gerar because of a famine, and just as his father had done, he told Abimelech that his wife was his sister (26:7), and Abimelech protested (verse 10).

Jacob was deceived by Laban, and ended up marrying two sisters. Leah had four children, and Rachel demanded that Jacob sleep with her handmaid so that she could have a surrogate family. Leah did the same, and at one point she paid Rachel for the opportunity to sleep with Jacob (30:16). There are plenty of wrong examples in this history. Rachel stole her father's household idols and lied to her father (31:35).

In the city of Shechem, there was a prince named Shechem who slept with Dinah, the daughter of Leah, which caused her to be defiled and shamed in the eyes of her brothers. Shechem offered to pay as much as was wanted, but "the sons of Jacob answered Shechem and his father Hamor deceitfully" and slaughtered the city, taking women and children as slaves (34:13, 29). Jacob complained about this, but Simeon and Levi responded, "Should he treat our sister like a prostitute?" (34:31). Yet it was their mother who had purchased a night with their father.

Rachel had said, "Give me children, or I shall die!" (30:1). And indeed, when she had her second child, she died. She named him "Ben-oni[2]," but Jacob renamed him Benjamin, son of the right hand (probably a reference to Rachel). She was buried near Bethlehem (35:19).

Reuben, the firstborn son of Leah, had sex with Bilhah, the handmaid of the now-deceased Rachel (verse 22). As firstborn, he would have eventually inherited his father's concubines, but because of his premature action, he lost his status as firstborn (1 Chron. 5:1).

Genesis 38 tells the story of Tamar. Judah had married Shua, and they had sons named Er, Onan, and Shelah. Judah got a wife for Er named Tamar. God killed Er, and in keeping with ancient custom, the next brother was supposed to sleep with the widow to produce offspring in Er's name (verse 8; cf. Deut. 25:5). But Onan did not want to make offspring for Er (because Onan would then get a smaller inheritance), and God killed him, too. But even after Shelah had come of age, he was not sent to Tamar to give her children. So Tamar pretended to be a prostitute and became pregnant by her father-in-law, Judah. When the pregnancy became known, Judah threatened to burn her to death, but when she proved that Judah was the father, he said, "She is more righteous than I, since I did not give her to my son Shelah" (verse 26). She had upheld her duty to her family, but he had not.

Women play a smaller role in the Joseph story. Joseph had a dream in which the sun, moon, and eleven stars bowed before him. The moon was interpreted as his mother (37:10), even though she was dead. Potiphar's wife wanted to sleep with Joseph, but when Joseph refused, she accused him of attempted rape (39:14). But she has no further role in the story. Pharaoh gave Joseph a wife—Asenath, the daughter of an Egyptian priest, and they had two sons, Manasseh and Ephraim (41:45-52).

Exodus-Deuteronomy — narratives

Exodus begins with the initiative of some women. The Hebrew midwives Shiphrah and Puah refused to kill Israelite boys. They lied to

---

[2] ESV footnote: "Ben-oni could mean son of my sorrow, or son of my strength." The first seems more suited to the context.

Pharaoh, and God blessed them (Ex. 1:19-20). A Levite mother hid her son for three months, then put him in a basket on the Nile; his sister watched while Pharaoh's daughter rescued the boy. The sister offered to find a wet nurse, and the mother was paid to nurse her own baby (2:1-9).

After Moses fled to Midian, he came to the defense of seven women and watered their flock of sheep; he married one of them, Zipporah, and they had a son named Gershom (2:15-22). When God was about to kill Moses, Zipporah saved his life by circumcising Gershom and touching Moses with the foreskin (4:25). God told Moses to lead the Israelites out of Egypt, and he promised to make the Egyptians favorably disposed toward them. "Each woman shall ask of her neighbor, and any woman who lives in her house, for silver and gold jewelry, and for clothing" (3:22). Later he told Moses that both men and women should ask their neighbors for silver and gold (11:2).

Miriam the prophetess led the women singing and dancing in worship (Ex. 15:20). Later, she and Aaron spoke against Moses because of his Cushite wife, and Miriam was punished for a week (Num. 12:1-15), presumably because she was the chief instigator; no mention is made of her gender. Men and women alike were involved in the golden calf (Ex. 32:2-3), and both were involved in building the tabernacle (35:22-29).

In Numbers 27, the daughters of Zelophehad petitioned Moses for a change in inheritance laws, allowing daughters to inherit if there were no sons. Moses took the request to God, who said, "The daughters of Zelophehad are right," and their request was written into the law (verses 1-11). These women left a permanent mark in the laws of the old covenant.

Exodus-Deuteronomy — laws

Just as in other neighboring cultures, laws were normally written in the masculine, as if only men would commit crimes. For example: "If a man ['iysh] steals an ox or a sheep… If a man borrows anything… (Ex. 22:1-14). The NRSV rightly translates these to be inclusive: "When someone steals an ox or a sheep… Whenever someone borrows an animal…" Many additional examples could be given of laws that assume the person is a male; a few laws mention women as well. All the laws of incest are given from the male perspective (Lev. 18).[3]

---

[3] The law prohibits a man from sleeping with his aunt (verses 12-14), but

The laws of Israel sometimes apply to men and women equally, sometimes unequally. We will present some of them to illustrate points of equality and aspects of inequality. God said he punished the sins of the fathers to the third and fourth generation (Ex. 20:5), but nothing is said about the sins of the mothers. Women were specifically included in the Sabbath commandment (verse 10) and the commandment to honor parents (verse 12). Anyone who cursed or attacked either parent was to be killed (21:15, 17). But in the tenth commandment, the "neighbor" is presumed to be male—nothing is said about the possibility that the neighbor might be a widow who owned property (20:17).

If a Hebrew man became an indentured servant, he was to be set free after six years, and his wife would be free, too; but if the master gave him a wife, she and her children did not have to be set free (21:2-4). The man could stay with his family only if he became a servant for life (verses 5-6). Servants, whether male or female, were to be freed if injured. A bull that killed either a man or a woman was to be destroyed (verses 26-28).

If a female was sold as a servant,[4] she was not to be set free. (In that society, such "freedom" might force her into prostitution.) She could be sold to Hebrews, but not to foreigners. If she was purchased for a son, she had to be treated as a daughter. If the son married another woman, he must not deprive the first one of conjugal rights, or else he must set her free (21:7-11). The last verse may imply that sexual relations were involved in the previous situations as well; it was common for female servants to be concubines.

If men caused a premature birth through reckless behavior,[5] they could be fined "as the woman's husband shall impose on him" (21:22). No

---

nothing is said about a woman sleeping with her uncle.

[4] Fathers could also sell sons into slavery; men and women could sell themselves (Lev. 25:39; Deut. 15:12).

[5] But if they caused a stillbirth or serious injury, verse 23 would then apply. Christopher Wright argues that in this context, "life for life" does not mean a death penalty, but a living child given to compensate for one killed before birth. The death penalty was not appropriate for accidental homicide (verse 13). (*God's People in God's Land: Family, Land and Property in the Old Testament* [Paternoster, 1997], 212).

mention is made of what the woman wanted. If a man slept with a virgin, he had to pay a bride-price, even if the father did not allow the marriage (22:16-17).[6]

Women were unclean for a longer period of time after giving birth to a female (Lev. 12:1-5). After an emission of semen, men would be unclean until evening; but women would be unclean for seven days for menstruation, and her uncleanness was more transferable (Lev. 15:16-24).

For vow redemption, females were valued less than males were (Lev. 27:2-7). Both sexes could take Nazirite vows to dedicate themselves to divine service (Num. 6:1).[7] Women were permitted to take religious vows, but they would be valid only if the father or husband approved (Num. 30:3-14). A vow by a widow or divorced woman was automatically valid (verse 9).

Apparently women could not be priests, although no law specifically addresses that (but most men could not be priests, either). A priest could give sacrificial food to his daughters, even to those who had returned to the family after being widowed or divorced (Num. 18:11; Lev. 22:13).

Males were required to go to the festivals and give an offering three times a year (Deut. 16:16), but it was assumed that women, children and widows would normally go as well (26:12; 31:12).

When the Israelites captured women in war, they could take a woman as a wife. No restrictions about race are noted. She could be freed, but not sold or treated as a slave (Deut. 21:10-14). If a man married two women, he was to count the firstborn son (who got the larger inheritance) fairly, not based on which wife he liked more (verses 15-17).

If a betrothed woman voluntarily slept with another man, she was guilty of adultery and both people would be killed (22:23-24). But if it happened in the country, it was presumed to be a rape, and only the man was to be killed (Deut. 22:23-27). If the girl was not betrothed, the man would be forced to pay 50 shekels and marry her, without right of divorce (verses

---

[6] Deut. 22:28-29 is similar, but does not allow any refusal, and specifies that the woman can never be divorced.

[7] However, the rest of the chapter is written as if the Nazirite is a man, in keeping with the convention that laws are written as if for males even when they apply to females.

28-29). The law did not give the girl any say in this.

If a man suspected that his new bride was not a virgin, he could challenge her. If evidence of virginity could not be given, the woman was to be stoned at her father's house, for being promiscuous while under his care (22:13-21).[8] If a man had been married for a while and suspected his wife of infidelity, he could bring an offering to the priest and put her to a test (Num. 5:12-28); the law presumed her innocence and left the punishment up to God's intervention.

If it could be proved that a wife slept with someone else, she and the other man were to be killed (Deut. 22:22)—but it did not work the other way around. A husband who slept with a prostitute, for example, was not considered guilty of adultery. Similarly, laws did not require men to be virgins when they married. Men could have multiple wives, but women could not have multiple husbands. Laws regulated the sexual behavior of young women and wives, but they did not regulate the sexual behavior of widows; nor did they prohibit prostitution.[9]

If a man wanted to divorce his wife, he had to provide her with a paper that permitted her to marry someone else (Deut. 24:1-4). The woman was not given the right to divorce her husband. Wives were legally under the authority of their husbands, and were sometimes treated like property, but they were not in the same legal status as "property"—they were not part of an inheritance, although concubines were. "A wife could not be sold as an ox or a donkey could.... A woman's conjugal rights... distinguished her from the slave who was truly owned."[10]

---

[8] But if he falsely accused her, he could never divorce her. The "evidence of virginity" may have been a cloth stained by a recent menstruation, showing that the woman was not pregnant at the time of marriage.

[9] However, prostitution was regulated and discouraged. Religious prostitution was not permitted, and the wages of a prostitute could not be brought into the tabernacle (Deut. 23:17-18). The daughters of priests could not become prostitutes, and priests could not marry prostitutes (Lev. 21:9, 14). Fathers could not force their daughters into prostitution (Lev. 19:29). But there was no penalty for prostitution itself.

[10] Linda Belleville, *Women Leaders and the Church: Three Crucial Questions* (Baker, 1999), 77.

Conclusion

Women were usually better off under the laws of Moses than they would have been in other nations.[11] Nevertheless, many of the above laws still strike us as favoring men over women. How should we respond to these laws?

First, we must acknowledge that the laws, as part of the old covenant, are obsolete. Christians today are under no obligation to live by these laws.

Second, we must recognize that even when the old covenant was in force, these laws did not describe the ideal society. Jesus pointed out that the law of divorce was a *concession* that God allowed because the people were sinful (Matt. 19:8). An already existing custom was regulated to prevent flagrant abuses, but the law did not imply approval of the custom itself. The same is true for many of the other laws, such as those that implied a greater sexual freedom for men than for women. The *lack* of penalty for men should not be taken as a divine endorsement of their freedom to visit prostitutes, for example. It was a patriarchal culture, and God allowed some inequities to continue for a time.

We believe that *no one* should be bought or sold into slavery. We believe that the life-long commitment of marriage should not be arranged without the consent of both bride and groom. We believe that fornication and adultery do not merit the death penalty. We believe that men as well as women should be virgins when they marry, and we believe that men as well as women should refrain from sexual activity outside of marriage.

Yet we also recognize that we cannot always insist on these ideals. In many nations, marriages *are* arranged, and the couples have to live with the result. Many young people are not virgins, and adultery does happen. Even within the community of believers, there is sometimes "hardness of heart"—a hardness that calls for repentance, but also requires practical accommodation to what people have done.

This is not the place to spell out ethics for the diverse situations that people get themselves into—we are simply pointing out that these laws, although biblical, were given in a particular cultural context, and we

---

[11] For examples, see William Webb, *Slaves, Women & Homosexuals,* pages 76-80, and the articles on women in *the Anchor Bible Dictionary* and InterVarsity's *Dictionary of the Old Testament: Pentateuch.*

should not view them as timeless directives from God. Even in the New Testament, there are directives that have been shaped by culture—head coverings for women, greeting people with a kiss, making a roster of older widows, etc. We will discuss these in a later chapter, but for now it is sufficient to note that the Old Testament is culturally limited to a far greater extent than the New Testament is.

In our next chapter, we will look at women in Israel's history—from Rahab to Esther. Due to the volume of material, we will again have to be brief, but this survey will give some historical context to the ministry of Jesus and the writings of Paul.

WOMEN IN ANCIENT ISRAEL—
FROM THE CONQUEST TO THE EXILE

In the previous study, we noted that the laws of Moses must be evaluated by New Testament values, because many of those laws were designed for a patriarchal culture. We cannot take the inequities of the laws of Moses as models for male-female relationships today—and certainly not as rules about the role of women in the church.

In this chapter, we survey additional Old Testament material about the role of women in ancient Israel. Although this survey does not directly address our question about the New Testament church, it does provide background and provide examples that may help us better understand what the New Testament says.

The book of Joshua

After Moses died, Joshua led the Israelites into the land of Canaan, where God gave them military victories. A woman plays a prominent role in the beginning of the story. Joshua sent two men into Jericho to spy out the city, and they stayed at "the house of a prostitute whose name was Rahab" (Josh. 2:1).[1] When the king wanted to arrest the spies, Rahab hid them and lied to the king's agents.

Rahab then told the spies of her faith in the God of Israel: "I know that the Lord has given you the land…. The LORD your God, he is God in the heavens above and on the earth beneath" (verses 9, 11). She asked the Israelites to spare her, her parents, her siblings, and their families, and the spies agreed. She helped them escape the city and suggested a strategy for them to avoid the Canaanite soldiers. Joshua told his soldiers to spare Rahab and her family when the city was destroyed (6:17, 25).

---

[1] Some people wonder if Rahab was really a prostitute, or merely an innkeeper. But the law of Moses permitted prostitution, and there is no reason to think that this Canaanite woman had a higher standard of morality. The New Testament remembers her as "Rahab the prostitute," and praises her faith but not her occupation. A person that is exemplary in one area is not necessarily a good model in others.

Whatever Rahab's faults might have been, she was a positive role model because she acknowledged the power of God. The New Testament praises her faith (Heb. 11:31) and her willingness to act on that faith (Jas. 2:25). She married Salmon and became an ancestor of Jesus Christ (Matt. 1:5).[2]

Judges

After Joshua died, Israel was ruled by various judges. One judge was a woman. "Deborah, a prophetess, the wife of Lappidoth, was judging Israel at that time. She used to sit under the palm of Deborah between Ramah and Bethel…and the people of Israel came up to her for judgment" (Judg. 4:4-5). As prophetess, she had a religious role, and as judge, she had a civil role in a public place.[3] Even in this patriarchal society, the people looked to her for leadership and wisdom, and the text does not imply any dishonor for Israel in being led by a female.

She apparently became a judge because of her role as prophetess (most other judges rose to prominence through military victories). As a prophetess, she gave orders from God: "She sent and summoned Barak…and said to him, 'Has not the LORD, the God of Israel, commanded you, 'Go, gather your men at Mount Tabor….'" Barak refused to go unless Deborah went with him, and she agreed, but noted that the honor of victory would then go to a woman (verse 9).

Sisera, the Canaanite general, gathered his army to attack. Deborah ordered Barak, "Up! For this is the day in which the Lord has given Sisera into your hand" (verse 14). So Barak attacked and killed the Canaanites. Sisera escaped to the tent of Jael, Heber's wife, who gave him a false sense of safety, then killed him while he slept (verse 21). Deborah and Barak then sang praises to God—a song that at least in parts was composed by Deborah (see 5:7). This is another religious role for her: public worship.

When God gave Deborah his words, she spoke with the highest

---

[2] Although it is possible that Matthew's Rahab is a different woman, it is not likely. Only one Rahab would be known to Matthew's readers, the one mentioned in Joshua.

[3] Since various people came to the Palm of Deborah, it must have been a public place. Israel did not yet have any official government buildings.

possible authority. Although God could have led Israel through a man (as he usually did), in this case he chose to give authority to a woman, even though Barak was enough of a leader that he could raise an army of 10,000 men.[4]

Nevertheless, Deborah set a precedent for women to be able to sing praises in public, for women to tell men what God has commanded (cf. Matt. 28:10), and to have certain kinds of authority, even spiritual authority in some situations. But none of those roles necessitates ordination in the role of elder or pastor.

Another notable woman in Judges is the daughter of Jephthah, a man who made a vow to offer "whatever comes out from the doors of my house to meet me when I return in peace from the Ammonites" (11:31). The exact nature of this offering is debated, but the daughter's willingness to cooperate is not: "My father, you have opened your mouth to the LORD; do to me according to what has gone out of your mouth, now that the LORD has avenged you on your enemies."

Delilah, another famous woman from the book of Judges, set an example of deceit and betrayal. However, her example was no worse than what Samson did.

Judges 19 tells us about a man and his concubine who spent the night in Gibeah. In a story reminiscent of Sodom, the men of Gibeah wanted to have sexual relations with the man, but he gave them the concubine instead (verses 22-25). They raped and abused her, and she died. The man cut her body into 12 pieces and sent them throughout Israel. The Israelites were outraged at what the people of Gibeah had done and they went to war, nearly exterminating the tribe of Benjamin (20:46-48). Then, to give wives to the surviving Benjamites, they killed everyone in Jabesh Gilead except for the virgin women; then they arranged for other Benjamites to seize women at a festival (21:10-22).

---

[4] Deborah was not working in the tabernacle—she was a civil leader as well as a prophetess. We should also acknowledge that some of the prophets and judges would not be qualified to be church pastors. God can choose to speak through a young boy, but that does not mean that we should consider boys as likely candidates for ordination (a point made by Bruce McNair in an unpublished paper). We must look to the New Testament for the qualifications of a New Testament office.

The book ends with this sad commentary: "In those days there was no king in Israel. Everyone did what was right in his own eyes" (verse 25). They lacked a king to maintain civil order and promote righteousness. They knew that this behavior, including the mistreatment of women, was scandalous. The text does not tell us which aspects of the sordid story they wanted to correct—but later books show that a king was not the answer to the problem.

Ruth

The book of Ruth provides a positive example from the same time period. Ironically, the example of faith and loyalty was set by a woman from Moab, even though the Torah said that Moabites could not yet become part of the people of Israel (Deut. 23:3). Nevertheless, three generations later, a descendant of that Moabite woman became king of Judah and Israel.

Elimelech and Naomi moved to Moab, and their sons married Moabite women. After Elimelech and his sons died, Naomi and Ruth moved back to Bethlehem, where the nearest male relative was asked to serve as a "kinsman-redeemer." Naomi owned rights to the field of Elimelech, and she could transfer it to the nearest male relative. However, that relative would also have the obligation to marry Ruth[5] in order to create a son for the family of Elimelech, and the field would eventually be given to that son (4:5).

The nearest kinsman did not want that part of the duty, so Boaz (son of Rahab and descendant of Tamar) not only bought the field, he also bought a wife: "Ruth the Moabite, the widow of Mahlon, I have bought to be my wife, to perpetuate the name of the dead in his inheritance" (Ruth 4:10). His child, Obed, became the legal inheritor of Elimelech's land.

The main characters in this story behave honorably. Naomi is faithful to the family she married into; Ruth has the frequently quoted statement of loyalty to Naomi and her God (1:16-17). Boaz is a model of charity, good manners, and proper conduct. Even though everyone did what was right in their own eyes, some people did what was right in the eyes of God, too—and it was from that family that the king eventually came.

---

[5] Naomi was apparently past the age of child-bearing, so Ruth was the only appropriate widow.

Historical books

The next book explains how Israel received its first king. The story begins with a woman—Hannah, who desperately wanted a son. "She was deeply distressed and prayed to the Lord and wept bitterly. And she vowed" to give her son to God (1:10-11). Eli, the high priest, accused her of being drunk, but she explained what she wanted, and he blessed her. God caused her to have a son, whom she named Samuel (verse 20).

Hannah is an example of a woman of faith, of prayer, of sincerity. She made a vow and kept it—and that became a pivotal moment in Israel's history. After Samuel was weaned, she took him to the tabernacle, gave him to Eli, and brought offerings. She prayed again, praising God with a psalm that became part of the Bible and therefore part of Israel's public worship (2:1-10). Hannah had an exemplary relationship with God that did not depend on men, but she did not have a leadership role.

1 Sam. 2:22 mentions women who served at the entrance to the tabernacle, but we do not know what role they had.

Women played a prominent role in the story of David. Like men, they were sometimes good, sometimes bad, and sometimes victims of injustice. Interesting character vignettes can be written for Michal, Abigail, Rizpah, Tamar, and Bathsheba, but they are not relevant to our study about women in leadership.[6]

The Queen of Sheba was a female leader in her own nation, and there is no hint in the Bible that her leadership was in any way inappropriate (1 Kings 10).[7]

The widow of Zarephath was an exemplary woman from the region of Sidon. She fed the prophet Elijah, swore by the name of God, and received her son back from the dead (1 Kings 17). Similarly, the wealthy woman of Shunem gave Elisha room and board, and also received her son back from the dead (2 Kings 4).

Jezebel, also from Sidon, set an opposite example—of Baal worship, theft and murder. As queen of Israel, she was an influential civil and

---

[6] Bathsheba played a key role in ensuring that Solomon would inherit the throne, but the story does not portray *public* leadership.

[7] If the king was alive, then the queen was serving as an important emissary to the most powerful nation in the area.

religious leader for evil. In the same way, Athaliah (although originally from Israel) usurped the throne in Judah and ruled for six years (2 Kings 11).

An example of good religious influence was given by Huldah, a prophetess. When Josiah's workers found the book of the law and saw that they had violated the covenant with God, they asked Huldah about what they had found in the book, and she prophesied, giving authoritative words to the high priest and several men (2 Kings 22:14-20). There was nothing inappropriate about asking a woman about the Bible. Even though Jeremiah was then alive, he lived further away than Huldah did. The word of God delivered through a respected older woman, a prophetess, was authoritative.

Later, a woman named Noadiah was hired to prophesy against Nehemiah (Neh. 6:14). Although she was a false prophetess, the fact that she was hired—and her name is mentioned—shows that the people respected the word of a prophetess just as much as the word of a prophet. Women in ancient Israel had less authority when it came to laws, customs, and Levitical worship, but they had equal authority when it came to prophecy.[8]

Other books

The book of Psalms is almost entirely written from a male (often a warrior's) perspective. When women are portrayed, they are usually mothers, and rarely in the role of worship. Psalm 68:11 is an exception: "The Lord gives the word; the women who announce the news [of military victory] are a great host" (verse 11[9]). Women played tambourines in the worship processions (verse 24-25; cf. 148:12-13).[10]

In Proverbs, women are used to symbolize wisdom (the Hebrew word for "wisdom" is feminine[11]), and are also used to symbolize folly and sin.

---

[8] False prophetesses are also mentioned in Ezek. 13:17-24; Isa. 8:3 mentions a true prophetess.

[9] Some other translations obscure the fact that the Hebrew word for "host" is in a feminine form.

[10] The female singers mentioned in Ezra 2:65 were probably part of the temple choir.

[11] The fact that the Hebrew word for wisdom is feminine suggests that the

The Proverbs 31 woman shows that Hebrew society praised highly competent women who were able to teach — but the context is in the family, not the religious assembly.

Near the end of the biblical period, approximately 478 B.C., a Jewish woman became queen in Persia. Although Esther hid her ethnic identity for a while, she eventually revealed it and thereby saved her people from genocide. However, she had limited formal authority. She was given access to the king only as a special favor, and the official decrees were his. However, she and Mordecai wrote an authoritative letter requiring Jews in the Persian Empire to celebrate a festival (Esther 9:29). "The command of Esther confirmed these practices of Purim" (verse 32). She had authority over the Jewish people to command a new religious festival.

Conclusion

The Bible provides some excellent models for women of faith, as well as some examples to avoid. Some of these involve a woman's personal relationship with God, and others involve a more public role, including leadership. For our study, the following are notable:

- As prophetess, Deborah spoke the word of God, giving an authoritative message to Barak. Huldah the prophetess gave the king an authoritative message based on Scripture. These women had spiritual authority.
- Deborah wrote a worship song and sang it in public; women were later involved in music at the temple.
- As judge, Deborah had civil authority; Esther also had authority over the Jews.
- These women were given authority by God, and the Bible does not imply that there was anything inappropriate about a female having these roles, even though it was not common for women to have these roles.

However, the New Testament church is a different social and spiritual reality, and it may have different rules about roles. Our next study will examine the ministry of Jesus and the early church.

Israelites did not view women as inherently gullible. Wise women are mentioned in 2 Sam. 14:2-20 and 20:16-22.

WOMEN IN THE MINISTRY OF JESUS

Conservative and liberal commentators are generally agreed on this: Jesus treated women well—despite the male-dominated culture in which he lived. He treated them respectfully, was sensitive to their needs, used them as good examples of faith, and included them in his ministry in several important ways. Nevertheless, when it came time to name 12 apostles, Jesus included only men. This fact is an important part of the debate about whether women may lead in the church today.

Women are prominent in the story of Jesus—he was born of a woman, had numerous interactions with women, and was seen first by women after his resurrection. Although these incidents do not tell us much about women *in leadership,* we will survey the Gospels to see 1) what Jesus taught about women, 2) how he interacted with women, and 3) why the apostles were all men.

Jesus' teaching about marriage

As far as the Gospels report, Jesus did not teach on male and female roles.[12] He never explicitly taught women to submit to men, nor did he explicitly say that they were equal in every way.[13]

However, he did teach about marriage. Some religious leaders asked

---

[12] Stanley Grenz writes, "Jesus gave no explicit teaching on the role of women in the church. In fact, he left no teaching at all concerning women as a class of people…. He treated every woman he met as a person in her own right" (*Women in the Church: A Biblical Theology of Women in Ministry* [InterVarsity, 1995], 71).

[13] "Jesus stopped short of ever making any explicit pronouncements about the equality of men and women (even to the extent that Paul does in Galatians 3:28), to say nothing of attempting to overthrow sociocultural conventions on gender roles…. Jesus cannot fairly be co-opted for modern liberationist or egalitarian agendas…. Neither the Gospels nor the book of Acts can prove decisive in answering the question of whether the first generation of Christians in general or Paul in particular reserved any leadership roles for men. For that one must turn to Paul's writings themselves" (Craig Blomberg, "Neither Hierarchicalist Nor Egalitarian: Gender Roles in Paul," in *Two Views on Women in Ministry* [ed. James R. Beck and Craig L. Blomberg; Zondervan, 2001], 335-37).

him, "Is it lawful to divorce one's wife for any cause?" (Matt. 19:3). The question concerned the interpretation of Deut. 24:1, which says, "When a man takes a wife and marries her, if then she finds no favor in his eyes because he has found some indecency in her, and he writes her a certificate of divorce..." Some rabbis thought that a man could divorce his wife if she displeased him in any way; others thought a man could divorce only if the wife did something indecent.

Jesus responded by quoting Genesis, basically saying that God intended marriage to last for life, and people should not break their vows. Moses allowed divorce, even for "indecency," because the people had hard hearts (Matt. 19:8). Jesus was strict: "Whoever divorces his wife, except for sexual immorality, and marries another, commits adultery...and if she divorces her husband and marries another, she commits adultery" (v. 9; Mark 10:12).[14]

In the Jewish world, only men could initiate divorce, and women were at a disadvantage. Jesus was removing this male advantage. Further, he said that *men* could be guilty of adultery if they married another woman— something the laws of Moses did not say. This response dismayed the disciples, and Jesus responded that celibacy was an honorable option for some (verse 12). As Mark 10:12 makes clear, the prohibition on divorce applies equally to women (Roman law allowed women to initiate divorce).

Tom Schreiner writes, "Jesus upheld the dignity of women by speaking out against divorce, which particularly injured women in the ancient world."[15] James Borland notes, "In his treatment of divorce...Jesus clearly regards women not as property but as persons. They have legitimate rights and should be respected."[16]

---

[14] Under Old Testament law, an adulterous wife would have been stoned. 1 Cor. 7 implies that additional exceptions are sometimes appropriate. However, this is not the place to discuss the ethics of divorce and remarriage. Those who want a more detailed discussion of this issue should see https://archive.gci.org/articles/what-the-bible-says-about-divorce-and-remarriage/ and https://archive.gci.org/articles/what-about-divorce-and-remarriage/.

[15] Thomas R. Schreiner, "Women in Ministry," in *Two Views on Women in Ministry* (ed. James R. Beck and Craig L. Blomberg; Zondervan, 2001), 185.

[16] James A. Borland, "Women in the Life and Teachings of Jesus," in *Recovering Biblical Manhood and Womanhood* (ed. John Piper and Wayne

Jesus also commented on male-female relations in the Sermon on the Mount, when he said, "Everyone who looks at a woman with lustful intent has already committed adultery with her in his heart" (Matt. 5:28). Again, Jesus was saying that *men* could commit adultery; although the law of Moses did not prohibit all extramarital affairs, Jesus said it was adultery to even desire another woman, whether she was married or not. Jewish rabbis were well aware of lust, but they usually blamed the women for being seductive. Jesus blamed the man, and the solution to lust is not to restrict women,[17] but for men to restrict their own thoughts (verse 29).

Although this teaching is stated for a male, as rules usually were, we believe that it also applies to females. That is, a woman who looks lustfully at a man has also committed adultery in the heart, and the best solution is not to segregate the sexes but to control the thoughts.

Last, Jesus mentioned that marriage is not applicable to the age to come (Mark 12:25). This does not explicitly say that males and females will be equal, but that is the probable implication.

Women as positive spiritual examples

"Women were employed by Jesus quite freely as illustrations in His

---

Grudem; Crossway, 1991), 115.

[17] "The approach most often taken by rabbinic Judaism to sexual temptation seems to have been the reduction to a minimum of any sort of contact between the sexes" (James Hurley, *Man and Woman in Biblical Perspective* [Zondervan, 1981], 64). Hurley's book was an influential scholarly presentation of the restrictive position, and has recently been reprinted by Wipf & Stock. Examples of rabbinic teaching:

- "He that talks much with women brings evil upon himself" (*mAb.* 1.5; cf. *Ned.* 20a)...
- "These are the women that may be put away without giving them their dowry: a wife that transgresses the law of Moses and Jewish custom, or if she goes out with her hair unbound, or spins in the street, or speaks with any man" (*mKet.* 7:6).

The social reality was probably that men did not talk with women unless necessary—see the disciples' surprise to find Jesus talking with a woman (John 4:27). In this discussion, we do not want to portray Judaism as bad or backwards—in its attitude toward women, it was average for its time. Greek authors generally had worse attitudes, Latin authors slightly better.

teaching," Borland notes.[18] "This is in stark contrast to the rabbis of the day. One looks in vain in their teachings for even one story or sermon illustration that mentions women," Linda Belleville adds.[19] In many of Jesus' illustrations, women are presented as positive role models of faith, which men should follow. For example:

- The Queen of the south, who was wiser than the first-century Jews (Matt 12:42)
- The woman mixing yeast into dough (Matt. 13:33), who is presented as an illustration of the way that the kingdom of God works[20]
- Women working when Christ returns, some of who are ready and others are not (Matt. 24:41)
- Ten virgins, of whom five were prepared and five were not (Matt 25:1-13)
- The widow of Zarephath, whom Jesus used as an example of a Gentile that God favored (Luke 4:26)
- The woman who found the coin she had lost (Luke 15:8-10). In this parable the woman plays the role of God, just as the shepherd did in the preceding parable and the father does in the following parable.[21]
- A persistent widow (Luke 18:1-8), a model for disciples to imitate in prayer
- A widow who gave everything she had (Luke 21:1-4)
- In Luke 11, an anonymous woman called out, "Blessed is the womb that bore you, and the breasts at which you nursed!" (verse 27). Jesus did not deny that his own mother was blessed, but he said that the real blessing is given to "those who hear the word of God and keep it!" (verse 28). A woman's spiritual worth is based on her response

---

[18] Borland, 117.

[19] Linda Belleville, *Women Leaders and the Church: Three Crucial Questions* (Baker, 1999), 48.

[20] Some scholars interpret the yeast as a bad thing, like tares in the wheat, but most scholars conclude that the parable of the yeast is intended to portray the growth of the kingdom in good ways.

[21] Jesus cast himself in the role of a female when he compared himself to a mother hen (Matt. 23:37).

to God, not in performing biological functions. Women are saved by faith, not by bearing children.

"Jesus did two important things" for this woman, Borland writes. "He gave her His undivided attention by listening to her comment, and He mildly corrected her and pointed her toward further spiritual understanding.... Jesus does not deny His mother's place of importance, but goes beyond it to a wider spiritual truth."[22]

"Christ never belittled the role of a mother," JoAnn Davidson observes, but he "refused to limit a woman's horizon to nurturing family and cooking."[23]

Jesus made a similar point when people told him that his mother and brothers wanted to speak to him (Matt. 12:47). He replied that the disciples were his real family: "Whoever does the will of my Father in heaven is my brother and sister and mother" (verse 50). Spiritual response is more important than biological origin. Jesus expanded the response to include "sister," even though the original comment did not mention sisters; by doing so he implied that women were spiritually on an equal footing with men.

Shortly before Jesus was arrested and killed, a woman[24] anointed him with a large amount of expensive perfume. The disciples grumbled about the expense, but Jesus praised the woman: "She has done a beautiful thing to me.... Truly, I say to you, wherever this gospel is proclaimed in the whole world, what she has done will also be told in memory of her" (Matt. 26:10, 13). What she did is a great illustration for *all* disciples: unrestrained devotion. Jesus said to the woman who anointed him, "Your faith has saved you" (Luke 7:50), and the fact that this story is preserved in the Gospels means that her faith is an example to us today.

Similarly, a Canaanite woman was praised for having great faith (Matt. 15:28).[25] As a non-Israelite, she had no claim to any favors from him, but

---

[22] Borland, 116.

[23] "Women in Scripture," in *Women in Ministry: Biblical and Historical Perspectives* (ed. Nancy Vyhmeister; Andrews University Press, 1998), 175.

[24] John 12:3 identifies her as Mary, sister of Martha and Lazarus. Luke 7 may report a different anointing.

[25] Jesus' initial reluctance to help the woman had nothing to do with her sex—

she appealed for grace and mercy. Hurley writes, "He shows respect for the faith of this woman and for her argument. He took women seriously."[26]

Women in the ministry of Jesus

James Hurley writes,

The most striking thing about the role of women in the life and teaching of Jesus is the simple fact that they are there.[27] Although the gospel texts contain no special sayings repudiating the view of the day about women, their uniform testimony to the presence of women among the followers of Jesus and to his serious teaching of them constitutes a break with tradition which has been described as being "without precedent in [then] contemporary Judaism."[28]

As Schreiner says, "Jesus treated women with dignity and respect and

---

it was simply that she was a Gentile. Jesus would have known about her faith from the start, but went through the conversation to help the disciples realize that it was right to heal a Gentile.

[26] Hurley, 85.

[27] Borland agrees: "Jesus regularly addressed women directly while in public. This was unusual for a man to do" (114).

[28] Hurley, 82-83, citing W. Forster, *Palestinian Judaism in New Testament Times* (London, 1964), 124. Some example of Jewish views of women:
- "Any iniquity is small compared to a woman's iniquity…. From a woman sin had its beginning, and because of her we all die" (Sirach 25:19, 24; 2nd century B.C.).
- "Better is the wickedness of a man than a woman who does good; it is woman who brings shame and disgrace" (Sirach 42:14).
- "The woman is inferior to the man in every way" (Josephus, *Against Apion* 2:201).
- "A hundred women are no better than two men" (Talmud, *Ber.* 45b) Although the Talmud was written well after the New Testament, in this case it is probably in agreement with first-century attitudes.
- "A man is required to say the following three blessings every day: 'Blessed are you who have not made me a heathen, who have not made me a woman, who has not made me illiterate" (*bMen.* 43b; *Ber.* 7.18).
- "There is no wisdom in woman except with the spindle" (*bYom.* 66b).]

he elevated them in a world where they were often mistreated."[29] Hurley writes that Jesus did not perceive women "primarily in terms of their sex, age or marital status; he seems to have considered them in terms of their relation (or lack of one) to God."[30] Borland's summary is a good one:

Numerous healings and the casting out of demons from women display Jesus' care and concern for women. Several such incidents are only briefly recorded. Jesus healed Peter's mother-in-law and allowed her in return to minister to Him (Mark 1:30-31; Matthew 8:14-15; Luke 4:38-39). Jesus also was concerned for a widow in Nain (Luke 7:11-15). He met her as she was weeping just before burying her only son. With compassion, He spoke to her and raised her son to life.

Later, Christ healed a woman who was hopelessly bent over for eighteen years (Luke 13:10-17). Courageously, on the Sabbath and inside the synagogue before hostile religious leaders, Jesus helped and defended this poor woman. He spoke to her, tenderly placed His hands on her, and caused her to stand erect, for which she glorified God. He then acknowledged her equal standing with men in Israel's religious heritage by referring to her as a daughter of Abraham (cf. John 8:33, 39).[31]

Sheila Graham writes,

Jesus' honor and respect was...extended to all women—an attitude largely unexpected and unknown in his culture and time. Jesus, unlike the men of his generation and culture, taught that women were equal to men in the sight of God. Women could receive God's forgiveness and grace. Women, as well as men, could be among Christ's personal followers. Women could be full participants in the kingdom of God.... These were revolutionary ideas. Many of his contemporaries, including his disciples, were

---

[29] Schreiner, 184.

[30] Hurley, 83.

[31] Borland, 115.

shocked.[32]

Elizabeth

We begin our brief survey of women in the ministry of Jesus with a woman whose role occurred before Jesus was born. Elizabeth, wife of the priest Zechariah, was noted to be "righteous before God, walking blamelessly in all the commandments" (Luke 1:6).[33] When Mary visited Elizabeth, "the baby leaped in her womb. And Elizabeth was filled with the Holy Spirit" and pronounced a blessing on Mary—words that are now part of Scripture (verses 41-45).

Mary

The mother of Jesus set a marvelous example with her words, "I am the servant of the Lord; let it be to me according to your word" (verse 38). Mary was also inspired to say a poem of praise that is now part of Scripture (verses 46-55). She again set a good example when she "treasured up all these things, pondering them in her heart" (2:19, 51). She was instrumental in Jesus' first public miracle (John 2:1-11). She may have been among the "family" who thought that Jesus had lost his sanity (Mark 3:21). At the cross, Jesus assigned John to take care of his mother, and Mary was counted among the disciples after his resurrection (Acts 1:14).

Borland writes,

> The woman whom God chose to have the most extensive association with Jesus was His mother, Mary.... Mary's life was significant for at least three reasons. (1) She was a first-hand witness of Jesus' divine origin and true humanity. (2) She was a tremendous model of godliness, faith, dedication, and patience, among other good qualities. (3) She, along with other women, was incorporated into the new life of the church at Pentecost.[34]

---

[32] "Jesus and Women"; see above, page 34.

[33] Luke may have stressed this because some people might assume that sin had caused Elizabeth to be barren. She refers to the "disgrace" of being barren in verse 25.

[34] Borland, 118-119.

Anna

When Jesus was taken to the temple to be dedicated, an elderly prophetess named Anna "began to give thanks to God and to speak of him to all who were waiting for the redemption of Jerusalem" (Luke 2:38). Unfortunately, we do not know what she said or how she spread the news.

Mary and Martha

Although the rabbis said that men should not talk with women, Jesus counted women among his friends. "Jesus loved Martha and her sister and Lazarus" (John 11:5). Once when Jesus was visiting Bethany, "a woman named Martha welcomed him into her house" (Luke 10:38). Since Martha owned a home, she may have been a widow. Her sister Mary "sat at the Lord's feet and listened to his teaching" (verse 39). But Martha was busy preparing the meal, and asked Jesus to tell Mary to help her.

The rabbis said that women should not be taught the Torah,[35] so Mary was shirking a typically female role in order to do something that was normally restricted to males. But Jesus did not "put her in her place." Rather, he said that she had chosen the right place at the time. "one thing is necessary. Mary has chosen the good portion, which will not be taken away from her" (verse 42). Spiritual growth is more important than domestic duties.[36]

Borland notes, "Jesus did not order [Martha] to stop serving but gently corrected her attitude about Mary."[37] Graham writes,

> Jesus did not feel that women's work—or men's work, for that matter—wasn't important. He was not saying it is wrong to be diligent and careful about our responsibilities. Christ was saying we should get our priorities straight. Women were called to be disciples of Jesus, just as men were, and women were expected to fulfill their

---

[35] "It is better that the words of the Law should be burned than that they should be given to a woman" (*jSot.* 3.4; 19a). "If a man gives his daughter a knowledge of the Law, it is as though he taught her lechery" (*bSot.* 4.3).

[36] This does not mean that domestic duties should never be done. Jesus himself washed feet and cooked fish. Jesus never assigned (nor does the Bible assign) domestic duties to women only.

[37] Borland, 119.

spiritual responsibilities, just as men were.[38]

Borland further notes that Mary set a great example for all of us today:

Women are to learn and apply the Word of God. This is vitally important. But actually, the application is much broader.... Every believer must make countless decisions throughout life, constantly choosing to act as a pupil with Jesus as the teacher. It does not mean that other duties or Christian graces are to be ignored, but it does imply that some things...are more important than other things. There are no role distinctions for learning from Christ.[39]

In that incident, Mary set a better example than Martha did. But Borland notes that Martha should be remembered for another incident as well: "On a later visit of Jesus to Bethany, it was Martha who was taught by Jesus while Mary sat in the house (John 11:20).... Martha gave a superb confession about Christ, saying, 'Yes, Lord, I believe that You are the Christ, the Son of God, who is to come into the world' (John 11:27, NKJV)."[40]

Samaritan woman at the well

"The conversation with the woman at the well is the longest recorded discussion Jesus had with anyone—and she, a Gentile woman."[41] Further, the lesson Jesus gave her about living water was just as profound as the lesson he gave Nicodemus—and the woman had a better response. Unlike Nicodemus, she was willing to be associated with Jesus. She told her neighbors about Jesus, and many of them believed in Jesus "because of the woman's testimony" (John 4:28-29, 39).

Davidson observes that this implies something *positive* about the reputation of the woman in the community:

It is unlikely that the men of a town would believe a prostitute's word about the Messiah or anybody, and go openly with her to see

---

[38] Graham, 16-17.

[39] Borland, 118.

[40] Ibid.

[41] Davidson, 173.

him. Perhaps this woman has not been given due credit for her true social position in Samaria. The narrative seems to indicate that she was a knowledgeable, informed woman. Her discourse with Christ reveals an intelligent familiarity with the foremost theological issues of the day.[42]

A daughter of Abraham

When Jesus was teaching in a synagogue, a woman who had been crippled for 18 years came in, and Jesus healed her (Luke 13:10-13). The synagogue ruler criticized Jesus, but Jesus defended himself, saying that the woman was "a daughter of Abraham" (verse 16).

Graham writes,

Before his most venomous critics, Jesus publicly showed his concern and high regard for this woman, someone whom others had probably seen for years as she struggled in her affliction to come to the synagogue to worship God. Someone whom they may well have shunned because she was a woman and because she was disabled.[43]

By using the rare phrase "daughter of Abraham," Jesus was reminding the people that women were also among the descendants of Abraham and eligible for the blessings.

Joanna and Susanna

Luke tells us that several women who had been healed helped support Jesus "out of their means" (Luke 8:3). These included "Joanna, the wife of Chuza, Herod's household manager, and Susanna, and many others."[44] Although they were probably involved in meal preparation, Luke indicates that their most significant role was to provide financial support.

Graham writes,

---

[42] Davidson, 173. Scholars often assume that the woman was immoral. She had five previous husbands, yes, but they may have died or divorced her due to no fault of her own. She was not married to the man she was living with, but the law of Moses did not regulate the sexual behavior of unmarried nonvirgins.

[43] Graham, 18.

[44] Mary Magdalene is also mentioned, but we will discuss her separately.

Some of these women—possibly widows—had control of their own finances. It was out of their generosity that Jesus and his disciples were at least partially supported. Although Christ worked with the cultural traditions of the first century, he ignored the limitations that had been placed on women by their culture. Women were free to follow him and to take part in his ministry to the world.[45]

Belleville further observes,

They are the *only* supporters mentioned. Also, they did not merely write a check to cover the expenses but accompanied Jesus and the Twelve as they traveled from place to place.... Jesus welcomed women among his traveling coterie, allowing them to make the same radical commitment in following him that the Twelve did.... That married women would be traveling with Jesus' group is striking indeed."[46]

"Jesus expected men and women to mix freely," Mary Evans writes.[47] The solution to lust was not to segregate women, but for men to control themselves.

Matt. 27:55-56 also mentions that "many women...had followed Jesus from Galilee, ministering to him, among whom were Mary Magdalene and Mary the mother of James and Joseph and the mother of the sons of Zebedee." (Mark 15:41 reports that the latter's name was Salome). Luke 23:27 reports that many women from Jerusalem followed him after his arrest, and he turned to them and taught them, saying that even worse times would come for Jerusalem.

A woman with bleeding

While Jesus was on his way to the home of Jairus, a woman who had been hemorrhaging for 12 years touched him, and was healed (Mark 5:22-29). She was afraid that Jesus would be angry (rabbis normally avoided women, especially unclean ones), but Jesus was not angry. He said,

---

[45] Graham, 18.

[46] Belleville, 51.

[47] Mary J. Evans, *Woman in the Bible* (InterVarsity, 1983), 47.

"Daughter, your faith has made you well" (verse 34)—addressing her with a term of affection and publicly praising her faith. Similarly, Jesus was not afraid of touching another unclean daughter, the dead child of Jairus (verse 41).

Mary Magdalene

Luke tells us that Mary of Magdala had seven demons cast out of her (Luke 8:2), but Mary should be better known as the first to see the empty tomb, the first to carry the good news to the disciples. Graham writes:

> Mary is almost always mentioned first in a list of the female disciples of Jesus Christ. She may have been one of the leaders of that group of women who followed Jesus from the outset of his ministry in Galilee to his death and afterward. The risen Jesus appeared to her first. It's ironic that in a time when women could not be legal witnesses, Jesus Christ chose women as the first witnesses of his resurrection.[48]

Although the men fled for their lives, the women faithfully followed Jesus to the cross (Matt. 27:55-56), and Mary sat nearby while Joseph of Arimathea put Jesus' body in the tomb (verse 61). Mary led the women who came to anoint Jesus early on Sunday morning (Mark 16:2), and an angel told them that Jesus had been raised (verse 6). They then told the news to the 11 disciples (Luke 24:10). Jesus appeared first to Mary (John 20:14), and told her to tell the disciples, which she did (verses 17-18).

Schreiner writes, "Even though the testimony of women was not received by courts…Jesus appeared to women first, showing again their significance and value as human beings.[49] Borland, another conservative, comments on the significance:

> Why were the women chosen as witnesses of the resurrection?

---

[48] Graham, 15. Josephus wrote, "From women let no evidence be accepted because of the levity and temerity of their sex" (*Antiquities* 4:219).

[49] Schreiner, 185-86. However, Evans writes, "It would be a mistake to over-emphasize the point, as it is quite possible that the women received the message first simply because they happen to have been there first" (p. 54). Unlike the men, the women were not hiding.

Was God bestowing a special honor on these women? Was God trying to indicate larger roles for women in His new community of believers? I believe both were intended. All four Gospel writers bestow a great honor on the women who lovingly and with servant hearts came early to the tomb to anoint Jesus' body, thus paying their last respects…. These women led the way in proclaiming the gospel…. The duty and high privilege of witnessing for Christ is still open to every believer, without distinction as to gender.[50]

Some scholars have noted that the women were told to bear witness to the fact that Jesus had risen—and this is one of the criteria for an apostle (Acts 1:22). But there is no evidence that any of these women ever functioned as witnesses of the resurrection in the public preaching of the church. Although their role in the resurrection was an important precedent for women speaking with authority, it was a restricted role for a specific need within the church.

The all-male apostles

As the evidence above indicates, scholars are generally agreed that Jesus treated women with respect, as people of the same spiritual significance as men. On this point, scholars who favor women's ordination are agreed with those who oppose it. There is one significant aspect of Jesus' ministry on which they do not agree, and that is the implications of the fact that Jesus chose only men to be among the Twelve. For example, James Borland writes that Jesus

demonstrated a clear role distinction between men and women. Nowhere is this issue seen more clearly than in Jesus' selection of only men for the role of apostle…. When moral issues were at stake, Jesus did not bend to cultural pressure. It was not social custom or cultural pressure that caused Jesus to appoint an all-male group of apostles. Had He so desired, He could easily have appointed six men and their wives as apostles….

Jewish culture did accept women into positions of leadership. Just three decades before Herod the Great took over as king, Israel was ruled for years by Queen Alexandra. The fact that an occasional

---

[50] Borland, 120.

judge (Deborah, Judges 4-5), or ruler (Athaliah, 2 Kings 11:3) was a woman also demonstrates that female leadership was possible.[51]

Since Jesus was willing to break social customs, and Jewish culture sometimes allowed female leaders, Jesus must have had a good reason to choose only men—and that reason, Borland argues, is because church leaders should all be men. "Even though many women have excellent leadership qualities, God still has clear role distinctions in mind when apostleship and eldership are considered."[52]

However, egalitarians respond that not only were the apostles all men, they were also all Jewish, and that indicates a cultural limitation that does not apply to church leadership today. Jesus did not pick any Samaritan men to be apostles, either, because of the cultural limitations he worked in.

The Jewishness of the disciples was necessitated by a theological fact: Jesus was sent only to the Jews (Matt. 15:24), and we have good biblical reasons for understanding that to be a temporary limitation. The Bible shows that the church began as all Jewish; it is no surprise that the leaders were all Jewish.

However, Borland points out an important fact: "The church did not start as all male and then later become both male and female. Christ's followers were both male and female from the beginning," and yet women were not chosen as leaders. Second, unlike the all-Jewish leadership, "male leadership was perpetuated by those whom Christ initially taught, trained, and to whom He committed the future leadership of His church."[53]

Twelve Jewish men

When Jesus chose only men as apostles, was he reflecting a permanent restriction on leadership within the church, or was it due to a temporary need? Jesus was willing to teach women in public and in private, and women were among his disciples, but he did not include them in the

---

[51] Borland, 120-21.

[52] Ibid.

[53] Borland, 121. Here he cites Acts 1:21; and 6:3, both of which specify males. We also note that Acts 6:3 calls for males even though the immediate need was for people to minister to women.

Twelve. There *are* good reasons not to have a Gentile in the Twelve, but why not any women?

Some egalitarians have answered that Jesus was limited by his culture, but as Borland noted, it seems unlikely that Jesus, who broke many religious conventions, was that limited by his culture.

However, Jesus did not challenge *all* the imperfect social customs of his day. He did not attack the Roman government, nor the custom of slavery. Instead, he used slaves in some of his parables without even a hint that such a custom was anything less than what God wanted. Yes, Jesus was willing to challenge culture on certain points, but we cannot assume that he agreed with everything that he let stand. Nevertheless, we must agree that when it came to choosing disciples, Jesus had an opportunity to challenge culture, but did not. He treated women as equals in other respects, but not for being in the Twelve.

Egalitarians often argue that equal worth requires equal access to all roles, but that does not seem to be a valid assumption. The Christian who has the gift of leadership is not more valuable to God than a Christian with the gift of service. One gift is more valuable for certain *functions* of the church than the other gift is, but the persons are of equal value even though the same *roles* are not open to both. The example of Jesus suggests that at least in certain situations it is not a sin to discriminate on the basis of gender when choosing church leaders.

Borland summarizes the argument:

> We can conclude that in the choice of the twelve apostles…in the pattern of male leadership followed by those whom Jesus taught most closely, and even in the twelve names inscribed on the foundations of the heavenly city, Jesus clearly affirmed an abiding role distinction between men and women and an abiding leadership role for men.[54]

John Piper and Wayne Grudem write,

> We would *not* argue that merely because Jesus chose twelve men to be His authoritative apostles, Jesus must have favored an eldership of only men in the church. But this argument would be at

---

[54] Borland, 122.

least as valid as arguing that anything else Jesus did means He would *oppose* an eldership of all men.[55]

In other words, Jesus didn't directly *talk* about eldership, but what he *did* supports the conservative conclusion. Schreiner writes, "A male apostolate does not prove that women should not serve as leaders, but when combined with the other evidence, it does serve as confirmatory evidence for the complementarian view."[56]

However, there is another factor to consider: the disciples were not only all Jewish, there were exactly 12. When there were only 11, Peter said that it was necessary to bring the number back to 12 (Acts 1:22). Jesus was forming a new people of God, and the 12 disciples represented the 12 tribes of Israel, and for that reason they had to be 12 men.[57] For the symbolism of this group, it was necessary for Jesus to discriminate against Gentiles and women. One of the discriminating factors is now obsolete, so it is possible for the other to be obsolete, too. The example set by Jesus in this matter is therefore of uncertain significance.

Belleville comments on the biblical symbolism:

> Twelve Jewish males...represent the twelve tribes and their patriarchal heads. It is the twelve apostles who will sit on thrones, judging the twelve tribes of Israel (Matt. 19:28; Luke 22:30). The new Jerusalem will have twelve gates, twelve angels, twelve foundations, and on them the names of the twelve apostles (Rev. 21:12, 14). It is important not to make a leap from the twelve apostles to male leadership in the church. The leap, instead, should be from twelve apostles to the [entire] church of Jesus Christ. It is

---

[55] John Piper and Wayne Grudem, "An Overview of Central Concerns," 67-68, italics added.

[56] Schreiner, 196.

[57] Davidson, 176, citing Evelyn and Frank Stagg, *Women in the World of Jesus* (Philadelphia: Westminster, 1978), 123. The weakness in this explanation is that the disciples were not one from each tribe, and if they did not accurately represent the 12 patriarchs in genealogy, then it could be argued that they did not have to be accurate in gender, either. But the conclusion is still the same: Since one factor is obsolete, the other may be as well. Whether it is obsolete must be discerned from the epistles.

not male leaders who will serve as judges in the future, nor, for that matter, is it female leaders. "Do you not know," Paul says, "that *the saints* will judge the world?... Do you not know that we will judge angels?" (1 Cor. 6:2-3).[58]

Further, the 12 apostles do not set a pattern for future church leadership.[59] After James was killed, there was no effort to bring the number back to 12. We should not assume that the choice of 12 male Jewish apostles constituted a pattern for future church leaders—we know that it did not establish a pattern in its number or its ethnicity, so we should be open to the possibility that it did not establish a pattern in gender, either. We need to see what the church actually taught about leadership, and what women actually did in the early church.

Summary

In scholarly debates about the ordination of women, scholars on both sides of the question often try to argue that *every* bit of evidence supports their particular view, and in some cases it seems that they try to make particular scriptures say something they do not clearly say.

Instead, it seems better to acknowledge that some aspects of the argument lean one way, and some lean the other, and others are simply inconclusive. We hope that this admission allows us to look at the evidence more objectively, allowing each verse or passage to convey its own message. Here we can summarize some of what we have found in this and previous studies:

- In Genesis 1, men and women alike are made in the image of God, thus favoring but not proving the egalitarian view.
- In Genesis 2, conservatives have a reasonable (although not conclusive) argument that the man was created before the woman and therefore may have authority.
- In Genesis 3, man's dominance over woman is presented as part of

---

[58] Belleville, 149.

[59] "The Twelve did not constitute or provide the model or framework for leadership or authority in the early church, apart from the very earliest days in the Jerusalem church" (David Scholer, "Women," in *Dictionary of Jesus and the Gospels* [ed. Joel Green et al.; InterVarsity, 1992], 886).

the consequence of sin, suggesting that such dominance was not God's original intent.

• In the Old Testament in general, women sometimes shouldered civil leadership roles and sometimes spoke the word of God, which by definition is authoritative. This favors the egalitarian view. However, women were never in the priesthood, supporting the conservative view that God does not allow females to have certain religious roles.

The example of Jesus challenges the view that women are subordinate, but it does not specifically address gender roles in the church. Conservatives are supported by the fact that Jesus *did* make gender distinctions in selecting only males as apostles, but as conservative scholars admit, this does not conclusively prove their view that women may not serve as elders, for other explanations are possible as to why Jesus chose 12 Jewish men as apostles.

In coming chapters, we will turn our attention to what actually happened in the early church, and what the rest of the New Testament says about women in the church.

WOMEN IN THE EARLY CHURCH

In this chapter, we survey biblical evidence on the role of women in the apostolic church. We will see that in the New Testament, various women are named as having key roles within the work of the church, but few are given titles, just as few men are given titles. All this evidence is (as we expected from the start) inconclusive for our ultimate goal, which is to decide whether the Bible prohibits or allows women to be ordained as elders in the church.

Let us say a few words about why our study has spent so much time on what might seem to be inconclusive research. Although various believers (on both sides of the question) would like for us to "get to the bottom line" and deal with the controversial texts first, we believe it would be a disservice to the church for us to do that. It would place readers in the position of having to react to the conclusion without having walked through the steps by which that conclusion was reached.

For example, if we had started with a text such as 1 Timothy 2:12 (which many people *do* see as conclusive), we would still need to confront a whole host of questions: What about Genesis, and what about Deborah, and what about women in the ministry of Jesus? We would still need to deal with all the auxiliary questions anyway, so we thought it best to survey the entire Bible before we focus on specific passages. The question concerns not merely one verse, but the whole message of the Bible.

Further, we cannot conclude whether various bits of evidence are relevant until we have actually studied them. We are sharing this learning process with you so that you can study along with us. This will help people see that the various questions *are* being considered.

The evidence that seems irrelevant to one person is sometimes considered important by another. You may have no questions about Phoebe, for example, but our chapter needs to deal with her because other people *do* raise questions about her. Therefore, we hope that you are studying along with us.

Women were important in the leadership of the early church, but the Bible does not give us as many specifics as we might like. In many cases we have to read between the lines to see the role that they had. This chapter will survey the evidence in Acts and the epistles. Some of the more controversial passages (1 Cor. 11, 14, and 1 Tim. 2) will be dealt with in later chapters.

Acts

Although Acts is traditionally called "the Acts of the Apostles," it ignores most of the apostles, focusing instead on Peter and Paul. In keeping with that focus, we catch only brief glimpses of the roles of women in the church, just as we catch only glimpses of John and others.

The first mention of women comes in Acts 1:14, which states that the original nucleus of the church included the apostles, "together with the women and Mary the mother of Jesus, and his brothers.." "The women" may refer to wives of the apostles, or to the women who followed Jesus (see Luke 8:2-3, for examples).

The next mention comes in Acts 2. The disciples were meeting on the day of Pentecost, and "they were all filled with the Holy Spirit and began to speak in other tongues" (verse 4).[1]

Peter explained to the crowd that this happened in fulfillment of Joel's prophecy:

> And in the last days it shall be, God declares, that I will pour out my Spirit on all flesh, and your sons and your daughters shall prophesy, and your young men shall see visions, and your old men shall dream dreams; even on my male servants and female servants in those days I will pour out my Spirit, and they shall prophesy. (verses 17-18)

In this early church meeting, God was causing women to speak in tongues and prophesy in a place where men and women had gathered to pray and worship. Nevertheless, women are not portrayed as public speakers in the remainder of Acts. Jewish and Greco-Roman society had few if any precedents for women to speak in public settings. The attitudes of Jewish men toward women can be seen in the fact that they did not permit women to testify in court. It is therefore not likely that men would view female preachers as credible sources for new religious ideas. Because of those attitudes, women had to support the gospel in other ways.

In one place, Luke describes the growth of the church in terms of "the number of men" (4:4); in another place he mentions both "men and

---

[1] We have no reason to think that women were not at this Pentecost meeting. Acts 1:14 says that men and women "joined constantly in prayer."

women" (5:14).[2]

Some of the women were widows who depended on support from the church. When Greek-speaking widows were neglected in the daily distributions, seven men with Greek names were chosen to resolve the problem (6:1-6). Luke tells us that the apostles asked specifically for men (verse 3), but we do not see any theological reason to prohibit women from being in charge of a widow-assistance program. We conclude that the apostles asked for men due to sociological reasons.

We next hear of women when Luke tells us that Saul "dragged off men and women and committed them to prison" (8:3; 9:2; 22:4). In a society that often ignored women and probably did not have prisons for women, it is striking that Luke tells us three times that Saul persecuted women as well as men. Saul apparently viewed Christian women as a serious threat to Jewish orthodoxy, probably because they were spreading the gospel to other women.

In Samaria, "both men and women" believed and were baptized (8:12). In Joppa, God used Peter to raise a hard-working disciple named Tabitha back to life (9:36-41). In Jerusalem, the disciples gathered for prayer at the home of Mary the mother of John Mark (12:12). Mary was apparently a widow who owned her own property and was wealthy enough to have a servant girl (verse 13).

After Paul preached in Pisidian Antioch, "the Jews incited the devout women of high standing and the leading men of the city, stirred up persecution against Paul and Barnabas, and drove them out of their district" (13:50). Here the women were influential as enemies of the gospel.

In Philippi, women came to the "place of prayer" outside the city (16:13). A wealthy woman named Lydia became a believer and invited them to her home (verse 15). Paul and his companions stayed there for some time, accepting her hospitality.[3]

---

[2] This might be explained by the fact that Luke was not there and had to rely on sources. The source for the earlier number may have been a count of men, and Luke did not speculate on what the total number of people might be. But when he wrote Acts 5:14, he was describing growth in his own words, and so he mentioned women.

[3] In ancient terminology, Lydia was a patron, with the traveling evangelists as

After Paul cast a demon out of a slave girl, he was beaten, thrown into jail, rescued by an earthquake, and befriended by the jailer. Shortly before Paul and Silas left the city, they "visited Lydia. And when they had seen the brothers, they encouraged them and departed" (verse 40). The group of disciples had grown to include men, and the new church apparently met at Lydia's house. Since Lydia had a successful business and owned the meeting location, it is probably safe to say that she was influential in the church, but Luke does not give her a formal title.

In Thessalonica, Paul preached in the synagogue, persuading some of the Jews and "a great many of the devout Greeks and not a few of the leading women" (17:4, 12). (Ancient writers say that women were socially more prominent in Macedonia than in other parts of Greece.[4]) In Athens, a woman named Damaris became a believer (verse 34).

In Corinth, Paul met Aquila and Priscilla, Jews who had been forced to leave Rome. They were tentmakers, and Paul worked with them for a while (18:3). They traveled to Ephesus with Paul (verse 19). After Apollos came to Ephesus, "Priscilla and Aquila...took him aside and explained to him the way of God more accurately" (verse 26).

When both husband and wife are named in Greek writings, the man is usually named first. Most Protestant scholars conclude that Luke, by naming Priscilla first, is indicating that she was the more prominent of the two.[5] This suggests that Priscilla was an excellent teacher, well versed in

---

her clients. It was common for wealthy people to support traveling teachers with room, board and salary.

[4] Craig Keener writes, "It is possible that Philippi allowed more prominence to women because of traditional customs in that region" (*Paul, Women, and Wives* [Hendrickson, 1992], 243). Gordon Fee writes, "Macedonia was well-known as an exception to the norm; from way back women held significant positions in public life" (*Listening to the Spirit in the Text* [Eerdmans, 2000], 73, citing W. W. Tarn, *Hellenistic Civilization* [World, 1952], 98-99).

[5] They are named three times in Acts and three times in Paul's letters. Priscilla is named first four of those times. Conservative James Hurley writes, "Commentators have, I suspect correctly, inferred that she was the more prominent" (*Man and Woman in Biblical Perspective* [Zondervan, 1981], 119). But John Piper and Wayne Grudem do not agree (*Recovering Biblical Manhood and Womanhood* [Crossway, 1991], 69).

Christian doctrine, but it does not say whether a woman may have a public teaching role.

Luke mentions that four daughters of Philip prophesied (21:9), presumably on a regular basis, but we do not know where or how they prophesied.

Romans

Most of Romans is a doctrinal exposition, but Paul does give us clues about the believers in Rome when he greets many of them by name in the final chapter. The first person mentioned is Phoebe, whom Paul introduces and commends, probably because she carried the letter to Rome. Paul calls her a *diakonos* "of the church at Cenchrea" (16:1).

Since *diakonos* can mean either deacon or servant, some translations have chosen "deacon" (e.g., NRSV), while others have chosen "servant" (ESV) or "minister" (NAB). If a man had been called "a *diakonos* of the church," most translators would have used the word "deacon,"[6] but some translators do not believe that the early church had female deacons and therefore choose "servant."

When Paul gives a function followed by "of the church in Cenchrea," it appears that he is giving Phoebe a title.[7] However, even if she is a deacon, we do not know what range of responsibilities she had.

As the person who carried the letter to Rome, Phoebe may have been asked to read the letter aloud to the assembled believers, and she may have been expected to convey verbal greetings from Paul and answer questions about what Paul may have meant by any phrases the audience found confusing.[8]

---

[6] "If the name in the text were Timothy or Judas, ninety-nine per cent of the scholars would presume that diakonos meant 'deacon' and a few footnotes would remark that it could mean 'servant'" (Hurley, 124).

[7] Origen (3rd century) and Chrysostom (4th century) both understood Phoebe to be a deacon (Belleville, "Women in Ministry," in James Beck and Craig Blomberg, editors, *Two Views on Women in Ministry* [Zondervan, 2001], 101).

[8] Craig Keener writes, "Since she bears Paul's letter, she may be called upon to explain anything ambiguous in the letter when the Romans read it, and Paul wishes them to understand that she is indeed qualified to explain his writing" ("Women in Ministry," in Beck and Blomberg, 238).

Paul asks the Roman Christians to "help her in whatever she may need from you, for she has been a *prostatis* of many and of myself as well" (verse 2). What is a *prostatis?* Some translations render it "helper," but the word usually meant "benefactor" or a "patron," a wealthy person who supported other people—a common arrangement in the first-century Roman Empire.[9]

Phoebe was apparently a wealthy woman who helped take care of some of the poorer believers in Cenchrea. She had some business in Rome, and Paul asked her to carry his letter to the believers there, and in turn he asks the believers to help her accomplish whatever she came to do. She was a trusted person, well respected in the church at Cenchrea.

Paul then greets Priscilla and Aquila and calls them "my fellow workers [*synergoi*] in Christ Jesus" (verse 3). He is not referring to their tentmaking work, but to their work in the gospel (he uses the same Greek word for Timothy in verse 21). They had moved back to Rome, and a church met in their home (verse 5).

Paul sends his greeting to "Mary, who has worked hard for you" (verse 6). He does not say when, where, or what the work was, but apparently it was something notable.

Paul greets "Andronicus and Junia,[c] my kinsmen and my fellow prisoners" (verse 7). They were Jews, probably imprisoned for preaching the gospel along with Paul. That much is often accepted, but Paul's next statement is vigorously debated: "They are well known to the apostles" (ESV) or "who are outstanding among the apostles" (NASB). Some take it to mean that they are outstanding in the eyes of the apostles; others say that they are outstanding apostles.[10]

---

[9] "Phoebe is commended here as a patroness" (Thomas Schreiner, 197). "In the culture of the day, a prostatis was a 'benefactor' (NRSV, revised NAB)—or as we would say today a 'sponsor'" (Linda Belleville, *Women Leaders and the Church* [Baker, 1999], 53). Some people have claimed that *prostatis* meant "to be a leader," but it is unlikely that Paul would say that Phoebe had been his leader.

[10] Hurley points out that "It is unlike Paul to make something like acquaintance with the apostles a matter of praise. It is therefore more likely that he intended to say that they were outstanding as apostles" (121). However, Wayne Grudem has recently argued that the Greek construction can legitimately mean "well known to the apostles" (*Evangelical Feminism and Biblical Truth* [Multnomah, 2004],

Further, there was some controversy as to whether Junia(s) was female. Some scholars, believing that apostles could not be female, suggested that Junias was a shortened form of the masculine name Junianus. However, there is no evidence that Junianus was ever shortened in that way, whereas there is abundant evidence that Junia was a woman's name.[11]

It is possible that Andronicus and Junia, Jews who came to Christ before Paul did (verse 7b), were known by the original apostles and commended by them. But it is also possible that they were apostles in their own right—apostles in the sense that they were official representatives sent from one church to another (see 2 Cor. 8:23 for an example of that use of the word; an ESV footnote says that "messengers" may be a good translation).

Church history knows nothing of what Andronicus did, so it is doubtful that he could be considered an outstanding apostle in the sense that the Twelve were. The more general sense of "apostle"—messenger—is the more defensible meaning for both Andronicus and Junia.[12] We conclude that Junia was a notable woman who probably represented a church in some official capacity along with her husband, but the evidence does not permit us to say that she was an apostle in the way that Paul and the Twelve were.

Paul also greets three women: Tryphena, Tryphosa, and Persis, who worked "in the Lord" (verse 12). Paul does not give details, but it was apparently religious work. He also greets Julia, the sister of Nereus, and the mother of Rufus (verses 13, 15). Paul has mentioned 10 women—a high percentage for literature of that era.

224-25). The precise meaning does not affect our study.

[11] Linda Belleville writes that the masculine name "does not exist in any extant Greek or Latin document of the Greco-Roman period. On the other hand, the feminine name Junia is quite common and well attested in both Greek and Latin inscriptions. Over 250 examples to date have been documented in Rome alone" ("Women in Ministry," 85).]

[12] Hurley points out that if "apostle" designated the most important office in the church, it would be odd to put these two people in the middle of the list of greetings (122). Fee writes, "The term in this case, as it almost surely does in 1 Corinthians 12:28 as well, refers to a 'function,' not an 'office'" (74).

Other letters

Paul mentions a report from "Chloe's people" (1 Cor. 1:11), but he does not indicate whether Chloe herself is a believer.

For sexual relations within marriage, Paul teaches that a wife has just as much authority as the husband (7:2-5). For that society, this teaching was amazingly egalitarian, but it says nothing about a woman's role in the church. The same is true of Eph. 5:21-33, where Paul tells wives to submit to their husbands and husbands to love their wives in a self-sacrificial way. He notes that other apostles were accompanied by their wives when they traveled (1 Cor. 9:5), but he does not say what role the wives had.

In chapter 11, Paul gives instructions about head-coverings for women who prophesy or pray. Because of the complexity of this passage and its importance in the debate, we will address it in a separate chapter. Paul's comments in 14:34-35 will also be addressed in a future chapter.

Paul does *not* mention the role of women as first witnesses of Jesus' resurrection (15:5). He is probably citing a tradition in the way that it was given to him, and the tradition probably did not include the women because they were not legal witnesses in Jewish society.[13]

Galatians 3:28 has been an influential verse in the debate about women: "There is neither Jew nor Greek, there is neither slave nor free, there is no male and female, for you are all one in Christ Jesus." Paul has taken three major social divisions of the first-century church and united them. Technically, he is speaking about unity, not equality, and he is speaking of salvation, not leadership.[14] Even after writing this verse, Paul is able to give different directives to men, women, and slaves.

However, equality in salvation *can* have implications for social relationships.[15]

---

[13] "The testimony of women carried little weight in Judaism, and it was evidently for that reason that they are not included in this earliest extant confession of the Church" (Richard Longenecker, *New Testament Social Ethics for Today* [Eerdmans, 1984], 77).

[14] Mary Evans agrees, but points out that both men and women are given the same status before God: "sons" (*Woman in the Bible* [InterVarsity, 1983], 64).

[15] Thomas Schreiner concedes this: "Klyne Snodgrass argues that Galatians 3:28 cannot be confined to salvation but also has social implications.... I believe Snodgrass is correct" ("Women in Ministry," in Beck and Blomberg, 186,

For example, we believe that Jews and Gentiles should have equal opportunity for leadership. It would be wrong to say, "Gentiles are equal when it comes to salvation, but if anyone in the congregation is Jewish, then the pastor must be Jewish, even if he is poorly qualified." Some people argue that it is wrong to have similar rules that favor men over women, but personal equality does not *always* necessitate equal roles. When it comes to salvation, the pastor is on the same level as everyone else, but he does not have the same *role* as everyone else. Similarly, Christian business owners and employees are equal when it comes to salvation, but that does not require equal roles in the business. There are limits to the social consequences of our unity in Christ.

Egalitarians sometimes conclude that Gal. 3:28 is a call for equal roles within the church, whereas traditional scholars usually do not.[16]

In Philippians, Paul pleads for two women to agree with one another (Phil. 4:2). They had "labored side by side with me in the gospel together with Clement and the rest of my fellow workers [*synergoi*]" (verse 3). These women were not just serving behind the scenes—Paul indicates that they were at his side, apparently doing the same sort of gospel work that Paul, Clement, and other co-workers did.[17]

---

referring to Snodgrass's article in Alvera Mickelson, ed., *Women, Authority, and the Bible* [InterVarsity, 1986], 161-81). But Schreiner points out that we must read Paul to see what the social implications are, rather than imposing modern ideas about equality. He cites Judith Gundry-Volf as an egalitarian who "rightly argues that Galatians 3:28 does not abolish all gender differences" (187).

[16] Beck and Blomberg observe that neither Keener nor Belleville put much stress on this verse (166), and it seems to be less used in recent egalitarian works. Stanley Grenz and Denise Muir Kjesbo note that "the egalitarian case may be overstated" on this verse (*Women in the Church* [InterVarsity, 1995], 107).

[17] David Scholer writes, "The term 'coworker' (synergos) appears to be what in the Pauline churches would be a veritable 'official' term for a person who works with leadership and authority in the gospel. Paul uses this term only for such persons, which includes Urbanus (Rom 16:9); Timothy (Rom 16:21); Titus 2 Cor 8:23); Philemon (Phlm 1); Demas (Phlm 24); Apollos (and himself, 1 Cor 3:9); Prisca and Aquila (Rom 16:3; here is the other instance of the use of this term for a woman); Epaphroditus (Phil 2:25); and Clement (Phil 4:3) (see also the general use of the term in Col 4:11)" ("Euodia and Syntyche: Bishops at Philippi?" in *Selected Articles on Hermeneutics and Women and Ministry in the New Testament*

The fact that Paul uses his letter to address the quarrel between these women suggests that their quarrel was affecting other people in the church—that the women were influential in some way.[18] They might have had a formal role in the church, but Paul does not give them a title.

In Colossians 4:15, he says that a church met at the home of Nympha, who was wealthy enough to own a house large enough for the church to meet in. In Philemon 2, he greets Apphia, probably the wife of Philemon.[19]

The pastoral letters

Paul's letters to Timothy and Titus say several significant things about women. The most controversial passage, 1 Tim. 2:11-15, will have to wait for another chapter.

In 1 Tim. 3:1-7, Paul gives characteristics of a good overseer.[20] In verses 8-10 he lists desirable traits of deacons. In verse 11, he says, "Women must likewise be dignified...."[21] Commentators debate whether "women" here means female deacons, or the wives of the deacons described in verses 8-10 and then again in verse 12.

The use of "likewise" in verse 11, just as in verse 8, could suggest that female deacons are in view. On the other hand, the fact that male deacons are again described in verse 12 could suggest that male deacons are in view throughout the passage. In this latter interpretation, verse 11 gives

---

[Fuller Theological Seminary, 2003], 146).

[18] The women "had gained a position of such influence as to make their present conflict a risk to the well-being of the church" (Evans, 129).

[19] Belleville says, "The fact that she appears in the letterhead indicates she was a leader of the church at Colossae" (53). Paul did not greet women in the introduction of any other letter.

[20] These should not be viewed as absolute requirements for church leadership, for Paul himself was not "the husband of but one wife," nor did he have a family to manage well (verses 2, 4). Similarly, in new churches, it would have been necessary to appoint recent converts (cf. verse 6) as leaders. Paul is giving guidelines, not requirements.

[21] We have used the fairly literal NASB for this verse. The ESV and NIV have "their wives," but the word "their" is not in the Greek. The NRSV has "women."

desirable traits of deacons' wives, just as verse 4 gave desirable traits of children for the overseers. But it would be odd to specify traits of a deacon's wife but say nothing about an elder's wife, unless the deacon's wife had a special role, such as assisting women in baptism.[22]

Walter Liefeld concludes, "It is impossible to tell whether these were the wives of the deacons or women who were serving as deacons."[23] Rom. 16:1 offers better support for female deacons, although it has another possible interpretation as well.[24]

Paul says that deacons should "each be the husband of one wife" (verse 12). As we discussed in an earlier chapter, Paul is giving desirable traits for a deacon, not absolute requirements. We allow single men to be deacons or ministry leaders, and similarly, we allow remarried men to be deacons, whether they remarry after a divorce or after their first wife dies. The Greek phrase apparently meant "a one-woman man"—that is, one who did not have a mistress, one who was faithful to the wife he had.[25] We

---

[22] "Whichever position is adopted as to whether women are to be 'deaconesses,' there is still consensus that women should be involved in 'diacononal' or service ministries in the church" (George W. Knight III, "The Family and the Church," in Piper and Grudem, 354).

[23] Walter Liefeld, *1 and 2 Timothy, Titus* (NIV Application Commentary; Zondervan, 1999), 134. Hurley points out that since the masculine word diakonos was used for both males and females, "the fact that Paul used diakonos to introduce the men in 1 Timothy 3:8 explains the necessity of another word in verse 11 if he wished to turn attention to women deacons" (231-32).

Conservatives who accept female deacons include Thomas Schreiner (in Piper and Grudem, 505, n. 13), Walter Neuer (*Man and Woman in Christian Perspective* [Crossway, 1991], 121), and Ann Bowman ("Women in Ministry," in Beck and Blomberg, 283).

[24] There is evidence that the early church had female deacons. In one of the earliest nonbiblical references to Christians, Pliny the Younger (governor in Asia Minor A.D. 111-113) reported to Emperor Trajan that "I judged it all the more necessary to find out what the truth was by torturing two female slaves who were called deaconesses" (*Letters* 10.96-97). The text is available online in several places, such as http://www.earlychristianwritings.com/text/pliny.html.

[25] Craig Keener, *And Marries Another: Divorce and Remarriage in the Teaching of the New Testament* (Hendrickson, 1991), 94.

do consider *this* to be a requirement.

We also believe that a similar rule should apply for female deacons: They should be faithful. If they are remarried, they should be faithful to the husband they now have. When Paul said that male deacons should be faithful to their wives, it would have gone without saying in that culture that a similar rule would apply to female deacons. As discussed in a previous chapter, biblical rules are often phrased from the male perspective even when they apply to females as well. (A later chapter will discuss whether this might apply to verse 2.) The main point is that female leaders should be of good character.

In 1 Tim. 5:3, Paul addresses another group of women: "Honor widows who are truly widows." He notes that widows should be supported by their families—"if anyone does not provide for his relatives, and especially for members of his household, he has denied the faith" (verse 8; cf. Mark 7:11-13). But if the widow did not have family support, the church apparently provided support.

"Let a widow be enrolled if she is not less than sixty years of age" and of good character (verses 9-10). Younger widows should not be put on the list, he says, "for when their passions draw them away from Christ, they desire to marry and so incur condemnation for having abandoned their former faith" (verses 11-12).

Timothy already knew what this "list of widows" was, but today we have to read between the lines to see what Paul was talking about. Apparently the widows made a life-long pledge to serve the church in return for its financial support, and remarriage was a violation of that pledge. Paul felt that women under age 60 might be so anxious to marry that they could not be trusted to keep a pledge of celibacy.

How much of this is applicable to the modern church? Did Paul intend for his letter to Timothy to become a manual of church organization for subsequent centuries and cultures? Should churches have a roster of older widows pledged to celibacy? Although it is permissible for churches to have such a list, we do not believe that the Bible requires this. There is wisdom in Paul's letter, but he wrote to a specific church, and the specific admonitions he gives must be evaluated to see whether they are appropriate in other settings.[26]

---

[26] We noted in an earlier chapter that the instruction Paul gave in 1 Tim. 3:6

Paul praised the faith of Timothy's mother and grandmother (2 Tim. 1:5), but we are not told whether they brought Timothy to faith in Christ. However, Paul also warned Timothy that women were targets of false teachers "who creep into households and capture weak women, burdened with sins and led astray by various passions, always learning and never able to arrive at a knowledge of the truth" (2 Tim. 3:6-7). These women had apparently heard the gospel but had not accepted it.

Paul told Titus, "Older women likewise are to be reverent in behavior.... They are to teach what is good, and so train the young women to love their husbands and children...and submissive to their own husbands, that the word of God may not be reviled" (Titus 2:3-5). Paul trusted older women to teach younger ones, and at least one purpose of this instruction is cultural, so that outsiders would have less to criticize about the gospel.[27]

General epistles

The remaining books of the New Testament say little about women and little about leadership in the church. Hebrews mentions Sarah, though scholars debate whether she is mentioned in passing or is commended as having faith (11:11). The author implies that faith inspired the women who received the dead raised back to life again (verse 35). James mentions that Rahab had exemplary faith (2:25).

Peter, after advising everyone to submit to government authorities, and slaves to submit to their masters, also advises women to be submissive to their husbands (1 Peter 3:1); he cites Sarah as exemplary in this respect (verse 6). He advises men "likewise" to treat their wives with respect, "as

---

would not apply to the church in Crete (cf. Titus 1:6-9); he did not intend his letter to be a manual for all churches. The point is that unless we believe that all instructions in 1 Timothy apply to the church today (which we do not), then we must discuss each instruction to ask whether it applies, or how it might be adapted. A later chapter will discuss whether 1 Tim. 2:11-12 is a directive for all subsequent centuries.

[27] Similarly, he advises slaves to be subject to their masters so that "they will make the teaching about God our Savior attractive" (verse 10). His advice is culturally appropriate, but we cannot assume that it implies an endorsement of the cultural setting in which it was given.

GRACE COMMUNION INTERNATIONAL

the weaker vessel," because they are equal heirs of salvation (verse 7).[28]

John greets a "chosen lady and her children" (2 John 1), but this is usually interpreted as a metaphor for the church (the Greek word *ekklesia* is feminine, and the church is considered the bride of Christ—2 Cor. 11:2; Eph. 5:25-27).

Revelation has both positive and negative imagery of women. The church is described as a woman (12:1-17) and as a bride (21:2)—a bride who joins the Spirit in inviting people to come to Christ (22:17). A more negative view is seen in 14:4, which says that the 144,000 "have not defiled themselves with women, for they are virgins." It is debatable whether we can ascertain anything about gender roles in the real world from these apocalyptic symbols.

Conclusion

Women had various important functions in the early church. Some taught, some prophesied, some provided financial support, and many worked in the gospel. Various people are called apostles, but rarely is anyone, whether male or female, given any other title. We know the names of only two men who are called "elder" and one woman who was called a "deacon."[29]

Since titles are rarely given, it is important to look at what people did, not what titles they had, and it is significant to see that in several cases, women worked alongside men in spreading the gospel, and the same Greek words are used to describe their work as are used for male leaders.

In our next chapter we will examine 1 Cor. 11, which refers to women in the church at Corinth who prophesied and prayed.

---

[28] Paul is making a general observation—he is not implying that all husbands are stronger than their wives. Nor is he saying that women are weaker intellectually or spiritually. On average, men are physically stronger than their wives, but, according to Peter, that should lead men to respect their wives, not abuse them.

[29] Peter and John call themselves elders in 1 Peter 5:1 and 2 John 1. As we concluded above, Romans 16:1 probably calls Phoebe a deacon; the seven men of Acts 6:5 are not specifically called deacons. It may have taken some time for terminology to become standardized.

160

WOMEN WHO PRAY OR PROPHESY
1 CORINTHIANS 11:3-16

One commentator wrote, "This passage is probably the most complex, controversial, and opaque of any text of comparable length in the New Testament."[30] And he may be right—but in our denomination, we have had far less controversy about it.

In our fellowship, we have long agreed that women do not need to wear head coverings in church today—these specific instructions do not apply in our culture. Having "solved" that question, we felt little need to dig into the passage any deeper. In decades past, our main use of the passage was to say that men should have short hair and women should not (verses 14-15).

When we asked members to submit papers concerning the role of women in the church, few had anything to say about this passage. Almost no one disagreed with our previous conclusion about head coverings—nor did they disagree with the article we published in 2001, which observed that the passage assumed that women could speak in church.[31]

Nevertheless, this passage raises some important questions about how we interpret the Bible, and how to decide whether a particular command is based in culture, or in creation.[32] Our old decision about head coverings was probably based more on what made "sense" to us than it was based on

---

[30] Craig Blomberg, *1 Corinthians* (The NIV Application Commentary; Zondervan, 1994), 214. Another scholar writes, "Commentators vary widely in their understanding of the background of the problem" (Richard Longenecker, *New Testament Social Ethics for Today* [Eerdmans, 1984], 80). They are trying to guess what kind of situation, and what cultural background, would cause Paul to write what he did. The variety of suggested solutions shows how hard it is to understand the background of the passage.

[31] "Women Who Spoke the Word of God"; see pages 58-62.

[32] Blomberg writes, "A passage such as 1 Corinthians 11:2-16 reveals the need for all believers to have a relatively sophisticated grasp of principles of biblical hermeneutics, so that they can sift through the historical-cultural background, understand the meaning of key terms and grammatical interrelationships within a passage, and fit this passage in with Paul's other teaching on the topic" (226).

a study of the text. We did not have a good explanation for why head coverings were obsolete but hair lengths were not. We were unwittingly basing our beliefs on assumptions that were rooted in modern culture.

In this study, we discuss numerous questions about this passage, but we cannot answer them all—nor do we need to. However, we do try to answer some key questions for us concerning the role of women in the church today.

1 Corinthians 11

In his first letter to the church in Corinth, Paul deals with several problems that the local church had. One of the issues he deals with is whether people should cover their heads when they pray or prophesy. Although he briefly addresses what men should do, most of his comments concern women.[33] We will survey the chapter and examine certain questions in greater detail.

Verse 1 says: "Be imitators of me, as I am of Christ." This is Paul's conclusion to his comments about meat in chapter 10—he encourages the Corinthians to do everything for the glory of God, to avoid causing offense, "just as I try to please everyone in everything I do, not seeking my own advantage, but that of many, that they may be saved" (10:33). In 11:1, he encourages them to follow this example. In chapter 11, too, he wants them to avoid causing unnecessary offense to the people around them.

Verse 2 says, "I commend you because you remember me in everything and maintain the traditions even as I delivered them to you." This may be a concluding comment for the previous topic, or it may be a general introduction to Paul's next topic, but either way, this verse does not seem to help us much in understanding what Paul writes in verses 3-16.

---

[33] David E. Garland writes, "Paul oscillates back and forth with statements about men and women, but this pattern is broken in 11:13 with a statement about the woman but none about the man." He also notes that Paul sometimes gives a supporting reason for his statements about women, without giving support for the corresponding statements about men—implying that he expects little resistance to his statements about men. "The best explanation for these breaks in the pattern is that the problem that Paul wishes to correct has to do with what the women were doing with their heads" (*1 Corinthians* [Baker, 2003], 507-8).

Women need a head covering

In the next verse, Paul begins addressing a new topic: "But I want you to understand that the head of every man is Christ, the head of a wife[34] is her husband,[35] and the head of Christ is God" (verse 3). Paul is using "head" as a metaphor, but the meaning of this metaphor is debated. Traditional scholars say that Paul is using the word "head" (Greek *kephalē*) as a metaphor for authority: Christ has authority over the male, the male has authority over the female, and God has authority over Christ. Other scholars argue that the metaphor means "source"[36] or "preeminence."[37] We will address this in more detail later.

No matter what the meaning, the sequence of "heads" is odd, since it goes down at first, and then up: Christ, man, God.[38] There is also some disagreement about whether the verse is talking about all men and women, or just husbands and wives. The NIV, for example, chooses the more generic meaning: "the head of every man is Christ, and the head of the woman is man."

---

[34] The ESV footnote says: "Greek *gunē*. This term may refer to a woman or a wife, depending on the context."

[35] The ESV footnote says: "Greek *anēr*. This term may refer to a man or a husband, depending on the context."

[36] For example, Mary Evans writes: "'Head' used in this context is a metaphor and there is no reason to suppose that the first century use of this metaphor will be identical with its twentieth century use, particularly as in the first century it was the heart not the head that was seen as the source of thought and reason, the head at this time being seen rather as the source of life" (*Woman in the Bible* [InterVarsity, 1983], 65).

[37] Garland, 516.

[38] "The odd sequence reveals that Paul has no interest [or at least it is not his main purpose] in establishing some kind of ascending hierarchical order to show the inferiority of women.... His purpose is not to write a theology of gender but to correct an unbefitting practice in worship that will tarnish the church's reputation" (Garland, 508, 514). Blomberg offers this suggestion: "Since the problem in Corinth involved men and women (but not Christ) dishonoring their heads, it is natural that he should refer to the heads of the man and of the woman first" (209).

Paul then moves to a more specific application: "Every man who prays or prophesies with his head covered dishonors his head" (verse 4). It is generally agreed that the second occurrence of "head" in this verse should be taken metaphorically: The covered man dishonors Christ.[39] Paul has begun the discussion by speaking metaphorically in verse 3 so he can use the metaphorical meaning in verse 4.

What does Paul mean when he says "with his head covered"? The Greek words mean something like "on the head." Is Paul referring to a hat, a turban,[40] an Arabic *kaffiyeh*, a prayer shawl (such as those used by some Jewish men today when they pray, or something else?[41]) In some pagan religious rites, Roman men covered their heads with part of their toga.[42] That may be what Paul is referring to—but he does not explain why this custom was dishonorable.[43] Some symbolism was probably involved, but

---

[39] "What individuals do to their physical head in worship reflects negatively or positively on their metaphorical head" (Garland, 514). Linda Belleville writes, "A man praying or prophesying with his head covered...disgraced Christ (1 Cor. 11:3-4). We cannot know for certain why this was" (*Women Leaders and the Church* [Baker, 1999], 129).

[40] "The fact that Jewish priests officiating in the temple wore turbans makes Paul's statement doubly surprising (Ezek. 44:18; cf. *m. Yoma* 7.5)" (Belleville, 129). We do not know why a turban would be appropriate for a priest but not for a man who is praying.

[41] "The Jewish practice of covering a man's head during worship did not become widespread before the fourth century A.D." (Blomberg, 221).

[42] "The statue from Corinth of a veiled Augustus—with his toga pulled over his head in preparation to offer a libation—may offer an important clue.... Wearing the toga over the head at pagan sacrifices was a familiar practice" (Garland, 517). Ben Witherington III points out that this was a Roman custom, not a Greek one (*Conflict and Community in Corinth: A Socio-Rhetorical Commentary on 1 and 2 Corinthians* [Eerdmans, 1995], 234). Corinth was in Greece, but a Roman colony, so it is not certain which culture predominated.

[43] Garland surmises that Paul objects to "the associations of the headdress with pagan sacrifice" (518). However, the Corinthians do not seem to be so naturally opposed to pagan practices that they would automatically agree that this practice was dishonorable (and the fact that Paul does not explain his logic indicates that he expects his readers to agree with his point). Non-Christian Greeks apparently did not think that pagan priests dishonored the gods by covering the head. Rather,

it is difficult for modern readers to know what it is.[44] It is especially difficult for us to know why a covering was considered dishonorable for a male but required for a female.[45]

Some scholars have suggested that the head covering is long hair pulled up and bound on the top of the head[46]; that when long hair was let down, it suggested rebellion or sexual availability.[47] Support for this is seen in verse 15, which says that a woman's long hair is given to her *instead* of a veil.[48] However, it is difficult to make this interpretation work in verse 4:

---

they probably assumed the opposite, that the custom honored the gods in some way. "It appears that such headcoverings were worn in Roman contexts to demonstrate respect and subservience to the gods" (Witherington, 234). In Garland's view, Paul objected to covered men for religious reasons, but bare-headed women for sexual reasons. Blomberg writes, "What the Corinthians did with their heads mattered because of either the sexual or the religious implications of their appearance (or both)" (215).

[44] Evans writes about customs of head coverings: "The evidence we do have seems to indicate that there was a great deal of variation in different regions and between town and country" (87). It difficult for us to know what the customs were; it is even more difficult to know what the customs meant to the people.

[45] Hurley argues that the symbol meant "being submissive to the authority of a man"—hence was appropriate for woman but not for a man (170). However, most men are under the authority of, and should submit to, male civil authorities. Women wore a head covering in public but male slaves did not; this suggests that the primary connotation was gender, not authority.

[46] Belleville does not have this view, but she describes the custom: "The typical hairstyle shown in portraits of upper-class Greek and Roman women involved twisting the hair into a roll at the top of the head and then looping it to form a raised ridge" (*Women Leaders,* 128).

[47] "For a Hebrew woman to go out uncovered was widely regarded as a disgrace...because a covered head was a sign of modesty.... To go out with loose hair in public...was a greater disgrace and considered grounds for divorce" (Garland 520, citing the *Mishnah Ketub.* 7:6; and Babylonian *Talmud Ned.* 30b, *Yoma* 47b, and *Ketub.* 72a).

[48] Paul uses a different word in verse 15 than previous verses. Long hair is given to the woman instead of some sort of clothing (*peribolaion*), but she needs to be covered (*katakalypta,* from the words for down and covered, verse 6). The

If a man had hair long enough to pull onto the top of the head, it seems that Paul would begin by saying that the long hair was disgraceful in itself—he would not start by criticizing an attempt to pull it up onto the top of the head.[49] Also, if the hair is pulled up, it would seem inappropriate for the Greek phrase to use the word *kata,* meaning down. And it would be odd to say that if the hair hung down loose, it might as well be cut off (verse 6).[50] Schreiner writes, "The verb translated as 'cover' in the NIV (*katakalypto*) occurs three times in verses 6-7…most often refers to a covering of some kind."[51] On the other hand, if the hair was covered, there would be little need to specify its length.

In verses 5-6, Paul writes, "Every wife [or woman] who prays or prophesies with her head uncovered dishonors her head, since it is the same as if her head were shaven. For if a wife will not cover her head, then she should cut her hair short. But since it is disgraceful for a wife to cut off her hair or shave her head, let her cover her head."[52] Again, it is not clear what type of head covering Paul is referring to—some say it is a

---

significance of these terms is debated.

[49] "If an 'uncovered' head simply means 'having her hair down,' how is 'the man's not covering his head in verse 7…the opposite of this?'" (Keener 22, quoting Gordon Fee's commentary). Witherington writes, "Plutarch uses the same phrase that Paul does, *kata kephalēs,* to refer to something resting on the head, not hair" (233).

[50] Robert Peterson writes, "In 1 Cor. 11:6, does it make sense to say a woman should have her hair cut short because her hair is already short? No." ("Women's Roles in the Church, What Does the Bible Say?" unpublished paper).

[51] Schreiner, 126. He notes that Philo uses the word for "uncovered" to mean with a cloth removed.

[52] The Greek word for "if" here (ei) implies a positive answer—that it is indeed a disgrace for a woman to have a shaved head. But it is not clear whether this disgrace falls on herself, on her metaphorical head, or both. Gordon Fee writes, "It has often been asserted that the shaved head was a sign of prostitution in Corinth; but there is not a known piece of evidence for such in the literature of antiquity" (*Listening to the Spirit in the Text* [Eerdmans, 2000], 63). He says that a shaved head was shameful because it indicated "the 'male' partner in a lesbian relationship."

woman's long hair (cf. verse 15b); others say it is a shawl.[53]

Paul does not say why it is shameful, and scholars have suggested several possibilities. Garland lists these: "somehow blurs gender distinctions, is a symptom of disorderly behavior, has links to pagan cultic activity, disavows the authority of the husband or paterfamilias, or is a cultural sign of immodesty."[54]

Paul apparently wrote this because some women in Corinth were breaking social custom and speaking without a head covering.[55] Why were they breaking social custom? Several reasons have been proposed: 1) They believed that gender-based restrictions did not apply in the church[56] or 2) They believed that when they were in church, they were no longer in public, but in a family, and women did not need to wear head coverings when in their own homes.[57] Keener writes, "Paul calls on them to submit

---

[53] In a few denominations today, a small piece of cloth is deemed sufficient even though it is not large enough to "cover" the head or hang "down" from it.

[54] Garland, 519. Richard Davidson writes, "The wearing of the head covering...was a sign of the wife's submission to her husband's leadership, not to the headship of all men" (in *Women in Ministry,* edited by Nancy Vyhmeister [Andrews University, 1998], 275).

[55] "That Paul is likewise upholding a firmly established social custom seems clear from terms like shameful...proper...disgraceful.... Even so, Paul's appeal to the creation order of Genesis 2 shows that something more than unbefitting behavior is at issue.... Some sort of sexual identity confusion lurks in the background" (Belleville, *Women,* 127-28).

[56] "Antoinette Wire's reconstruction of the situation that generated Paul's correctives has...gained a fair measure of acceptance and remains plausible. Some Christian women (and maybe some men!) were interpreting their freedom in Christ to mean that they could flout social convention concerning public appearance" (Blomberg, in *Two Views,* 341; see also Hurley, 170).

Evans suggests that women thought they had to dress like a man in order to prophesy, and Paul explains to them that women did not have to dress or act like men in order to be free, but that they were free to pray and prophesy as women (Evans, 90).

[57] "Christian women may not have thought of themselves as going out in public when they worshiped in homes and called one another 'brother' and 'sister'" (Garland 521, citing Fee and Winter). Against this view it can be noted

to the head coverings so as not to cause offense"—Paul does not want the women to bring shame on their husbands.[58] Others suggest that the women were copying practices found in some other religions.

Prophesying in public

Paul is saying that it is shameful for a woman to pray or prophesy with an uncovered head. We might ask three questions at this point: 1) What does it mean to prophesy? 2) Is this praying and prophesying done in public, or in private? 3) Should the church today require women to wear a head covering?[59]

To understand what Paul means by "prophesy," we do not need to refer to Old Testament customs (which are of debatable significance), for Paul himself tells us what he understands the word to mean. In chapter 12, Paul lists prophecy as one of the gifts of the Spirit. In chapter 14, Paul describes what he means: "The one[60] who prophesies speaks to people for their upbuilding and encouragement and consolation…. The one who prophesies builds up the church" (14:3-4).

Throughout chapter 14, Paul contrasts tongues and prophesying, and he concludes, "in church I would rather speak five words with my mind in order to instruct [*katecheō*] others, than ten thousand words in a tongue"

---

that the Corinthians were not treating one another like family in other respects.

[58] Craig Keener, *Paul, Women, and Wives* (Hendrickson, 1992), 21. He notes that Paul used himself "as an example of sacrificing one's own rights in chapter 9…. The principle he articulates could be applied to any of us. If our dressing a certain way in public will cause discomfort to our spouse, we ought not to do it. Paul is clearly less concerned with the particular apparel worn in a given culture than he is with its effects" (pp. 21, 36).

[59] If we took verse 6 literally, the church should give haircuts to women who speak without a head covering—but it seems clear that Paul does not intend this literally. "Paul is using here the ancient debating principle of reductio ad absurdum: reducing the position of his opponents to the absurd. If they want to bare their heads so badly, why don't they bare them altogether by removing their hair, thus exposing themselves to public shame?" (Keener, 35).

[60] The Greek word here (*anthrōpos*) refers to both men and women. The ESV accurately avoids the impression that only men are intended. At least in Antioch, prophets were part of the leadership of the church (Acts 13:1).

(14:19).[61] In this verse, he implies that someone who prophesies instructs the church. In verse 24 he says that if people are prophesying, an unbeliever can learn something: "he is convicted by all.... so, falling on his face, he will worship God." In verse 31 Paul says that people learn as a result of prophecy. Although prophecy is not exactly the same as teaching, it has similar results.[62]

According to Paul's definition, prophesying helps people in the church learn.[63] In Corinth, the Holy Spirit was inspiring both men and women to speak edifying messages during worship services. If the words were inspired by God, then they had authority.[64]

Women were speaking in a church meeting—there would be little need for Paul to address proper attire for something done in private. Blomberg gives seven lines of evidence that indicate that the passage is about a public setting:

1) Verses 2 and 17 are paired in content, suggesting that a similar setting is in view throughout,

2) The concern for appearance suggests a public setting,

3) The best analogies about men covering their heads are in a setting

---

[61] From the Greek word *katecheō,* we get the English word catechism, which refers to an organized system of instruction.

[62] Paul lists prophecy and teaching as separate gifts (Rom 12:6-7; 1 Cor 12:29; 14:6; Eph 4:11). One possible difference in the gifts is that teaching may involve advance planning, whereas prophecy is spontaneous. As mentioned in previous chapters, there are biblical examples of female prophets.

[63] Blomberg gives this description: "the proclamation of a message given by God to a Christian speaker for the benefit of a particular congregation. It may include both spontaneous utterances and carefully thought-out communication, so long as the prophet is convinced that God has led him or her to preach a certain message" (210). Grudem argues that prophecy is always spontaneous, and is not an exposition of Scripture (*Evangelical Feminism and Biblical Truth* [Multnomah, 2004], 229).

[64] People should not assume that every utterance claimed to be prophecy is actually inspired by God. Paul instructs the church to "weigh carefully what is said" (14:29; cf. 1 Thess. 5:20-21). Some theologians believe that God does not give the gift of prophecy to anyone in this era, but the example in Corinth still shows that God allows women to speak in worship services.

of (pagan) worship,

4) Paul discusses spiritual gifts primarily in a church setting,
5) Women had little opportunity to minister to men in private,
6) The mention of angels in verse 10 makes sense in a worship setting, and
7) Verse 16 refers to the practice of other churches, which suggests a setting within church.[65]

Thomas Schreiner gives four slightly different reasons: 1) The subsequent topics concern worship, 2) Prophecy is supposed to edify the community, 3) Meetings in a home would count as a church meeting, and 4) 1 Cor 14:34 is not intended to be a complete prohibition.[66]

Paul had to address the issue in this letter because some Corinthian women had been speaking in church without a head covering.[67] In some

---

[65] Blomberg, 219.

[66] Thomas Schreiner, *Recovering Biblical Manhood and Womanhood* (Crossway, 1991), 132. That 1 Cor. 11:3-16 concerns worship settings is the consensus of most traditional and egalitarian scholars. James Hurley says that the "women were praying and prophesying, to some sort of meeting of the church" (180). John Piper and Wayne Grudem say that verse 5 addresses "women prophesying in church" (*Recovering,* 69, 85). Walter Neuer also accepts "the church" as the setting for this passage, though he later qualifies it to say it was "small house groups," not the "whole church" (*Man and Woman in Christian Perspective* [Crossway, 1991], 112, 118). However, in many cities, a small house group was the whole church, so it would be artificial to try to distinguish them. As Schreiner says, "the distinction between public and private meetings of the church is a modern invention" (*Two Views,* 228).

Harold R. Holmyard argues, based largely on 1 Cor 14:34, that the women were not speaking in a church meeting ("Does 1 Corinthians 11:2-16 Refer to Women Praying and Prophesying in Church?" *Bibliotheca Sacra* 154 [Oct. 1997]: 462-73). He agrees that a public setting is meant, but not church: "The issue of head coverings implies a public setting, not prayer in private" (472). He does not address the above lines of evidence. In our own fellowship, Peterson claims that church settings are not discussed until verse 17, but he does not address the evidence given above for a public setting. He also argues that women still need to wear a shawl on their head when praying. We reject that, and believe that the evidence favors a church setting.

[67] "While it not likely that the Corinthian men were in fact putting coverings on, it would seem quite likely that the Corinthian women had concluded that,

societies, a head covering is a sign of submission or modesty; in others (e.g., Saudi Arabia) even the king wears a head covering in public. No matter what the head coverings symbolized in Corinth, it is clear that they do not symbolize the same thing in all cultures, and we conclude that they are not required as a sign of submission for all Christian men and women in all regions and centuries. There seems to be a consensus[68] that Paul's instruction here was based primarily on culture—he was applying a general principle to a specific situation, and although the principle is still valid, the specific application is not. But what *is* that "general principle"? Scholars debate whether it is to maintain a distinction in *authority* between males and females, to maintain a distinction in *appearance* between the sexes, or simply to avoid doing something the surrounding culture considered scandalous.

The glory of man

Paul now gives a reason for men to uncover their heads: "A man ought not to cover his head, since he is the image and glory of God, but woman is the glory of man" (1 Cor. 11:7). Unfortunately, we do not understand Paul's reasoning here. We note the following questions:

If being in the image and glory of God means that a man should not cover his head, then this would apply to *all* situations, not just speaking in

---

having been raised with Christ (1 Cor. 4:8-10), their new position in Christ and their resultant freedom to participate in the worship by prayer and prophecy was incompatible with wearing a sign of submission to their husbands" (Hurley, 170). They thought that something in the gospel had liberated them from gender-based social conventions. However, Witherington speculates that some men were following Roman custom and wearing a headcovering, while women were following Greek practice, and the variations were causing controversy (Witherington, 238).

[68] Hurley concludes that "her hair is a sufficient sign; no shawls are needed" (184). Neuer likewise does not advocate coverings today, although he notes that women who "think that they should follow Paul's instruction about covering the head…should not be made fun of, but respected for their stand" (114).

Piper, Grudem, and Schreiner all conclude that Paul commanded head-coverings for the culture he was in, but that they are not required today (75, 138). They see a timeless principle behind Paul's teaching: a requirement to "use culturally appropriate expressions of masculinity and femininity."

church. In other words, the reason given here proves more than Paul intended, and we cannot make the same argument today. We do not know why it would be inappropriate for "the image and glory of God" to wear a hat, whether on the job or in the church. Further, we do not know what Paul means by woman being "the glory of man."[69]

Paul's next verse says that the female came from the male, but the male's role in her creation was totally unlike God's role in the creation of the male. Is man the "pride and joy" of God, and woman the "pride and joy" of man? Perhaps that is what Paul means, but that would not explain why one must cover the head and the other must not. Blomberg notes that "in verses 14-15 'glory' is the opposite of 'disgrace,' so in both places it probably carries the sense of 'honor.'"[70]

Last, we note that women are also made in the image of God (Gen. 1:27), a point that Paul did not mention. It seems clear that he is using the evidence from Genesis selectively, not in a comprehensive way. He is not trying to present a theology of gender behavior—he is simply dealing with one particular practice.[71] But it is not clear why he brought the word

---

[69] Schreiner says that "the focus here is on the word glory.... Paul's point is that one should always honor and respect the source from which one came" (133). Garland suggests that "if a woman were to appear in worship with her head uncovered, the splendor of her tresses (11:15) should bring honor to her husband" (523). The idea is that each gender brings honor to the metaphorical head, but in worship it would be inappropriate for a woman to bring glory to her head, man. So by wearing a head covering, she can point to God rather than man. However, others argue that the problem with her tresses is lust, not misdirected glory. William Webb writes, "This proposition related to the question of how much of a woman's beauty/glory should be visible in a worship setting—an issue of modesty" (*Slaves, Women, and Homosexuality*, 274).

Hurley suggests that "the glory of a thing is...that which points to or manifests its dignity, honour, or station. Man is relationally the glory of God when he is in an appropriate relation to him: under God, thereby pointing to God's dominion" (174). He suggests that a man gives God glory "as he exercises his leadership role and the woman is the glory of the man as she appropriately responds" (206). But this definition of "glory" seems to be tailored for Hurley's interpretation of this passage, rather than being based on the way the word is used elsewhere.

[70] Blomberg, 211.

[71] Hurley suggests a narrow context: "The woman is not called to image God

172

"image" into the argument at all.

In verses 8-9, Paul appears to explain the way in which woman is the glory of man: "For man was not made from woman, but woman from man. Neither was man created for woman, but woman for man." The man was the source of the woman, and the woman was created for the man.[72] Is woman the glory of man because she *came* from man? If so, then all of creation, including the woman, would be the glory of God, for everything came from him. Paul seems to be reasoning on the basis of which sex was created first, but we do not understand how he goes from his reason to his conclusion. Moreover, in verses 11-12 Paul seems to modify the argument (just as he clarified his statement in 1 Cor 1:14), perhaps because the evidence does not say as much as his first comment might imply.[73]

In the next verse, Paul goes back to his main topic—the need for women to have a head covering. "That is why [because woman was created from man and for man] a wife ought to have a *symbol* of authority on her head, because of the angels" (verse 10). Scholars do not know what the angels have to do with this subject. Paul is alluding to something, but we do not know what it is.[74]

---

or Christ in the relation which she sustains to her husband. She images instead the response of the church to God.... There need be no implication whatsoever that women are not the image of God in other senses" (173).

[72] As we covered in a previous chapter, the woman was made for the man because he was alone and did not have a mate, unlike all the animals. She was made to be his companion, not his servant. The man did not lack for creatures to have authority over—what he needed was someone who was like himself.

[73] Paul says one thing in 1 Cor 1:14 but retracts it in verse 16. He is thinking out loud, and his secretary wrote it down, and rather than delete the incorrect statement, Paul added a correction. It would be a mistake for us to focus on the first statement and not on the correction.

[74] Scholars have made a variety of suggestions, such as 1) angels attend worship meetings and are sensitive to misbehavior in the worship service, 2) some angels are sexually attracted to women and the head coverings keep the angels in line, 3) the head covering is a sign that woman has authority over angels, or 4) angels are an example of beings who refused to submit to their place in creation. The Corinthians might have known what Paul meant, but we do not. An ESV footnote suggests another meaning for *angelos:* "Or messengers, that is, people

The word "symbol" in the last part of the ESV translation of this verse is in keeping with the traditional interpretation, that the covering is a sign that the woman is *under* authority, but the Greek literally says "the woman ought to have authority on her head." In all other uses, *exousia* means having authority; it never means "a symbol of being *under* authority."[75]

If we take the verse literally, it means that the head covering *gives* the woman authority to speak—that by putting on the appropriate attire, she is permitted to pray and prophesy.[76] Because she was created from and for the man, she needs this head covering to authorize her to speak in the worship assembly.[77] Another possible interpretation is that the phrase means "to have authority over"—that she is "to have control over her head" by wearing the customary covering.[78]

In verses 11-12, Paul appears to qualify or clarify part of his previous argument.[79] He writes, "Nevertheless, in the Lord woman is not

---

sent to observe and report."

[75] Hurley writes, "The term does not mean 'sign of (someone else's) authority.' It has instead an active sense and, apart from the context, would be taken as pointing to the authority of the woman herself" (176). He suggests that the appropriate hairstyle "marked her as one possessing authority, as viceregent of creation, one who would join in the judgment of rebellious angels" (177). However, Schreiner gives a vigorous defense of the traditional view, saying that the word "ought" signals "an obligation, not a freedom" (135).

[76] Neuer writes, "If the women pray or prophesy before other members of the church, then they possess the spiritual authority to do so only if they do it obediently, accepting the position assigned to them at creation" (115). Richards writes, "The most natural meaning would be that a woman has 'authority,' that is, the freedom to act or to worship, simply by following proper decorum" (320). A point against this view is that Paul tells the woman what she "ought" to have; it does not appear that he is extolling her freedom.

[77] Against this view, Garland notes, "The introductory phrase 'because of this' means that Paul is drawing a conclusion from what has been argued in 11:3-9, and these verses emphasize the woman's secondary place as the glory of man, not her authority to pray and prophesy" (525).

[78] Blomberg, 212, and Garland, 525. A similar thought may be in 14:32, where Paul uses different Greek words to say that prophets should control their spirits.

[79] "He backtracks lest the Corinthians become confused and think that he

independent of man nor man of woman; for as woman was made from man, so man is now born of woman. And all things are from God." Just as the original man was the source of the first woman, all subsequent men have come from women, and God is the source of everything. This verse seems to reduce the strength of the argument from priority or source.

Why does Paul say that this interdependence is "in the Lord"? Why does he begin the sentence with the contrastive word "nevertheless"? This seems to imply that aspects of the previous argument were *not* based "in the Lord."[80] Belleville draws this conclusion: "In the final analysis, whatever meaning we attach to the man is 'the head of the woman' (1 Cor. 11:3), this state of affairs does not hold true 'in the Lord.' Mutual dependence is what should characterize life in community, for 'in the Lord' a 'woman is not independent of man, nor is man independent of woman' (1 Cor. 11:11)."[81]

After this, Paul gives another reason for his instruction that women should wear a head covering when they speak in church: "Judge for yourselves: is it proper for a wife to pray to God with her head uncovered? Does not nature itself teach you that if a man wears long hair it is a disgrace for him, but if a woman has long hair, it is her glory? For her hair is given to her for a covering" (verses 13-15).

Paul apparently believes that he has given the Corinthians enough information to make the answer obvious. Even though Corinth was saturated with sin, he appeals to the Corinthians' own sense of propriety, as if they would all sense the disgrace of a woman speaking without

---

implies that women are inferior to men" (Garland, 508). "These two verses clearly form a tension on a theoretical level with his previous arguments" (Webb, 87).

[80] Blomberg suggests that the contrast is between Christ and creation: "'In the Lord,' that is, among Christians, the nature of creation is substantially qualified but never erased altogether" (216). But it seems problematic to posit a large difference between creation and Christ, as if Christ changed God's original design for humanity. This may instead be a hint that Paul's argument, although it alludes to creation, is actually based in culture. The word "however" in verse 11 implies that he is giving a contrast or correction, not reinforcing the previous point.

[81] Belleville, *Women Leaders,* 131. Webb writes, "Not only do his 'in the Lord' comments take the abrasive edge off of the patriarchy of Paul's day, but resident within them are seed ideas for future development" (278).

anything on her head.[82]

When Paul writes "nature," he uses the word *physis,* which usually referred to the way the physical and biological world was, but sometimes referred to social custom.[83] Paul apparently uses it in the latter meaning here, for biological facts do not teach people that long hair is a "disgrace" for one sex and a "glory" for the other.[84] Rather, our physiological nature teaches us that a man's hair grows as much as a woman's. The word "disgrace" indicates a social stigma and a cultural convention.[85]

Paul is not saying that men who took a Nazirite vow were a disgrace—he was writing to the Corinthian situation and not trying to make a

---

[82] Paul's purpose throughout this passage, Neuer notes, is to preserve female honor, not to demean her. "The woman upholds her dignity and glory by preserving her womanly character and her position in the creation" (Neuer, 115).

[83] The BDAG lexicon lists four meanings: "1) condition or circumstance as determined by birth.... 2) the natural character of an entity.... 3) the regular or established order of things.... 4) an entity as a product of nature" (Walter Bauer et al., *A Greek-English Lexicon of the New Testament and Other Early Christian Literature,* third edition [University of Chicago Press, 2000], 1069-70).

[84] Hurley says that it means "God's design for nature rather than simply the way things happen to be" (178). By defining the word as "God's design," Hurley can then say it means whatever he wants it to mean. Schreiner says that Paul "is referring to the natural and instinctive sense of right and wrong that God has planted in us" (137)—but it is doubtful that gender-based hair lengths are an instinct found in all cultures. Cultures do have concepts of right and wrong, and of "masculine" and "feminine" behavior and attire, but discrimination by hair length is an illustration of how the custom is applied in some societies; it is not an instinct in itself. Hair does not grow very long in either sex in some ethnic groups, and there is nothing "feminine" about the long braids of early Native American warriors.

[85] Blomberg takes the word *physis* to refer to a "long-established custom" (213). Keener is not sure, saying that Paul may have believed that "women's hair naturally grows longer than men's" (43). He finally concludes, "Whether Paul's argument is that women by virtue of creation have longer hair than men, or that the social norms of his day demand women's hair to be longer under normal circumstances, does not in the end need to be decided. In either case, Paul would seem to be making an argument that addresses symbolic gender distinctions, and requiring men and women to recognize those differences between them" (45).

universal, timeless statement.[86]

Since Paul can appeal to the Corinthians' own sense of what is proper and natural, it is apparent that he is asking for behavior in conformity to normal custom—for women to have their heads covered while speaking in the church, and for men to avoid the custom that was appropriate to females.[87] Although some of the Corinthian women had apparently concluded that the gospel freed them from gender-based restrictions, Paul says that they should conform to this particular custom.[88]

In verse 16, he gives one more reason: "If anyone is inclined to be contentious, we have no such practice, nor do the churches of God." None of the churches threw social custom to the wind and encouraged women to act like men, and vice versa, so the Corinthians should not, either. Garland writes, "His comment has the same force as that of Josephus's conclusion to an argument: 'None but the most contentious of critics, I imagine, could fail to be content with the arguments already adduced.'"[89]

Conclusion

Paul has given six reasons for women to wear a head covering:
- The head of the woman is man (verse 3).
- Speaking without a covering is as dishonorable as shaving the head (verse 5).
- Woman was made from and for man, so she should wear a head covering (verse 9).
- Because of the angels (verse 10).

---

[86] "When he speaks explicitly of length of hair, he grounds his arguments in what is proper (verse 13), normal practice (verses 14-15) and contemporary custom (verse 16). None of these verses...implies a timeless, transcultural mandate" (Blomberg, 215).

[87] Witherington concludes that it is "unlikely that Paul would impose any foreign or specifically Jewish custom on the ethnically mixed *ekklēsia* in Corinth" (235).

[88] "When a wife converts to Christianity and learns that she is set free in Christ so that she can pray and prophesy in public, it does not mean that she can disregard social conventions" (Garland, 509). She is not free to bring shame and dishonor on her husband.

[89] Garland, 532, citing *Against Apion,* 1:21.

- It is not socially proper for a woman to speak uncovered (verse 13).
- The church has no precedent for breaking this tradition (verse 16).

Today, we cannot confidently use any of these reasons. Even if we could agree about the meaning of "head," we cannot explain why it has to be symbolized by a head covering in one case but the lack of a head covering in another case. In most modern societies, there is little or no stigma attached to women speaking without a head covering, and we cannot say that it is as shameful as shaving the head. Third, we cannot offer any reason why the priority of creation should be forever symbolized by a head covering. Fourth, the presence of angels in this list makes it obvious that we do not have a complete understanding of the context in which Paul was working. Fifth, what is "socially proper" is different today than in first-century Greece. And today, there are many precedents against this tradition.

Paul's arguments do not make sense to us primarily because his reasons are based in beliefs found in first-century Corinth; they are not designed for cultures like ours that do not share those same beliefs.[90] Although Paul cites biblical evidence and spirit beings, it appears that the real basis of his argument is cultural—he was explaining the attire that was appropriate for women and men *in that culture.* We further suspect that if Paul knew of a reason that would apply in all cultures and all ages, then he would have used it, rather than ending up with social custom and "we've never done it that way before."[91]

Our doctrinal review team concludes that women are permitted to speak in church without head coverings.[92]

---

[90] "Paul, a pastor and a missionary, is concerned about getting his point across to his people, not with impressing modern Western readers with arguments that would work transculturally. Paul employs a transcultural argument only when he is making a transcultural point" (Keener, 31-32).

[91] "Had any one of his arguments here been an absolute, unambiguous, universal proof, Paul could have settled for one argument instead of four" (Keener, 22).

[92] In making this decision, it was not necessary for us to rule on the exact meaning of *kephale,* the precise nature of the head covering, or the significance of "authority" in verse 10. We do not have the expertise in Greek literature and language to provide conclusive answers to those questions. We also note that this

Paul apparently believed that men and women should respect social conventions about gender-specific attire.[93] Men should not try to look like women, nor should women try to look like men. God created male and female different, and he declared that to be good, but the Bible does not specify the characteristics of masculine and feminine attire. That changes from one nation to another, one culture to another, and from one century to another. In Paul's day, it meant that women should wear head coverings when speaking in public, but it does not mean that today.

In conjunction with this conclusion, we also make the following observations about the *reasons* that Paul offered:

Someone might argue that we should accept Paul's arguments even though we do not understand them. Angels are the same today as when Paul wrote, so we should accept his argument as valid today, and women should be covered by cloth when they speak in church. We reject that approach to Scripture. Paul gave *reasons* for his directive; he did not demand obedience without understanding.

The fact that Paul's arguments do not make sense to us is a hint that he was basing his arguments on cultural customs. Even in a city renowned for sin, he appeals to the readers' sense of propriety and disgrace. His argument from "nature" in verse 14 is actually an argument from custom; the "glory" that Paul speaks of in verse 15 is also a cultural matter.

Whether Paul uses *kephalē* in the sense of authority, or to refer to source, either way, women are allowed to pray and prophesy in church. Whether she has a sign of authority on her head, or has a sign of being

---

passage is not about ordination or appointing people to church leadership. We want to base our policies on scriptures that are clear, and this passage is not clear.

[93] "Most interpreters agree that one timeless principle that may be deduced from this passage is that Christians should not try to blur all distinctions between the sexes" (Blomberg, 214). "The fundamental principle is that the sexes, although equal, are also different" (Schreiner, 138). "Paul takes issue not with what women are doing but with how they are doing it. Women (and men for that matter) can pray and prophesy in the church, but they must not flaunt the social conventions of the day in so doing" (Belleville, Women Leaders, 153). "Paul's view is that the creation order should be properly manifested, not obliterated, in Christian worship.... Male-female differentiation is part of what God intends to redeem, not transcend or supersede" (Witherington, 236-37).

under authority (everyone is under *some* authority), the most significant part of this passage is that women *do* have the authority to speak spiritual words in public worship. This passage does not restrict her words in any way; it is only a matter of attire.

Paul is apparently applying a general principle to the situation in Corinth. However, from the passage, it is not clear what the principle is. Here are some possibilities:

All women are under the authority of all men, because woman was created from and for man. Women should therefore wear a symbol of submission, which in Corinth was a head covering, but in other cultures may be something else. However, this does not explain why it is wrong for men to wear a head covering, because they are also under authority. Nor do we believe that all women are under the authority of all men.

Married women are under the authority of their husbands, because woman was created from and for man. Therefore all women, married or not, should wear a symbol that they are submissive to that principle.[94] Again, this does not explain why it would be disgraceful for men under authority to wear a head covering, and it does not explain why Paul is concerned about head coverings only when people pray and prophesy. The head coverings apparently had significance in public worship, but not in a woman's private relationship to God.

Men and women should dress in ways appropriate to their gender in that culture, and when they are speaking in public, they should not dress in such a way that distracts from the words they speak. This would explain why Paul is concerned about attire of both men and women *when speaking*.[95] We conclude that this suggestion has the most merit.

---

[94] Keener responds to this by saying, "Nothing in this passage suggests wives' subordination. The only indicator that could be taken to mean that is the statement that man is woman's 'head,' but 'head' in those days was capable of a variety of meanings, and nothing in the text indicates that it means subordination.... The only clear affirmations here, besides that men and women are different and should not conceal that fact, is the equality and mutual dependence of men and women" (47).

[95] Keener concludes, "We can notice some transcultural points in his argument: one should not bring reproach upon one's family or upon the Christian gospel; one should not seek to destroy symbolic gender distinctions by pioneering unisex clothing styles; one should respect custom and do one's best to avoid

Since we conclude that women do not have to wear head coverings in church today (a conclusion we have held for decades), we also conclude that Paul has alluded to evidence from Genesis to support a cultural custom. The fact that Paul is selective in his use of the evidence from Genesis shows that he is not starting with Genesis and trying to explain its application in Greco-Roman society. Rather, he is starting with a custom in his culture and trying to find as many lines of support as he can think of for the people he was writing to. Since he was a rabbi steeped in Scripture, he begins with an illustration from Scripture, but he later has to qualify it, and he gives several comments based on what society considers honorable or disgraceful.

The important point is that women are permitted to pray and prophesy in church. Women may speak about spiritual topics and instruct the church as God leads them. Even if we use the most restrictive meaning of prophecy [that is, infallibly inspired words], and even if it rarely if ever happens today, the precedent is still set that God allows women to instruct and edify the church according to their gifts.

However, the mutual dependence of males and females does not mean that they must behave in identical ways. Paul made restrictions on *how* women prophesied in church—he required them to wear attire appropriate to women. We uphold this principle today, acknowledging that in most nations today, this does not mean a headcovering, but means that women should not try to look like men. The authority of their words does not rest in external appearance, but in conformity with the gospel of God.

Appendix A: The meaning of *kephalē*

Garland writes: "Three views commend themselves. First, 'head' has been traditionally understood to designate hierarchy and to imply authoritative headship."[96] In support of this view, Hurley writes, "The Greek versions of the Bible used *kephalē* (head) to translate the Hebrew word *r'osh,* which also means 'head.' The Hebrew word, however, was used to indicate one in a position of authority or command as well as origin or 'priority.'"[97]

---

causing someone to stumble" (46).

[96] Garland, 514.

[97] Hurley, 164. Unfortunately, Hurley left out an important point. Keener

Hurley argues that although *kephalē* may mean origin in some contexts (e.g., Col. 1:15-20), it does not mean that in marital contexts. "If 'head' means 'source' in 1 Corinthians 11:3, Paul's parallelism is poor and he virtually teaches that God made Christ."[98]

Blomberg agrees: "Its two main [metaphorical] meanings were either 'source' or 'authority.'... The other passage in which Paul calls a man 'head' over a woman refers as well to wives' subordination to their husbands (Eph. 5:22-24), so 'authority' seems somewhat more likely here too."[99] Egalitarian W. Larry Richards admits that although the meaning of "source" is attractive, Paul elsewhere uses *kephalē* "in the sense of authority, not source."[100]

Part of the difficulty in the discussion is that commentators who support the meaning of "authority" generally conclude that the male has

---

writes, "The Septuagint rarely translates *ros* (in the sense of leader) literally as 'head'; most often it uses other Greek words that mean 'leader.' It retains 'head' for leader less than one tenth of the time, despite the Hebrew usage" (32). Alan Redmond, a pastor in Winnipeg, has studied the words in some depth. He writes, "There are 547 occurrences of *ros* that I found in a Hebrew (BHS) search with Gramcord.... The instances where *ros* has the meaning of chief or ruler are of special interest to us. These number about 180. The majority are translated as *archē*.... I found 9% of the time that *ros* has the sense of chief or ruler where it is translated by *kephalē*." Although it is not a common meaning, it is a possible meaning of *kephalē,* and he concludes: "The sense of authority could not likely have been excluded from the metaphor without special comment from Paul."

[98] Hurley, 166. Schreiner argues strongly for the meaning of "authority" (127-28).

[99] Blomberg, 208-9.

[100] Richards, in *Women in Ministry,* 318. He limits that authority to marriage. "Paul never, here or elsewhere, widens the wife's subordination to her husband within the family circle to a general subordination of women to men's authority, in the church or in society" (319). Witherington has a similar view: "Paul does not simply equate the family structure, which in the household codes is somewhat patriarchal, with the structure of the family of faith" (238, n. 26). He argues that *kephalē* probably connotes authority, but notes: "Paul's vision of headship or leadership involves the leader in being the head servant.... It is difficult to come to grips with a Paul who is neither a radical feminist nor an ardent patriarchalist.... Paul, like Jesus, was a man who was not and is not easily pigeonholed (240).

authority because he is the *source* of, or is prior to, the woman. "Source" and "authority" are related concepts, so "source" often makes sense. However, they argue that the primary connotation of *kephalē* is authority (the result) rather than source (the cause). Blomberg says that no one has shown that *kephalē* can mean source "without simultaneously implying some dimension of authority."[101]

However, Perriman questions the logic, "The question of authority is irrelevant to a discussion of the proper manner in which men and women should pray and prophesy; nor is it a valid deduction from the idea that man has authority over the woman that she should veil herself in worship."[102] It is not clear why the woman must honor the man by being covered, when the man has to do the exact opposite in order to honor Christ. The passage is not about authority *per se,* and although verse 10 uses the word "authority," the meaning there is not clear.

The second suggestion is that *kephalē* means "source." Mary Evans writes, "In Colossians 1:18 Christ is spoken of as 'the head' of the church in the context of his being before all things and the source of creation."[103] However, "the 'paucity of lexicographic evidence'—no Greek lexicon offers this as an option…makes this meaning for 'head' highly suspect…. Although the idea of source may fit the account of the woman's creation from the man's rib, it does not fit God as the source of Christ."[104] Some egalitarians respond that God is indeed the source of Christ in his messianic role, and Paul is speaking only of a function, not the source of being.[105] They also point out that "source" is clearly part of the context

---

[101] Blomberg, *Two Views,* 342.

[102] A. C. Perriman, "The Head of a Woman: The Meaning of Kephalē in 1 Cor. 11:3" (*Journal of Theological Studies* 45 (1994): 620.

[103] Evans, 66. She also points out that earlier in this letter, Paul has balanced the authority of the husband and the wife (1 Cor 7:4, using the verb form of *exousia*); he does not seem to be combating a problem of women trying to exert authority over men.

[104] Garland, 515-16.

[105] "This objection fails if the text refers to Jesus' source as the Father from whom he proceeded at his incarnation as a human being" (Keener, 33-34). Keener also makes a suggestion about the unusual order in verse 3: "If the incarnation is

(see verses 8-9).

Garland agrees with Perriman in supporting a third view: "The best option understands *kephalē* to mean 'that which is most prominent, foremost, uppermost, pre-eminent' (Perriman 1994).... The 'head' denotes one who is preeminent, and though it may result in authority and leadership, that is not its basic denotation. It is not linked to ideas of obedience or submission."[106]

But Blomberg notes, "It is unclear if an entity can be most or even more prominent without implying some functional superiority."[107] Although Paul does give a requirement for men, the emphasis of this passage is to give a requirement for women, to stop women from doing something they had begun to do, and that requirement is based on the fact that the male is the *kephalē* of the female.

In short, it seems that most interpreters choose a meaning for *kephalē* based primarily on their beliefs about what *other* verses say about male authority. The interpreters are influenced by their own culture, either in assumptions about what it means to be a "head," or in beliefs about what it means to be "equal."

Appendix B: Head coverings in the Greco-Roman world

Craig Keener gives some detailed information about head coverings in the ancient world:

---

in view, then 11:3 is in chronological sequence."

[106] Garland, 516. Belleville agrees: "*Kephalē* is rarely used to describe the relationship of one individual to another.... Prominent is by far the most common [metaphorical] usage.... Source and leader, on the other hand, are quite rare— although examples can be found.... What all this means is that Paul's uses of *kephalē* must be decided on a case-by-case basis" (*Women Leaders,* 123). She also notes that "Now I want you to know that" is the way that Paul introduces new information (130). We cannot assume prior knowledge on the part of the Corinthians of man being the head of the woman. And since the metaphor had several possible meanings, the original readers would have to use the context to tell them which meaning was intended—and the context is not about authority and submission.

[107] Blomberg, *Two Views,* 343.

The practice of women covering their heads in public may be related to the old Greek tradition that restricted women in many ways to the domestic sphere. In theory, at least, women in fourth century BCE Athens could not go to the market and were not to be seen by men who were not their relatives.... This ideal seems to have continued to some degree in conservative parts of the Greek-speaking Mediterranean world [which would probably not include Corinth]....

Roman women were, however, much less secluded, although some moralists wished them to be more secluded than they were. It was reported that in an earlier period a husband might have divorced his wife for going into public unveiled, or disciplined his wife or daughter for conversing publicly with another man.... Plutarch goes on to explain that a woman's talk should also be kept private within the home...she 'ought to do her talking either to her husband or through her husband.'... We cannot suppose that all levels of society hearkened to the moralists (the moralists themselves were well aware that this was the case)....

Why would the Corinthian Christian women's uncovered heads have caused offense? One recurrent suggestion is that an uncovered head was the traditional garb of prostitutes. Dress could indeed sometimes indicate that a woman was a prostitute.... But the evidence for *head coverings* distinguishing wives from prostitutes is slender.... Head coverings typified married women in general in Jewish Palestine, so that an uncovered head could indicate a virgin seeking a husband as easily as it could connote a prostitute....

Others...have suggested instead that Paul may have been thinking of the 'uncovered and disheveled heads' of pagan prophetesses.... In most Greek religious activities women uncovered their heads, and this may be significant. But it is doubtful that Paul or the Corinthians would have thought specifically about pagan prophetesses' hairstyles; such prophetesses...were generally secluded from public view....

In general, Greek women were expected to participate in worship with their heads uncovered.... Men were also to worship bareheaded. In contrast, Roman women had to cover their heads when offering sacrifices.... Roman men would also pull the toga over their head at sacrifices. Corinth was a Roman 'colony' in Greece during this period....

Covering one's head was sometimes associated with mourning; the practice was a standard sign of grief, for both men and women.... During the funeral procession itself, Roman sons would cover their heads, while daughters would 'go with uncovered heads and hair unbound.'...

It is unlikely that most Palestinian Jews viewed the head covering as a symbol of women's *humiliation,* but at the least a head covering was a necessary sign of public *modesty* for all Palestinian Jewish women who could afford it. One story tells of a woman so destitute that she could not afford a head covering, so she had to cover her head with her hair before going to speak with Rabbi Johanan ben Zakkai.... A Jewish woman who ventured into public with her hair down and exposed to view, or who otherwise could be accused of flirtatious behavior, could be divorced.... Jewish teachers permitted loosing a woman's hair only in the case of an adulterous woman, who was publicly shamed by exposure to the sight of men....

Veiling customs varied geographically. Veiling seems to have prevailed in parts of the eastern Mediterranean.... Evidence for this custom in Greek life, however, is sparse....

It is probable that some well-to-do women thought such restrictions on their public apparel ridiculous, especially if they were from parts of the Mediterranean world where head coverings were not considered necessary. But to other observers, these women's uncovered heads connoted an invitation to lust. The issue in the Corinthian church may thus have been a clash of [class-related] cultural values concerning modesty, and Paul wants the more [wealthy] liberated elements within the church to care enough about their more conservative colleagues [the poor] not to offend them in this dramatic way.... Most women in Greco-Roman statues and other artwork from this period [generally the wealthy] have uncovered heads.... Nothing in 1 Cor. 11 suggests a practice that requires women's heads to be covered all day long.[108]

---

[108] Keener, 22-30; see also Cynthia L. Thompson, "Hairstyles, Head-coverings, and St. Paul: Portraits from Roman Corinth," *Biblical Archaeologist,* June 1988, 99-113.

"WOMEN SHOULD REMAIN SILENT"— A STUDY OF 1 CORINTHIANS 14:34-35

In 1 Corinthians 14:33-35, Paul wrote:

As in all the churches of the saints, the women should keep silent in the churches. For they are not permitted to speak, but should be in submission, as the Law also says. If there is anything they desire to learn, let them ask their husbands at home. For it is shameful for a woman to speak in church. (verses 33-35).

If we take this literally, it would mean that women are not allowed to sing in church nor respond when the pastor asks for comments or questions from the audience. Moreover, it would contradict what Paul said in chapter 11, where he said that women *could* pray and prophesy in church if they had the appropriate attire.

Common sense, church custom, and good principles of biblical interpretation all say that we should not take these verses literally—and almost no one does. Paul is not making a blanket prohibition that says that women can never speak in church. Rather, he was addressing his comments to a certain situation, and his comments are limited in some way. The question is, What are the limits of Paul's prohibition? In the this chapter, we examine the context and look at the details of these verses.

A call to order

In 1 Corinthians 11, Paul begins to instruct the Corinthian church about their disorganized worship services. As we studied in our previous chapter, he says that women should wear a head covering when they pray and prophesy; then he corrects the Corinthians on the way they had been observing the Lord's Supper. In chapter 12, he addresses the proper use of spiritual gifts in the worship service. He describes a number of gifts, and insists that all gifts are important to the Body of Christ; the variety of gifts calls for mutual respect and honor, not vanity or shame.

In chapter 13, he describes love as the best way, and in chapter 14 he makes an extended contrast between the gift of tongues and the gift of prophesying. Apparently some people in Corinth were extolling the gift of tongues as a mark of superior spirituality. Paul did not tell them to stop speaking in tongues, but he did put some restrictions on how tongues should be used in the worship service:

- There should be two or three speakers (14:27).
- They should speak one at a time (verse 27).
- There should be an interpretation (verse 27b). If no one can interpret the tongues, "let each of them keep silent in church and speak to himself and to God" (verse 28).

However, this requirement should not be lifted out of its context to create a complete prohibition on the person ever speaking, singing or praying.[1] Paul is apparently trying to give some organization to what had been a chaotic worship meeting—several people speaking at once, speaking words that no one could understand.

Paul recommends the gift of prophecy as a far more helpful gift, but he gives similar guidelines for those speakers, too:

- Only two or three should speak (verse 29). If someone else has something to say, the first speaker should be quiet.[2]
- They should speak one at a time (verse 31).
- People should "weigh what is said" (verse 29; cf. 1 Thess. 5:21).

Paul notes that "the spirits of the prophets are subject to the control of the prophets" (1 Cor. 14:32). That is, the speakers are able to stop; they cannot use "God made me do it" as an excuse for adding to the commotion.[3] When God gives a gift, he also gives the person the responsibility to make decisions to use that gift in an appropriate way. Simply having the gift is not an excuse to use it whenever and wherever the person wants to. Paul explains his reason: "For God is not a God of

---

[1] Paul uses the same Greek word that is translated "silent" in verse 34. James Hurley notes that "there is no intention that the first [person] should speak no more in the worship service. He or she may certainly sing hymns, pray, etc.... Paul left it to his readers to grasp the context" (*Man and Woman in Biblical Perspective* [Zondervan, 1981], 190).

[2] The NIV translation obscures the fact that Paul has used the same Greek word for silence. Here again, Paul did not intend to prohibit all subsequent speaking by the person—he called for silence only for the immediate situation.

[3] This point probably applies to tongues-speakers, too. The Greek verb is *hypotassō*, here translated as "subject to the control of," but more commonly translated as "submit."

confusion but of peace" (verse 33).[4] Paul then tells the women to be quiet, and to ask their questions at home (verses 33-35, quoted above). Let's examine some of the details in these verses.

Observations

1) Women are not the only people Paul tells to be "silent." He uses the same word in verses 28 and 30 to tell tongue-speakers and prophets to be silent when others speak. In both of those verses, he is calling for a temporary silence, not a complete and permanent prohibition.[5]

2) The word for "speak" (*laleō*) does not necessarily mean a formal role in the pulpit—it is a general word that can also be translated "talk." Paul used a general word to say that women should not talk, and we have to make an interpretive choice: Was he prohibiting formal speaking roles, or talk in the audience, or something else?[6]

---

[4] Gordon Fee and a few other scholars have suggested that Paul did not write these verses—a small number of old manuscripts have these verses in a different place, as if they have been added to the text from a marginal comment. However, all manuscripts *do* have these verses, and we accept them as part of the canonical epistle. Scribes occasionally made mistakes when they copied manuscripts, and corrections were written in the margin, and these corrections were sometimes incorporated into the text on subsequent copying, not always in the right place.

A few scholars have suggested that Paul is here quoting some Corinthians, and disagreeing with them, but this seems unlikely. These verses are neither stylistically or theologically like the other places where Paul probably quotes the Corinthians (e.g., 6:12-14). Neither hypothesis is necessary, for there are adequate explanations for why Paul would write these words.

[5] "The question is, what kind of 'silence' does Paul mean in 1 Corinthians 14:34? It cannot be silence of all speech... Paul says in 1 Corinthians 11, just three chapters earlier, that women who pray and prophesy should have their heads covered, which assumes that they could pray and prophesy aloud in church services" (Wayne Grudem, *Evangelical Feminism and Biblical Truth* [Multnomah, 2004], 232-33). Similarly, Craig Keener writes, "Once you protest that Paul did not mean to prohibit all speaking, you have already raised the interpretive question of what he actually did mean in his historical context and how it might be applied in our context today" ("Women in Ministry," in *Two Views on Women in Ministry* [ed. James R. Beck and Craig L. Blomberg; Zondervan, 2001], 41).

[6] Craig Blomberg suggests this possibility: "Perhaps they were 'chattering,'

3) Paul says that instead of speaking, women should be in submission. This implies that the Corinthian women were speaking in an insubordinate way. The fact that Paul said in chapter 11 that women could pray and prophesy, and in chapter 14 that two or three people could prophesy in a worship service, shows that women are allowed to have a slot in the speaking schedule. It is not insubordinate for them to speak prophecies; it is therefore likely that Paul is prohibiting some less-formal speaking, such as chatter or comments from the audience.[7]

4) Paul says that "the Law" requires submission. There are several options for what kind of submission is meant:

First, submission of all women to all men. However, as we saw in previous studies, the Old Testament does not require all women to submit to all men, nor does it require them to be silent. Nevertheless, some scholars believe that Paul is alluding to a "principle" derived from Genesis.[8]

---

or even gossiping, as some Jewish women...reputedly liked to do" in the synagogues (1 Corinthians [NIV Application Commentary; Zondervan, 1994], 280).

[7] Grudem writes, "There is nothing in 1 Corinthians that says women were being disruptive" (243). That is technically true—but it is also true that nothing in the epistle says that tongue-speakers were causing problems, either. Paul describes that problem in conditional clauses: "If I did this... If everyone spoke in tongues... If you are praising God with your spirit..." Despite this style of argumentation, scholars generally agree that Paul is dealing with a real situation. His instructions imply a problem that he was trying to correct; so also with his comments about women.

[8] Josephus says that Scripture taught women to submit (Against Apion 2:24), and it was probably widely assumed that it did, though specific verses could not be cited. The idea is that the male has authority over the female either because he was created first (Genesis 2) or because subordination was part of the curse against the woman (Genesis 3). Historically, most scholars have cited the curse, but traditional scholars today generally base their explanations on Genesis 2, perhaps because they do not want to say that women in Christ are subject to the curse. Garland writes, "Gen. 3:16 is predictive, not prescriptive, and Jewish exegetes did not ground the subordination of women in the creation narrative" (1 Corinthians, 672). Hurley says that Paul "uniformly appealed to the relation of Adam and Eve before the fall rather than after it, to Genesis 2 rather than to

Second, submission of wives to their husbands.[9] Although this command is not explicitly found in the Old Testament, the presence of the command in the New Testament suggests that it was based on Old Testament principles.[10] Further, verse 35 indicates that Paul may have been dealing with a husband-wife problem. However, if Paul is alluding to a rule about family relationships, it would not necessarily apply to authority in the church.

Third, submission to a Roman law that restricted women's roles in pagan worship.[11] Although Paul normally means the Mosaic law when he uses the word *nomos*, it is possible that he meant civil law in this verse; the Corinthians would know by context which law he meant.

Fourth, submission to themselves. Just as Paul told the prophets to control themselves (verse 32), he uses the same Greek word in verse 34 to say that women should be in submission; the proximity of these two uses suggests that Paul means for women to control themselves. The New

---

Genesis 3" (192).

However, even if the first man had authority because of being created first, it is far from clear in Genesis whether 1) all subsequent males have authority over all subsequent females, or 2) their authority is limited to spiritual matters, or 3) is limited to marriage. The Old Testament gives examples of women who had some authority over men in civil and religious matters.

[9] The Greek words for man and woman often mean husband and wife; the meaning is determined by the context. Gordon Fee notes that one ancient manuscript adds "to their husbands," but he comments, "It is not at all clear that this is what the author intended" (*The First Epistle to the Corinthians* [New International Commentary on the New Testament; Eerdmans, 1987], 699).

[10] For example, Eph. 5:22. Paul balances this command with the admonition for husbands to love their wives in a self-sacrificial way (verse 25).

[11] "Official religion of the Roman variety was closely supervised. The women who participated were carefully organized and their activities strictly regulated" (Linda Belleville, "Women in Ministry," in Beck and Blomberg, 119). Richard and Catherine Clark Kroeger cite Plutarch, Cicero, and Livy for evidence that Rome had laws regulating the behavior of women in worship ("Pandemonium and Silence at Corinth," *Reformed Journal* 28 [June 1978], p. 9). References are Plutarch, *Lives, on Solon;* Cicero, *Laws,* II.xv; Livy, XXXIX.xv; and Phintys, *Stobaeus,* IV.23.61.

American Standard Bible translates verse 34b in this way: "let them subject themselves, just as the Law says."[12] In this case the "law" could be either Roman law or general biblical principles of decency and order.

Fifth, Paul addresses the problem by saying, "If there is anything they desire to learn..." This implies that the problem in Corinth concerning the asking of questions with a desire to *learn* something.[13] Blomberg suggests, "Perhaps the largely uneducated women of that day were interrupting proceedings with irrelevant questions that would be better dealt with in their homes."[14] Belleville says, "Their fault was not in the asking per se

---

[12] "'Submission' and 'silence' are two sides of the same coin. To be silent is to be submissive—and to be submissive (in the context of worship) is to be silent. Control over the tongue is most likely what Paul is talking about" (Belleville, 119). The idea is that when Paul told women to be in submission, he meant the same thing as when he told prophets to be in submission. Ralph Martin writes, "What Paul is rebuking is the way women were upsetting the good order of the worship.... The merit of this view is that it enables us to take 'be in subjection' as referring not to their husbands but to their own spirits" (*The Spirit and the Congregation* [Eerdmans, 1984], 85).

[13] The Greek word is *manthanō,* usually translated "learn." The NASB translates it literally: "If they desire to learn anything..."

[14] Blomberg, 280. Although some first-century women were well-educated, most were not. They married young and stayed at home. Keener advocates this as the primary problem—the women were

speaking up, asking questions to learn what was going on during the prophecies or the Scripture exposition in church.... The women are interrupting the Scripture exposition with questions. This would have caused an affront to more conservative men or visitors to the church, and it would have also caused a disturbance to the service due to the nature of the questions....

Plutarch says that it is important to ask lecturers questions only in their field of expertise; to ask them questions irrelevant to their discipline is rude. Worse yet are those who challenge the speaker without yet understanding his point.... This principle is particularly applicable to uneducated questioners who waste everyone's time with their questions they have not bothered to first research for themselves.... So also those who nitpick too much, questioning extraneous points not relevant to the argument.

but in the inappropriate setting for their questions."[15]

Sixth, Paul says that the women "let them ask their husbands at home."[16] This may imply that the problems were caused primarily by women who were married to Christian men.[17] Grudem is probably right in

---

It was rude even to whisper to one another during a lecture, so asking questions of one another would also have been considered out of place and disrespectful to the speaker. Why would the women in the congregation have been more likely to have asked irrelevant questions than the men? Because, in general, they were less likely to be educated than men. (Keener, *Paul, Women and Wives,* 81-83)

Schreiner also notes that Plutarch encouraged students to interrupt lectures with questions, and says that Paul would have been unfair to silence only the women (350-351). But Paul said that only one person should speak at a time; he probably did not want anyone to interrupt the speakers; he was not following the advice Plutarch gave for lectures.

[15] Belleville, *Women Leaders and the Church* (Baker, 1999), 161.

[16] Grudem notes that this does not necessarily imply that the women were asking other men. "When Paul says that wives should 'submit to your own husbands, as to the Lord' (Ephesians 5:22), does that imply that the wives at Ephesus were all submitting to other women's husbands? Of course not" (244). However, 1 Cor. 14 is a more corrective passage than Eph. 5 is.

[17] D.A. Carson asks, "We must ask why Paul then bans *all* women from talking. And were there no noisy men?" ("Silent in the Churches," in John Piper and Wayne Grudem, *Recovering Biblical Manhood and Womanhood* [Crossway, 1991], 147). Grudem has a similar objection: "To say that only women and no men were disorderly is merely an assumption with no facts to support it" (246). However, we could equally ask why Paul forbids all questions, even though not all questions are disrespectful. See below for evidence that Paul sometimes gives commands to an entire class of people when only some of them are problems.

We can see in chapter 11 that Corinthian women had some behavioral problems that men did not have, and we have to consider the possibility that this might be true in chapter 14, too. We do not think that Paul unfairly singled women out; we therefore (in response to Carson's question) conclude that women were the ones who happened to be causing a problem in Corinth by talking and asking questions. Since Greco-Roman culture gave men many opportunities for public meetings, but women had few, it is to be expected that women would have the most problems in what was for them a new situation. L. Ann Jervis writes, "Paul evidently singled out 'the women' here simply because in his eyes, they were the culprits in the situation" ("1 Corinthians 14.34-35: A Reconsideration of Paul's

suggesting that Paul "assumes that the Corinthians can make appropriate applications for single women [or those married to pagans], who would no doubt know some men they could talk to after the service."[18] Paul is giving "husbands at home" as an illustration, not as a limitation on who can answer and where they must be. For example, it would be permissible to ask questions while walking home, or of other women, or of other men.[19] Paul's main point is, Don't talk in church, not even to ask questions.

7) Paul says that it is "disgraceful" for women to talk in church. This word appeals to the Corinthians' own sense of social propriety. He is saying that church custom (verse 33b), the law (verse 34), and social expectations (verse 35) all prohibit women from talking in church.[20] The questions themselves are not wrong, for they can be asked at home, but it is disorderly to ask them in the worship service.

8) It is not clear whether "s in all the churches of the saints" (verse 33b) introduces this topic, or concludes the previous one. Linda Belleville notes that in the other places Paul appeals to the practice of other churches, it is at the *end* of the discussion (1 Cor. 4:17; 7:17; 11:16), and it is redundant to have "in the churches" both in the introductory clause and at the end of the same sentence. As she notes, "'Let the women...' is a typical Pauline

---

Limitation of the Free Speech of Some Corinthian Women," *Journal for the Study of the New Testament* 58 [1995]: 71).

[18] Grudem, 235. 1 Cor. 7 shows that the congregation included widows and other single women. We should not expect Paul to address every possible situation when that is not his main point.

[19] If Paul is using "husbands at home" as an illustration, not as a prescription, which seems likely, then he is not dealing with a husband-wife problem.

[20] Craig Keener notes, "Whereas questions at public lectures were expected, ancient literature testified that unlearned questions were considered foolish and rude—and women generally possessed inadequate education and were most often unlearned" (51). Noisy or disorderly women would not be considered "in submission," even if they were not breaking any particular command. "It would be particularly embarrassing to a husband for his wife to transgress social boundaries and question him in public. This behavior still makes persons uncomfortable in cultures that have an unwritten rule between spouses that one does not shame or embarrass the other in public" (David Garland, *1 Corinthians* [Baker, 2003], 670).

start to a new paragraph."[21] However, this does not seem to affect the interpretation of the verses. Either way, it seems that other churches were already doing what Paul wanted the Corinthians to do.

Church, law, and society

Paul has already indicated that women can pray and prophesy in church (chapter 11), and a worship service includes two or three people prophesying in turn (14:29-32). This means that it is permissible for women to have formal speaking roles in the church. Paul was apparently forbidding some other type of speech. Just as he did not allow tongue-speakers or prophets to speak out of turn, he did not want women to speak out of turn, saying things in such a way that they were breaking social customs about what is appropriate.

Paul appealed to church custom, the law, and cultural expectations; we will consider how each of these is relevant to the problem that Paul is dealing with.

1) We know very little about how first-century churches functioned, except for what the New Testament tells us—and the picture is one of variety. Some churches were led by apostles and elders; others by prophets and teachers; some by overseers or elders or deacons. Although we know the names of a number of influential men and women, we can associate those names with specific titles in only a few cases. We know even less about how a typical worship service was conducted; 1 Cor. 14 is the primary evidence.

2) We have surveyed the Old Testament, and find no prohibition on women speaking in public.[22] Scripture provides examples of women who

---

[21] Linda Belleville, *Women Leaders,* 157-58. Garland expresses the majority view: "The repetition of *ekklesiai* seems clumsy, but it is easier to understand how church custom applies to a wife...than it does to the statement that God is a God of peace" (669-70).

[22] Grudem suggests that Paul "seems to be referring to the Old Testament generally as 'the Law,' probably especially the Creation order in Genesis 2, and understanding it as teaching a principle of male leadership" (234). But as we discussed in an earlier chapter, it is far from clear that Genesis 2 teaches a hierarchy based on sequence of creation. When scholars say that women are not allowed to have spiritual or ecclesiastical authority, they are basing that conclusion on 1 Tim 2:12. It may or may not be a valid conclusion (we will discuss

had leadership roles in civil government, in publicly praising God, and in giving authoritative answers about spiritual matters to male civil leaders (e.g., Deborah, Miriam, and Huldah). Scripture does not require all women to submit to all men.

The problem in Corinth probably involved either a) wives speaking against or dishonoring their husbands,[23] or b) more generally, women acting disorderly and for that reason considered "not in submission." The "law" that Paul mentions may be a civil law, or a New Testament rule.

3) In Greco-Roman society, women were given authority in the household, but rarely had opportunity for public speaking. Craig Keener notes a typical expectation: "Plutarch goes on to explain that a woman's talk should also be kept private within the home...she 'ought to do her talking either to her husband or through her husband.'"[24] The average woman was less educated and had little experience in public assemblies; this may have contributed to the problem in Corinth.[25]

---

that in our next chapter), but it is exegetically incorrect to say that this is taught in Genesis 2, which makes no such limitation.

Hurley writes, "It is difficult to figure out how it could be said that the Law (i.e., the Old Testament) taught that women should be silent at all times in worship. It teaches the opposite (Ex. 15:20-21; 2 Sa. 6:15,19; Ps. 148:12). It is not difficult to see that the Old Testament would support the silence of women in the judging of prophets, as its whole structure teaches male headship in the home and in worship" (191-192). Hurley appeals to a generality because there is no particular verse that says what he wants it to say.

[23] Blomberg observes, "If 'women' is better interpreted as 'wives,' then these restrictions would not bar single women from the eldership, nor husbands and wives from positions of joint leadership, nor wives from offices of oversight in churches in which their husbands are not members" (286)—because none of those situations would involve wives ruling over their own husbands. He later suggests, "In Presbyterian or Episcopalian forms of church government, even senior pastors submit to larger structures of authorities over them, so presumably women's subordination could be preserved even with a female senior pastor" (291).

[24] Craig Keener, *Paul, Women, and Wives* (Hendrickson, 1992), 23.

[25] Blomberg writes, "If one of the cultural explanations for Paul's silencing the women is accepted, then contemporary Christians will silence women only where comparable problems—lack of education, interfering chatter, or the promotion of false teaching—still exist. And they will impose silence on men who

196

It is sometimes suggested that synagogues had separate seating for men and women, and that the early church continued this custom—hence when women asked questions of the men, it was necessary to shout across a barrier, and that is why Paul prohibited such questions in church. Although the hypothesis is attractive because it would provide a motive for Paul's directives, there is little proof for gender-separated seating for first-century synagogues.[26]

Weighing the prophecies

Several scholars have argued that Paul is saying that women should not be involved in the "weighing" of prophetic messages (verse 29)—only men may determine whether a message is in accordance with sound doctrine.[27] In this view, men and women may prophesy, but only men may

---

fall victim to one of these problems as well" (286).

[26] Keener, 76. Donald Binder writes, "Our only clear evidence for the division of the sexes in a synagogue comes from Philo's writings about the practices of the Therapeutae…. We can only guess to what degree these customs reflected those held outside this specialized community" (*Into the Temple Courts: The Place of the Synagogues in the Second Temple Period* [Society of Biblical Literature, 1999], 378-9). The Therapeutae were a religious sect and their practices were not necessarily representative of other synagogues.

[27] The view was suggested in 1965 by Margaret Thrall, professor at Cambridge, in a commentary on 1 and 2 Corinthians. It was defended in detail by three Cambridge students: James Hurley in a dissertation in 1973, Wayne Grudem in a dissertation in 1978, and by D.A. Carson (Ph.D., Cambridge, 1975) in a book in 1987.

Thomas Schreiner, another traditionalist scholar (Ph.D., Fuller, 1983), expresses reservations about this view (in a book review in *Trinity Journal* 17 [spring 1996]: 120). More recently, he notes that "the specific situation that called forth these words is difficult to identify" (in Beck and Blomberg, 231). Blomberg adopts Grudem's view, but admits, "The obvious drawback of this approach is that it must infer a meaning for 'speaking' which Paul never spells out. But that problem afflicts all of the views that take Paul's words as less than absolute" (ibid.).

Richard M. Davidson opts for his view, but restricts it to marital relations: "Paul's call for the wives to 'be silent' (*sigaō*) was a particular silence while their husband's prophecies were being tested, and did not indicate total silence in the worship service" ("Headship, Submission, and Equality in Scripture," in *Women*

comment on the validity of the prophecies, because only men have that authority. This interpretation has the advantage of keeping verses 34-35 on the same subject as the rest of the chapter: the orderly use of spiritual gifts.[28] In keeping with this view, they say that women may speak in church but (based largely on 1 Tim 2:12) may not have authority.

This interpretation has become almost unanimous among traditionalist scholars. They argue that prophecy (an unplanned comment) is not as authoritative as teaching (an explanation of Scripture); women can speak prophecies but should not have "ecclesiastical authority" in which they have the responsibility to teach or judge in an official way what men say.

Several points may be noted against this view:

1) When Paul says that "the others" should weigh what is said (verse 29), he may mean the entire congregation or the other prophets—either of which would have included females. Keener suggests that the "others" who weigh (*diakrinō*) the prophecies would be people with the gift of discernment (*diakrisis*) (12:10), but he notes that nothing suggests that only males are given this gift.[29]

2) When Paul wrote that they should "weigh what is said," it is by no means clear that he is advocating a formal discussion and pronouncement by leaders of the church. Rather, his meaning might more simply be that each person should *think* about whether the saying is true, much as people today might during sermons.[30] Contra Grudem, verses 34-35 are hardly an

---

in Ministry [ed. Nancy Vyhmeister; Andrews University Press, 1998], 277). Mary Evans suggests the same: "What is being prohibited is not the questioning of any man by any woman, but a wife taking part in the judging of her own husband" (*Woman in the Bible* [InterVarsity 1983], 99).

[28] "The discussion of women has a natural place and does not appear as a sudden intrusion or as a shift of topic" (Hurley, 190). Scholars who have a different view say that the verses "seem to rudely interrupt the topic at hand" (Belleville, *Women Leaders,* 155). Keener refers to "the awkward way it fits its context," and explains: "Paul frequently digressed, and digressions were a normal part of ancient writing" (*Paul, Women and Wives,* 74).

[29] Keener, *Paul, Women and Wives,* 79.

[30] Grudem admits that verse 29 implies that the women should be "silently evaluating the prophecies in their own minds" ("Prophecy—Yes, But Teaching—No" (*Journal of the Evangelical Theological Society* 30 [1987]: 21). There is no

adequate explanation of "how to proceed with 'let the others weigh what is said.'"[31]

3) There is no evidence that "all the churches of the saints" had any procedure for evaluating prophecies—or that this was done in *any* other church. None of the early interpreters suggested that verses 34-35 are guidelines for evaluating prophecy.[32]

4) Paul nowhere suggests that the weighing of prophecies, or discerning of spirits, is more authoritative than prophecy. Rather, throughout 1 Cor. 14 he extols prophecy as the most useful gift.

5) These scholars have reversed the natural meaning of verse 35, which suggests that the women want to *learn* something by asking questions. In contrast, these scholars say that the problem is that the women were expressing a judgment. It would be of dubious value for a woman with the gift of discernment to withhold her reservations about the message until she got home, where she would share her thoughts with her husband, who might not have the gift of discernment.[33]

6) It seems that worship services in Corinth were chaotic; they probably did not have a time designated for evaluating prophetic messages, so it is doubtful that Paul is addressing problems that the Corinthians already had with this evaluation time—nor is there evidence that Paul is anticipating a

---

indication in the text that the evaluation is ever done out loud. Paul said that only two or three tongues-speakers should speak, and only two or three prophets should speak; he would therefore not be likely to invite an unlimited number of men to comment verbally on the prophecies. He makes no regulations for prophecy-evaluators, which suggests that this was not a formal part of the worship service.

[31] Grudem claims that verses 33b-35 explain how to judge prophecies (234).

[32] Most early interpreters emphasized the silence of women, without providing for exceptions. The common complementarian interpretation and the common egalitarian interpretation are both relatively modern; both recognize that the traditional approach ignored the context.

[33] "If Paul is here referring to the 'weighing of prophecy' he would be advising 'the women' to carry out that function at home. Such private judging of prophecy would be in contravention both of the method Paul has just prescribed (the other prophets are publicly to discern prophecies) and the function of true prophecy as a community edifier (14.4) and public witness (14.24)" (L. Ann Jervis, "1 Corinthians 14.34-35," 61).

hypothetical objection. Verses 34-35 indicate that the problem concerned comments and questions that the women were making, perhaps to everyone at once, or to specific men.[34]

7) In the Grudem-Hurley view, it would not be insubordinate for a woman to ask questions or make comments about the prophecy given *by a woman*. But Paul does not address such a possibility.

8) Paul's call for women to be quiet comes five verses *after* he says that prophecies should be evaluated, and it uses a different verb. Paul does nothing to connect verse 34 with verse 29. Verses 34-35 may not be on the topic of spiritual gifts, but they *are* about order in the worship service, and it is not unreasonable for Paul to include these verses in this chapter, and then conclude his discussion of spiritual gifts in verse 36.

It is reasonable to suggest that Paul is prohibiting the same kind of speech that he prohibits for tongues-speakers and prophets: out-of-turn speaking. While someone has the podium, the others should be quiet, not making loud comments, not calling out questions (no matter how well intentioned[35]), and not having their own conversations, for any of those would be disgraceful in the eyes of the public, contrary to what God wants, and contrary to the way that other congregations functioned.[36]

---

[34] Grudem suggests that "Paul anticipates an evasion of his teaching" (234), as if women might say, If we can't evaluate the prophecies, can we at least ask questions? But throughout chapter 14, Paul seems to be addressing real situations, and there is no hint in verse 35 that he is switching to a hypothetical question. He does not anticipate "what if" questions about tongues-speaking, for example. If he simply wanted to silence women, verse 34 would have been sufficient.

[35] Keener says, "Paul here actually opposes something more basic than women teaching in public…he opposes them learning too loudly in public" (*Paul, Women and Wives*, 80).

[36] Grudem says that if Paul is addressing a problem unique to Corinth, then it would be pointless to say that "women should remain silent in the churches" (245). But it makes perfectly good sense to say that people should not interrupt worship services, no matter what church we are talking about, no matter whether it is a problem in other churches.

Grudem also objects to the idea that Paul's main concern is order in the church: "Paul himself says that his concern is the principle of submission" (247). Paul mentions submission, yes, but he does not say that it is his primary concern. His concern throughout the chapter is on order, and it is not unreasonable to think that

Ben Witherington suggests the following possibility: "It is very believable that these women assumed that Christian prophets or prophetesses functioned much like the oracle at Delphi, who only prophesied in response to questions, including questions about purely personal matters. Paul argues that Christian prophecy is different: Prophets and prophetesses speak in response to the prompting of the Holy Spirit, without any human priming of the pump. Paul then limits such questions to another location, namely home. He may imply that the husband or man who was to be asked was either a prophet or at least able to answer such questions at a more appropriate time."[37]

Noisy women

We believe that the "noisy meeting" theory makes sense of the biblical data: Women were disturbing the meeting in some way.[38] However,

---

this might be his primary concern in verses 34-35 as well. Carson, writing in a volume that Grudem helped edit, says: "Although the focus in the second part of the chapter is still on tongues and prophecy, it is still more closely related to the order the church must maintain in the enjoyment of those grace gifts" (152).

In verses 34-35, Paul's concern is the behavior of women, and his reference to submission and the law is only one of his lines of support. As we saw in 1 Cor. 11, Paul could gather support from several lines of evidence (including Scripture) for head coverings, a custom based in culture. His primary concern in that passage was not a doctrine of headship, or of God's image, or of angels in worship services (although he mentions them), but his primary concern is women's appearance. We should not confuse a supporting argument with the primary purpose of the passage. In 1 Cor. 14, order is the primary concern; submission is a supporting argument.

[37] *Conflict and Community in Corinth: A Socio-Rhetorical Commentary on 1 and 2 Corinthians* (Eerdmans, 1995), 287. Similarly, Richard Longenecker writes, "Paul's words here pertain to the topic of charismatic excess discussed in chapters 12-14, are meant to restrict certain aberrations which arose within the worship of the Corinthian church, and should not be turned into a general ecclesiological principle" (*New Testament Social Ethics for Today* [Eerdmans, 1984], 86).

[38] Paul does not provide enough information for us to be sure about the exact nature of the problem. It might involve rude comments, chatter, noisy questions, or ecstatic shouts (which characterized women in some Greek mystery religions). As Blomberg notes, "Egalitarians and hierarchicalists alike need to stop accusing

Hurley criticizes this view, and we will respond to his objections:

1) "There is no indication elsewhere in the letter that the women in particular were unruly."[39] We believe that this objection is not valid. An analysis of chapter 11 shows that women were the primary problem; Paul gives fewer supporting arguments for the way that men should appear, suggesting that he believes there is a greater need to correct the way women pray and prophesy.

2) "Paul does confront unruly situations in the letter (11:33-34; 14:27,29,31). He meets them by establishing order rather than by silencing the unruly completely." This is true, but it says nothing against the noisy meeting theory. No one believes that Paul silenced women completely.[40] The silence he commanded for women was a temporary silence, just as it was for prophets and tongues-speakers; the goal of all these commands was an orderly worship service.

3) "The rule which Paul sets out is one which he says applies in all his churches (14:33b). It seems unlikely that the problem of noisy women had arisen in all of them." However, Paul does not say that a *rule* had to be given in all the churches—it is enough that the churches were already doing what theology and culture said was proper. No matter how the problem is defined, it seems unlikely that the same problem had arisen in all the churches—if it had been that common, Paul would have given the Corinthians some guidance on it when he established the church in

---

each other of being unbiblical and instead acknowledge more humbly that the biblical data simply aren't clear enough to permit dogmatism on either side" (292).

[39] Quotes from Hurley are from page 188 of his book.

[40] Grudem has a similar objection: "If women were being disruptive, Paul would just tell them to act in an orderly way, not to be completely silent.... If noise had been the problem in Corinth, he would have explicitly forbidden disorderly speech, not all speech" (245). But not even Grudem believes that Paul tells people to be "completely silent." His objection can be turned on his own view: If Paul meant judging prophecies, then he would have said that, rather than forbidding all speech. It is not fair for people to object to proposed interpretations by saying that the text doesn't explicitly indicate that particular problem, because the text doesn't pinpoint *any* particular problem. It is unavoidable that we have to guess what problem best accounts for Paul's response.

Corinth, and on this matter he does not allude to any prior teaching.[41] Most churches were already orderly.[42]

4) "It seems unlike Paul to silence all women because some are noisy or disruptive. His actual handling of other disorderly people provides concrete grounds for arguing against wholesale action when only some individuals are in fact violators." This objection is groundless. Paul sometimes gives commands to an entire group even when it is unlikely that *every* member of the group had a problem:

In 1 Tim. 5:11, he writes as if *all* younger widows are unable to control their desires to be married; in Titus 1:12 he writes as if everyone on Crete is a lazy glutton. In 1 Tim. 2:8, he instructs *men* to pray "without anger or disputing." Apparently the problem about prayer in Ephesus was caused only by men, and probably only by some of them, so Paul gave instructions only for the men; in the same way, the problem with talking in Corinth happened to be caused by women. Paul was writing to specific churches, dealing with specific situations, not trying to write manuals for all churches in all times. Paul sometimes wrote principles that are of universal validity, but other instructions are an application of timeless truth to a specific situation.

Even in Hurley's interpretation, Paul was too sweeping in his

---

[41] "We may assume that the problem was specific to Corinth and perhaps a few other cities like it. After all, his other instructions in this chapter address specific abuses of the gifts at Corinth; had they obtained generally, we can be sure that Paul would have already given these regulations during his extended stay with them" (Keener, *Paul, Women and Wives,* 73). Verse 36 also implies that Paul is dealing with problems that are unique to Corinth.

[42] Grudem has a similar objection: "His rule cannot be restricted to one local church where there supposedly were problems.... Paul directs the Corinthians to conform to a practice that was universal in the early church" (245). But Grudem's objection applies to his own view, as well: There is no evidence that other churches were having problems with a prophecy-evaluation time in the worship service, nor evidence that most other churches had insubordinate women. Paul implies that a "rule" was not necessary in most churches; they were already doing what they were supposed to do. Everyone agrees that Paul is telling the Corinthians to conform to what other churches did; the question is whether the deviation at Corinth was disruption, or that women might be tempted to ask questions about the prophecies.

prohibition—he forbids all questions because *some* of them might not be submissive. However, Paul's command is quite reasonable if we understand Paul to be addressing a general commotion: People should not disrupt the service. Paul assumed that the Corinthians could figure out, just as we do today, that whispering is permissible, and that a woman can ask the pastor, not just her own husband. It is not disgraceful for women to pray and prophesy in church, but it is disgraceful for them (or anyone else) to cause a commotion, and that is Paul's main concern.

Conclusion

Although we cannot answer all questions about the specific situation Paul was addressing in Corinth, we do conclude that he was addressing a specific situation rather than making a general prohibition on women speaking in church. His intent was to prohibit disruptive and disrespectful questions and comments that were part of the chaotic Corinthian meetings—and in Corinth, these particular practices were coming from the women. Just as he told the disorderly tongues-speakers and prophets to control themselves because God is not a God of disorder, he also told the women to control themselves because the law teaches self-control. If they want to learn something, they can ask questions somewhere else.[43]

Only one person should speak at a time. Everyone else, whether male or female, should be quiet, for it is disgraceful for people in the audience to be talking while someone else is speaking to the group. Just as Paul's call for tongues-speakers or prophets to be silent should not be turned into a demand that they never say anything at all, so also his call for women to be quiet should not be turned into a demand that they never give messages of spiritual value in church. That is something that Paul specifically allows in 1 Corinthians 11.

---

[43] Eugene Peterson gives this paraphrase in *The Message:* "Wives must not disrupt worship, talking when they should be listening, asking questions that could more appropriately be asked of their husbands at home. God's Book of the law guides our manners and customs here. Wives have no license to use the time of worship for unwarranted speaking."

QUESTIONS ABOUT 1 TIMOTHY 2:11-15

For many people, 1 Timothy 2:12 is concise proof that women should not have authority in the church. Paul did not allow women to teach or have authority, they say, and neither should we.

However, almost no one insists on the last part of the verse: "she must be silent." Paul did not believe that women should be silent *at all times,* even in church. So in this chapter, we examine this verse more carefully in its context to see what Paul is really prohibiting. As we look more carefully, we discover questions about how we should apply these words to the church today.

These verses are important, so we must study them carefully, with prayer, to try to avoid mistakes. As we noted at the beginning of this series, we want to base our beliefs and practices on Scripture. We do not want to twist the Scriptures.

At the same time, we want to recognize that there are genuine difficulties in understanding this passage. One scholar wrote, "It is sometimes implied that the hierarchicalist's argument all boils down to 1 Timothy 2. This is patently not the case…. If anything, this passage complicates matters because the exegetical questions are so complex."[1]

Because of the difficulties in this verse, this chapter is quite long, even when some of the important supporting material has been moved into footnotes. We encourage you to read it carefully, and at least the summary at the end. We pray that we can all examine this passage of Scripture with a sincere desire to hear what God is saying to us through it.

Observations and questions

1 Tim. 2:11-12 says: "I do not permit a woman to teach or to exercise

---

[1] Craig Blomberg, "Neither Hierarchicalist Nor Egalitarian: Gender Roles in Paul," in *Two Views on Women in Ministry* (ed. James Beck and Craig Blomberg; Zondervan, 2001), 357-58. Craig Keener writes, "It would be surprising if an issue that would exclude at least half the body of Christ from a ministry of teaching would be addressed in only one text" (*Paul, Women, and Wives* [Hendrickson, 1992], 101).

authority over a man; rather, she is to remain quiet."[2] We will begin with a few observations about these verses, noting areas in which we need further clarification:

1. Paul did not believe that a woman must be quiet *at all times.* He says that women can pray and prophesy in a worship service (1 Cor. 11). There may be a difference between *prophecy,* which Paul allowed, and *teaching,* which he did not. Was there a special situation in Ephesus that called for women to be silent?

2. The Bible does not teach that females can *never* have authority over males. Scripture allows women to have civil authority over men, and to have authority over male children, male teenagers, and others.[3] Again, we'd like to find out what situation Paul was dealing with, and whether it applies to the church today.

3. When Paul says, "I do not permit...," he is stating his policy for churches in his area. This may imply that all churches in subsequent centuries should have a similar policy—or it may not.

4. 1 Tim. 2:11 says that a woman should learn "with all submissiveness." However, Scripture does not teach that a woman must be in total submission to *all* men. What kind of submission is Paul is talking about?

5. 1 Tim. 2:12 does not use the normal Greek word for authority (*exousia*)—it uses the rare Greek verb *authenteō.* Why? Is there is a difference in meaning between these two words?

6. In verses 13-15, Paul appears to give *reasons* for what he says in verse 12. But the reasons given create additional questions:

   a. Verse 13 says that Adam was formed first, but why should that be a reason for women to avoid authority specifically in church, when women can have authority in civil government?

---

[2] "Quiet" is the ESV translation of *hēsychia.* Paul used a different word, *sigaō,* in 1 Cor. 14.

[3] God gave Deborah authority as a prophetess and judge, and Esther as a queen.

    b. Verse 14 says that Adam was not deceived—implying that he sinned deliberately. Why would this be a reason for men to have authority?

    c. Verse 15 says that women "will be saved through childbearing," but this does not make sense for spiritual salvation *or* physical protection.

7. 1 Tim. 2 addresses several cultural matters: for people to pray for kings, for men to lift their hands when they pray, and for women to avoid braids, jewelry and expensive clothes. Can we can take verse 12 as a permanent guideline when we do not take verses 8-9 as permanent guidelines?

8. Paul's letter gives pastoral advice on a variety of topics to Timothy as he grapples with a controversy in Ephesus (1:3). Some of the advice seems applicable for any church in any age, but other remarks seem specific to Timothy's situation. (For example, 1:18; 4:12-14; 5:23.) Why should we take 2:12 as a permanent policy when we ignore Paul's advice in 1 Tim. 5:9 to maintain a list of widows over age 60?

9. In 1 Tim. 6:1-2, Paul counsels slaves to submit to their masters, especially if the masters are Christian. His teaching is based on a cultural situation that is no longer universally true. Is this also the case for his advice for women to be submissive?

Most of these observations and questions have come from people who disagree with the traditional interpretation. That is not surprising, because on almost any subject, people who are happy with the traditional view have little incentive to search for more details. However, the requests for clarification are legitimate, and we need reasonable answers. We will start by presenting the traditional or complementarian view.[4] Then we will

---

[4] The "complementarian" view is that men and women are complementary, having different roles in the family and in the church. The "egalitarian" view stresses the equality of men and women, saying that there is no role in the church restricted to one sex or the other. Both terms are less than perfect, since complementarians believe that men and women are equal in worth, and many egalitarians believe that men and women have different and complementary strengths.

present the egalitarian objections to that view, and finally discuss whether the objections are reasonable.

The traditional[5] view

James Hurley argues that 1 Timothy was designed to give instructions that would apply in all churches, in all ages:

> It is universally accepted that 1 Timothy was intended to provide a clear statement concerning certain issues which its author, whom I take to be Paul[6], felt needed attention....
>
> Paul wrote..."how it is necessary [*dei*] to conduct oneself" [3:15]. *Dei* is an impersonal verb meaning "one must" or "one ought.".... Paul's use of *dei* here is presumptive evidence that he considered what he said normative beyond the immediate situation.... Paul's abstract language indicates that his instructions should have a general rather than closely limited application..... He delivers "trustworthy sayings worthy of full acceptance.".... Only the last section of the fifth chapter is pointedly restricted to Timothy.[7]

Hurley ignores 1 Tim. 1:18 and 4:12-14, and says nothing about any modern application of 5:9-14.

Thomas Schreiner, another traditional scholar, is more cautious: "The letters should not necessarily be understood as timeless marching orders for the church but must be interpreted in light of the specific circumstances

---

[5] In some churches, "tradition" is that women never speak from the podium. Hurley, Moo, Piper, Grudem, and Schreiner present a moderated version of tradition, in that they argue that women may speak in church in some circumstances. The "tradition" is changing.

[6] Some scholars do not believe that Paul wrote the Pastoral Epistles, or that he had someone else formulate the wording. The exact authorship does not affect our study, since we accept these epistles as canonical and therefore authoritative for faith and practice. We will proceed on the basis of Pauline authorship.

[7] James Hurley, *Man and Woman in Biblical Perspective* (Zondervan, 1981), 196.

that occasioned them."[8] Although parts of the letters deal with deviant teachings found in specific situations, he says that the letters as a whole "reflect the pattern of governance that he expected to exist in his churches."[9] T. David Gordon writes, "The Pastoral Epistles are…written with the purpose of providing instruction of ordering churches at the close of the apostolic era."[10]

Hurley notes that 1 Tim. 2 deals with prayer and worship. Referring to "the prayer posture of the day," Paul exhorts the men to pray in a peaceable way. In particular, he wanted them to avoid anger and an argumentative spirit.[11] Paul then advises the women to avoid ostentatious hair and clothing styles. "Both sexes are to live holy lives of obedient works. The difference between the commands to the two sexes gives us some indication of besetting sins of the day."[12] Paul's instructions "are, to a certain extent, culturally relative," but they are based on timeless principles: humility and good behavior.

Paul does not forbid *all* braids and jewelry, Hurley says.

> He refers instead to the elaborate hair-styles which were then fashionable among the wealthy…. He probably meant "braided hair decorated with gold or with pearls."… Obedience to this command of Paul's requires no subtle exegetical skill or knowledge of the customs of Paul's day; it requires only an assessment of what

---

[8] Thomas Schreiner, "An Interpretation of 1 Timothy 2:9-15," in *Women in the Church* (2nd ed.; edited by Andreas Köstenberger and Thomas Schreiner; Baker, 2005), 87.

[9] Ibid.

[10] T. David Gordon, "A Certain Kind of Letter," in Andreas Köstenberger, Thomas Schreiner, and H. Scott Baldwin, eds, *Women in the Church* (1st ed., Baker, 1995), 59.

[11] Schreiner writes, "When Paul calls on men to pray 'in every place'… this is probably a reference to house churches" (91). First-century Jews sometimes recited various curses against apostates in their prayers. It is possible that some early Christians used similar curses against government officials or their religious opponents, and Paul tells them to stop.

[12] Hurley, 198.

adornment is excessively costly and not modest or proper. Christians…have no need to set aside Paul's instructions as somehow "culture bound."[13]

We agree that women may wear braids, gold, and pearls today, and should not flaunt their wealth. Schreiner writes,

> The similar text in 1 Peter 3:3 supports this interpretation, for read literally it prohibits all wearing of clothing, which is scarcely Peter's intention. The words on clothing provide help in understanding the instructions on braids, gold, and pearls. Paul's purpose is probably not to ban these altogether, but to warn against expensive and extravagant preoccupation with one's appearance.[14]

Paul then addresses another aspect of behavior appropriate for women: They should learn quietly and submissively. Douglas Moo observes, "That Paul wants Christian women to learn is an important point, for such a practice was not generally encouraged by the Jews."[15]

Paul is not just stating a personal preference, Hurley argues—Paul gives verse 11 as a command. The Greek word "does not mean silence but carries with it connotations of peacefulness and restfulness…. Paul is not…calling for 'buttoned lips' but for a quiet receptivity and a submission to authority."[16] Schreiner says, "Not absolute silence but rather a gentle and quiet demeanor is intended."[17]

---

[13] Ibid., 199.

[14] Schreiner, 95.

[15] Douglas Moo, "What Does It Mean Not to Teach or Have Authority Over Men?" in John Piper and Wayne Grudem, *Recovering Biblical Manhood and Womanhood* (Crossway, 1991), 183. But he also says that the stress is on the manner, not the command to learn. "It is not the fact that they are to learn, but the manner in which they are to learn that concerns Paul" (183; similar comment by Schreiner, 97).

[16] Hurley, 200. The Greek has a third-person imperative: "have a woman learn." He also claims that the verb in verse 12 is not just a personal preference, "but has overtones of command" (201).

[17] Schreiner, 98.

Why did Paul feel it necessary to write this verse? Moo says, "Almost certainly it is necessary because at least some women were *not* learning 'in quietness.'... The facts that this verse is directed only to women and that verses 12-14...focus on the relationship of men to women incline us to think that the submission in view here is also this submission of women to male leadership."[18] "It is certainly possible that the prohibition is given because some women were teaching men."[19]

Why silence only the women? Was it because the average woman was not as educated as the average man? No, because Greco-Roman society had some educated women and many illiterate men.[20] If education was the problem, then it would be inconsistent for Paul to silence women but say nothing about uneducated men.[21]

Some inscriptions in Asia Minor show that women functioned as high priests in some temples—therefore there was no *cultural* scandal involved in women being in religious authority, which leads Wayne Grudem to conclude that Paul's directive must have been based on God's law, not cultural sentiments.[22]

---

[18] Moo, 183. "We can also be fairly certain that women were functioning as teachers in the Ephesian community; otherwise, Paul would have no need for a corrective" (Linda Belleville, *Women Leaders and the Church* [Baker, 1999], 169).

[19] Schreiner, 112.

[20] Steven M. Baugh writes, "To say that Ephesian women were uneducated because they did not appear in 'graduate schools' of philosophy, rhetoric, and medicine is misleading. Few people in antiquity advanced in their formal education beyond today's elementary school levels, including men like Socrates, Sophocles, and Herodotus.... There were wealthy women in the Ephesian congregation. At least some of these women were educated" ("A Foreign World: Ephesus in the First Century," chapter 1 in *Women in the Church,* 2nd ed., 34).

[21] Wayne Grudem, *Evangelical Feminism and Biblical Truth* (Multnomah, 2004), 293.

[22] Grudem notes that "some women had prominent roles in pagan religions in Ephesus.... The idea that women could not hold church office because it would have been unacceptable in that society does not square with the evidence" (324). Nancy Vyhmeister notes, "On the western coast of Asia Minor there was a

However, this does not mean that women should not speak in church. Hurley writes: "Women were certainly free to speak in the Pauline churches (1 Cor. 11). Paul is speaking only of teaching situations here in 1 Timothy 2."[23]

In support of this interpretation, he notes that verse 12 is a conceptual repetition of verse 11. Learning corresponds to not teaching, and submission corresponds to not having authority. Just as Paul wants women to learn in a submissive manner, he does not want them to teach *in an authoritative manner.*[24]

---

tradition of dominant women" (*Women in Ministry* [Andrews University Press, 1998], 339). Clinton Arnold and Robert Saucy suggest that in Ephesus,

> women were converting to Christianity and desiring to attain leadership roles in the church similar to what they held in society. Aware of this situation, Paul addressed this issue because he did not want these churches to cave in to the cultural pressures of the day and violate a deep-set theological conviction about order between men and women" ("The Ephesian Background of Paul's Teaching on Women's Ministry," chapter 12 in *Women and Men in Ministry: A Complementary Perspective,* ed. Robert L. Saucy and Judith K. TenElshof [Moody, 2001], 287).

[23] Hurley, 201. Similarly, Piper and Grudem write,

> Paul endorses women prophesying in church (1 Corinthians 11:5) and says that men "learn" by such prophesying (1 Corinthians 14:31).... Teaching and learning are such broad terms that it is impossible that women not teach men and men not learn from women in some sense.... The teaching inappropriate for a woman is the teaching of men in settings or ways that dishonor the calling of men to bear the primary responsibility for teaching and leadership. ("An Overview of Central Concerns," in Piper and Grudem, 69-70)

[24] "Both verses have the same situation in mind, one in which women are not to teach authoritatively but are to learn quietly" (Hurley, 201). Blomberg also combines the two as "authoritative teaching" (364). However, Grudem (317) and Moo separate them: "We think 1 Timothy 2:8-15 imposes two restrictions on the ministry of women: they are not to teach Christian doctrine to men and they are not to exercise authority directly over men in the church" (Moo, 180). He says that these two prohibitions show us what Paul means by "full submission" (184). "Paul treats the two tasks as distinct elsewhere in 1 Timothy" (187). The fact that Paul twice calls for female silence (verses 11-12) suggests that he did not allow

Hurley concludes that the verse means "that women should not be authoritative teachers in the church," and he associates that with the office of elder. Paul did not forbid *all* teaching by women, Hurley claims. "What Paul disallowed therefore was simply the exercise of authority over men."[25] Werner Neuer writes, "Paul excludes women from the office of teaching because teaching the assembled congregation would necessarily place them over men."[26]

Moo acknowledges that the present-tense form of the verb "permit" *could* allow for a temporary situation, but a present-tense verb can also be used for a permanent command (e.g., Rom. 12:1).[27] Whether Paul indicates a temporary prohibition or a permanent rule cannot be decided by the grammar, but only by the context. Moo notes, "Paul's 'advice' to Timothy is the word of an apostle, accredited by God, and included in the inspired Scriptures."[28] Even an indicative verb—a statement—can be used to imply a command, as Paul does in verses 1 and 8.[29]

What sort of "teaching" is not allowed? The Greek word for "teach" *can* refer to a ministry that any believer might do (Col. 3:16), but it more often refers to a special gift associated with church leadership (Eph. 4:11). "In the pastoral epistles, teaching always has this restricted sense of

---

any form of teaching. Teaching usually involves some form of authority.

[25] Hurley, 202.

[26] Werner Neuer, *Man and Woman in Christian Perspective* (Crossway, 1991), 119. "Authorised teaching belongs… to the leadership and direction of the congregation and carries with it an obligation on church members to obey it" (ibid.).

[27] "As far as the present tense of the verb goes, this allows us to conclude only that Paul was *at the time of writing* insisting on these prohibitions" (185).

[28] Moo, 185. Moo does not explicitly draw conclusions from his statement, but he insinuates his conclusion. However, temporary commands such as "use a little wine" are also apostolic, inspired, and biblical.

[29] Schreiner, 99-100. He notes that this does not prove that the verb in verse 12 is a permanent command, but that the form of the verb does not prove that it is temporary.

authoritative doctrinal instruction" (e.g., 1 Tim. 2:2).[30] Teaching was an important part of the function of an elder (1 Tim. 3:2).

However, in Protestant churches, authority is based in Scripture, not in the preacher. Does modern preaching involve the same sort of authority? Moo argues that it does, since "the addition of an authoritative, written norm is unlikely to have significantly altered the nature of Christian teaching.... Any authority that the teacher has is derived...but the activity of teaching, precisely because it does come to God's people with the authority of God and His Word, is authoritative."[31]

What is the difference between prophecy (which women may do, according to 1 Cor. 11) and teaching (which they may not, according to 1 Tim. 2:12)? Neuer says, "In contrast to prophecy, which is related to specific situations and according to Paul is subject to assessment by the congregation, teaching is binding and of general validity, so that the congregation must submit to it (cf. Rom 6:17; 16:17; 1 Cor 4:17; 15:15ff.; Col 2:6-7; 2 Thess 2:15)."[32] Grudem says that teaching is based on transmitting apostolic teachings, whereas prophecies may have errors and

---

[30] Moo, 185, and Schreiner, 101.

[31] Moo, 185-86. Moo notes that "evangelistic witnessing, counseling, teaching subjects other than Bible or doctrine—are not, in our opinion, teaching in the sense Paul intends here" (186). Piper and Grudem say, "We do not think it is forbidden for women to tell the gospel story and win men and women to Christ" (77)—although that is a form of teaching, and it may involve doctrines about Jesus and salvation. They admit that there is a hazy line between a Priscilla-type role and an official teaching role (76, 85).

Moo says that women can vote in a congregational meeting, presumably even when women are the majority. He reasons that voting "is not the same thing as the exercise of authority ascribed, e.g., to the elders" (187). He thinks that women can perform administrative duties, and notes that the passage is only about the Christian community; it does not address business, government, and education. Neuer is more restrictive: "Women may give instruction, so long as it is not public teaching of the congregation, but takes place among small groups of women" (121).

[32] Neuer, 119. However, pastoral teaching should also be subject to assessment by the congregation, and if it violates Scripture, the congregation does not have to submit to it.

must be evaluated.[33]

Schreiner is reluctant to accept Grudem's definition of prophecy as "mixed with error," but he argues that it is different from teaching, vertical rather than horizontal, and more spontaneous. "Prophecy applies to specific situations and is less tied to the consciousness of the individual."[34]

What sort of authority is not allowed? Paul does not use the normal word for authority here (*exousia*), but a rare word (*authenteō*). Traditional scholars argue that the meaning is the same: to have authority over.[35] "The two words are used synonymously in at least eight different contexts."[36] Köstenberger analyzes all the "neither...nor" constructions in the New Testament, and finds that in all cases, both words are positive, or both are negative.[37]

---

[33] As summarized by Schreiner, 102.

[34] Schreiner, 102. This definition seems more speculative and precise than the biblical evidence warrants. Schreiner notes that the prophecies of women are just as authoritative as the prophecies of men, but they may nevertheless be given "without overturning male leadership, whereas 1 Timothy 2:11-15 demonstrates that women cannot regularly teach men" (ibid). One scholarly study of prophecy in the New Testament gives a broader definition: "What all manifestations of this gift have in common is the speaker's sense that they have a 'word from the Lord,' but a preacher who has meditated on a text or theme long enough to have had such an experience may well then qualify as one prophesying when he or she speaks to a Christian gathering or congregation" (David Hill, *New Testament Prophecy* [Marshall, Morgan & Scott, 1979], 213, cited by James Beck and Craig Blomberg, "Reflections on Complementarian Essays," in *Two Views on Women in Ministry* [ed. James Beck and Craig Blomberg; Zondervan, 2001], 308).

[35] For more on the meaning of *authenteō*, see the appendix at the end of this chapter.

[36] Schreiner, 103.

[37] Andreas Köstenberger, "A Complex Sentence: The Syntax of 1 Timothy 2:12," chapter 3 of *Women in the Church,* 2nd ed., 71. He notes that this observation has been accepted by egalitarian scholars such as Padgett, Keener, Marshall, and Giles, although some of them, in order to keep *authenteō* as negative, try to see "teaching" as also negative in this verse. Belleville objects to the principle, expressing some reservations about the method of Köstenberger's study, but not offering any counterexamples of her own.

Paul views "teaching" as a positive function.[38] This therefore suggests that Paul also viewed *authenteō* as a positive function: to lead, direct, or exercise authority. Although teaching is good, Paul said that women should not teach men; in the same way he said that women should not exercise authority over men even though authority in itself is not bad. Paul is making restrictions not because the activities are bad, but because the people are female. This is simply the counterpart to what Paul said in the earlier verse, that women should be submissive.

What "men" are in view here? Since the Greek words *gynē* and *anēr* can mean either woman and man, or wife and husband, depending on context, some have suggested that Paul did not make restrictions on all women, but only on women exercising authority over their own husbands. But Moo notes that Paul speaks of men in general in verse 8, and women in general in verse 9, and if he wanted to shift the meaning to wives in particular, he would need to supply a verbal indicator, such as by saying that he did not allow women to exercise authority over *their own* men.[39] Lacking such an indicator, and since the surrounding context is about church rather than family relationships, it seems best to conclude that Paul is speaking of men and women in general—or more specifically, the men who had authority in the church. As Schreiner writes, "The context of verse 12…suggests that the submission of all women to *all* men is not in view, for not all men taught and had authority when the church gathered."[40]

Paul's comments were motivated by a particular problem in the church

---

[38] "The verb *didaskō* (I teach) has a positive sense elsewhere in the Pastoral Epistles (1 Tim. 4:11; 6:2; 2 Tim. 2:2). The only exception is Titus 1:11, where the context clarifies that false teaching is the object" (Schreiner, 104). Saucy writes, "Further evidence for the positive understanding is seen in the fact that the prohibition of exercising authority is specifically said to be 'over a man.' Only a positive meaning makes sense of this addition, as surely the apostle would have prohibited women from 'domineering' or 'flaunting authority' over all people, not just men" ("Paul's Teaching on the Ministry of Women," chapter 13 in Saucy and TenElshof, 294).

[39] Moo, 188; see also Grudem, 296-99; Schreiner, 92-94; Belleville, 121.

[40] Schreiner, 99.

at Ephesus, but that in itself does not mean that his advice does not apply to other situations. He addressed the specific situation in verse 11, Moo says, and then supports it in verse 12 with a general statement about the way he wants all of his churches to function.[41] He is restricting women not because they are uneducated or deceived (a temporary situation); he is restricting them because they are women (a permanent situation). They are allowed to teach, but not to teach men.[42] They can have authority, but not authority over men.

Reasons for the prohibition

Hurley argues that Paul bases his view on Scripture, not on the cultural situation. By following his instructions with *gar* (usually translated "for"), Paul is expressing reasons for his command.[43] Paul makes no reference to social customs, or to the idea that most women did not yet have enough education to be teachers, or the idea that they were the chief proponents of false doctrine. Rather, he says that Adam was created before Eve, thereby giving him authority over her, just as the firstborn son eventually "became the head of his father's house and leader of its worship."[44]

---

[41] Moo, 189.

[42] Schreiner, 101.

[43] "When a command or other instruction is given in paraenetic material, it is highly unlikely that the expression *gar* is to be taken in any other way than causal" (Gordon, 61). "When Paul gives a command elsewhere in the Pastoral Epistles, the *gar* that follows almost invariably states the reason for the command.... Even in ordinary speech reasons often follow commands" (Schreiner, 105). Note the qualifying phrase "almost invariably," which suggests that a different use is possible.

Egalitarians often argue that verses 13-15 are illustrations, not reasons. Philip B. Payne writes, "It makes good sense to take *gar* in 1 Tim. 2:13-14 as explanatory since the example of Eve's deception leading to the fall of mankind is a powerful illustration of how serious the consequences can be when a woman deceived by false teaching conveys it to others" ("Libertarian Women in Ephesus: A Response to Douglas J. Moo's Article," *Trinity Journal* 2 [1981]: 176, citing Robertson's *Grammar*).

[44] Hurley, 207. He cites scriptures about inheritance by the firstborn son, but even though he is seeking an application for worship situations, he cites no

Moo writes, "For Paul, the man's priority in the order of creation is indicative of the headship that man is to have over woman."[45] He writes:

By rooting these prohibitions in the circumstances of creation rather than in the circumstances of the fall, Paul shows that he does not consider these restrictions to be the product of the curse and presumably, therefore, to be phased out by redemption. And by citing creation rather than a local situation or cultural circumstances as his basis for the prohibitions, Paul makes it clear that, while these local or cultural issues may have provided the *context* of the issue, they do not provide the *reason* for his advice. His reason for the prohibition of verse 12 is the created role relationship of man and woman, and we may justly conclude that these prohibitions are applicable as long as this reason remains true.[46]

Eve rather than Adam was deceived, Paul writes in verse 14—but how does that support a rule that women cannot teach men? Hurley asks, "Would you rather be led by an innocent but deceived person, or by a deliberate rebel?"[47] He dismisses the idea that women are too gullible to

---

evidence that the firstborn son necessarily had authority in worship. He does not attempt to explain why Adam's priority would give males authority over females in religious matters but not always in civil government. As evidence that priority is linked with authority, Hurley notes that Col. 1:15-18 connects Christ's authority with him being firstborn, before all things, and the beginning. Hurley argues that it is reasonable to conclude that Paul connected being first with implying authority.

[45] Moo, 190. "Paul maintains that the Genesis narrative gives a reason why women should not teach men: Adam was created first and then Eve. In other words, when Paul read Genesis 2, he concluded that the order in which Adam and Eve were created signaled an important difference in the role of men and women" (Schreiner, 105-6).

[46] Moo, 190-91. If the logic is extended, it would imply that women will be subordinate to men in all eternity, since verse 13 will always be true, but this is probably more than Moo wants to say. It does cast doubt on the validity of his reasoning.

[47] Hurley, 215. Hurley never suggests how we should answer the question. Schreiner notes that this "would seem to argue against men teaching women, for

be teachers (cf. Titus 2:3, 2 Tim. 1:5; 3:15).[48]

However, that interpretation is found in the early church fathers, and it is the simplest reading of the text.[49]

Neuer refers to "the greater susceptibility of women to temptation," and says that Paul, rather than oppressing women, is simply keeping them out of a situation they could not handle.[50] Grudem is not clear on this point, but says that Paul refers "to a characteristic of Eve that he sees as relevant for all women in all cultures."[51] Grudem writes, "Some complementarians understand this verse to be referring to the fact that Eve wrongfully took leadership in the family and made the decision to eat the forbidden fruit on her own, and other complementarians understand this to refer to a woman's 'kinder, gentler nature' that makes her less likely to draw a hard line when close friends are teaching doctrinal error."[52] Both of these ideas

---

at least the woman wanted to obey God, while Adam sinned deliberately" (113-14). But he never answers the question, either.

[48] Hurley (215) notes that Paul blames Adam for the entry of sin into the world (Rom. 5:12; 1 Cor. 15:21-22).

[49] If verse 14 gives a reason for verse 12, these verses say, in short, that women should not teach men because Eve was deceived. The easiest way to get from one concept to another is to assume that the characteristic mentioned for Eve is relevant to the prohibition because it somehow applies to all subsequent women. William J. Webb notes that the traditional teaching of the church is "that women are more easily deceived than men due to an inferior capacity to understand and make sound judgments.... The traditional rendering is the most supportable reading of the text" (*Slaves, Women, and Homosexuals: Exploring the Hermeneutics of Cultural Analysis* [InterVarsity, 2001], 225). Blomberg notes that the "common Jewish and Christian belief throughout history" is "that women are ontologically inferior to men" (365-66). He further notes, "Attempts, however sophisticated, to defend the view that women are inherently more gullible fly in the face of all contemporary social-scientific analysis and do not fit the context of 1 Timothy" (366).

[50] Neuer, 120.

[51] Grudem, 296.

[52] Ibid. The fact that these ideas are proposed, despite not being in the text, suggests that people are not comfortable with what the text seems to imply. Blomberg faults Schreiner for suggesting, without any biblical or contemporary

seem far from what the text actually says—it specifies deception, and says nothing about leadership or gentleness.[53]

Does the text imply that women are more easily deceived? Moo thinks that this interpretation is possible, but unlikely. "There is nothing in the Genesis accounts or in Scripture elsewhere to suggest that Eve's deception is representative of women in general."[54] Moreover, Paul allows women to teach other women—they are capable of teaching correctly. Schreiner also argues against female gullibility: "This interpretation should be rejected since it implies that women are ontologically and intellectually inferior."[55]

Schreiner notes that "all sin involves deceit," and Adam was therefore deceived; what verse 14 means is that Eve was deceived *first*—the word "first" is understood from an implied parallel with verse 13.[56] Schreiner writes:

> Paul's purpose is…to focus on the fact that the serpent approached and deceived Eve, not Adam…. The serpent subverted the pattern of male leadership and interacted only with Eve during the temptation. Adam was present throughout and did not intervene. The Genesis temptation, therefore, is indicative of what happens when male leadership is abrogated.[57]

---

evidence, that women are less able to discern doctrinal errors (366). Webb notes, "The revised historical position 'cleans up' the traditional view based upon their own social-scientific awareness" (227). He notes that since the text does not say how verse 14 is related to verse 12, some speculation is inevitable.

[53] Webb notes, "The role-reversal interpretation is convoluted; it requires the reader to bring unnecessary and unwarranted information to the text" (114).

[54] Moo, 190. In 2 Cor. 11:3, Eve provides an example for both men and women.

[55] Schreiner, 114.

[56] Ibid. Blomberg faults this view also: "There are no well-known principles from antiquity…that would make the order in which one was deceived in any way significant" (366).

[57] Schreiner, 115.

If this is Paul's thought, he picked a roundabout way of expressing it, one that requires the readers to fill in several steps of logic. Schreiner wants to cast blame on Adam, but the text says that Eve is the one who "became a sinner." Schreiner admits that his interpretation is weak, but says that the egalitarian view is weaker.[58]

In effect, Schreiner is blaming Adam for sinning first, for he failed to protect his wife from the serpent. Hurley also wants to blame Adam: "Paul seems to be saying that Eve was not at fault; she was deceived.... Could it be that his point in verse 14 is that Adam was the one appointed by God to exercise religious headship?"[59]

Moo makes a slightly different suggestion: Verse 14 "is intended to remind the women at Ephesus that Eve was deceived...precisely in taking the initiative over the man.... If the women at the church at Ephesus proclaim their independence...they will make the same mistake Eve made and bring similar disaster on themselves and the church."[60] In short, there is no widely accepted view among traditional scholars. The diversity of the suggestions may indicate that the original context is not known.

Finally, we will consider verse 15, which is not a reason for Paul's

-----

[58] "The verse is difficult" (112). "I can scarcely claim that I have given the definitive and final interpretation of this passage" (120). "The complementarian view stands on the basis of the clarity of verse 13 so that resolving the interpretation of verse 14 is not crucial for the passage as a whole" ("Women in Ministry," in *Two Views on Women in Ministry* [ed. James Beck and Craig Blomberg; Zondervan, 2001], 225).

[59] Hurley, 215-16. In this interpretation, too, readers would have to supply several steps of missing logic. "The headship of men in domestic and religious affairs continues from the pre-fall period through the time of Christ's advent" (220). Note that Hurley again specifies religious headship, without any evidence from Genesis for this specificity. Schreiner makes a similar unwarranted qualification: "The creation of Adam before Eve signaled that men are to teach and exercise authority in the church" (120, italics added).

[60] Moo, 190. Note in this view that Eve was not deceived into eating the fruit, but into taking initiative. But Genesis has the opposite emphasis: It is clear about the fruit but says little if anything against Eve taking the initiative.

prohibition, but a qualification for verse 14.[61] Nevertheless, it is part of the paragraph. Hurley says that if the verse "refers to salvation from sin, it is a flat contradiction of Paul's view of salvation by trust in Christ." Another option is that the woman will be kept safe in childbearing, but "this seems almost totally irrelevant to the context."[62] Moreover, as Schreiner says, "the fact that Christian women have often died in childbirth raises serious questions about this interpretation."[63]

The grammar allows another possibility: She (singular, referring to Eve) will be saved through *the* childbearing (the Greek text has the word "the," possibly referring to the birth of Christ), if they (plural, referring to all later women) remain in the faith. It is not that Eve's salvation is dependent on later women's faithfulness, but the thought is elliptical, requiring readers to supply a verb: Eve will be saved through the birth of Christ, and subsequent women *will be saved,* too, if they remain in the faith. This is a possible interpretation, Hurley says, but "it breaks with the flow of the passage."[64]

Schreiner argues against it: "Those who posit a reference to Jesus' birth have subtly introduced the notion that salvation is secured as a *result* of giving birth to him, whereas the text speaks not of the result of birth but of

---

[61] Schreiner, 115.

[62] Hurley, 221. Moo notes that this would entail an unusual meaning for *sozō,* normally translated "save" (192). Keener argues, "The most natural way for an ancient reader to have understood 'salvation' in the context of childbirth would have been a safe delivery, for women regularly called upon patron deities…in childbirth" (*Paul, Women, and Wives,* 118). Payne writes, "Paul's obvious concern is to highlight the role of woman both in the fall (2:14) and in salvation (2:15)" (178).

[63] Schreiner, 115. He also argues that the verb always has the meaning of spiritual salvation in the Pastoral Epistles.

[64] Hurley, 222. Hurley suggests another possibility: Women will be "kept safe from wrongly seizing men's roles by embracing a woman's role." This seems to read something into the text that is not there, and others have not accepted this meaning of "save." Schreiner notes that "verse 12 is too far from verse 15 for this latter interpretation to be plausible" (116).

the actual birthing process."[65] Moo suggests that the verse designates "the circumstances in which Christian women will experience their salvation—in maintaining as priorities" the role that Scripture assigns to women.[66] Paul has simply mentioned one role—bearing children—as a way of designating the female role in general.

Schreiner agrees, saying that childbearing "represents the fulfillment of the woman's domestic role as a mother in distinction from the man."[67] He notes that the verse mandates more than childbearing: "It is not sufficient for salvation for Christian women merely to bear children [i.e., accept the female role]; they must also persevere in faith, love, holiness, and presumably other virtues.... Women will not be saved if they do not practice good works."[68]

1 Tim. 4:15-16 provides a parallel—Paul says that Timothy will save himself by being a good pastor. An insistence on good behavior does not negate the doctrine of salvation by grace and faith. The point is that women do not need to take on a man's role in order to be saved. Despite what the false teachers might say against childbearing, women will be saved by staying in their traditional role.

There are some difficulties in this interpretation: First, it ignores the

---

[65] Schreiner, 116.

[66] Moo, 192. He speculates that "false teachers were claiming that women could really experience what God had for them only if they abandoned the home and became actively involved in teaching and leadership roles in the church."

[67] Schreiner, 118. "A woman should not violate her role by teaching or exercising authority over a man; instead, she should take her proper role as a mother of children." Paul is not saying that barren women cannot be saved—he is simply citing a common role of a woman that a man cannot possibly have.

[68] Ibid. Good works cannot merit salvation, but they "are a necessary consequence of salvation (e.g., Rom. 2:6-10, 26-29; 1 Cor. 6:9-11; Gal. 5:21).... Since Paul often argues elsewhere that salvation is not gained on the basis of our works (e.g., Rom. 3:19-4:25; Gal. 2:16-3:14; 2 Tim. 1:9-11; Titus 2:11-14; 3:4-7), I think it is fair to understand the virtues described here as evidence that the salvation already received is genuine" (ibid., 118-119). In other words, Schreiner wishes that Paul had stated things the other way around: women will be saved by faith, if they continue in good works.

change from singular to plural, requiring that women in general be represented first by a singular and then by a plural. Second, it makes the verse an odd tangential idea nearly irrelevant to the context: I do not permit women to have authority over men, because men were created first and Eve was a sinner, and oh, by the way, women will be saved by being good women.[69]

Third, if Paul wanted to refer to the female role in general, he would have been clearer if he had used a principle he had already mentioned—submission—rather than introducing the specificity of childbearing. Last, it speculates that the false teachings at Ephesus included a criticism of childbearing. This is a plausible suggestion, since the heresy included a rejection of marriage (4:3), but this speculative reconstruction of the setting is precisely the method that traditional scholars have criticized egalitarians for using.[70]

If verse 15 can best be explained by suggesting that it is a response to a particular false teaching in Ephesus, perhaps that approach can be used for the statements in verses 13-14, too.[71] Overall, we might find Paul's

---

[69] Susan Foh (who supports the traditional view) calls the verse "a sort of *non sequitur.*" Schreiner criticizes her for that (115), but his interpretation also amounts to a non sequitur, an aside designed to refute something that may have been a false teaching in Ephesus. Paul apparently feels no need to say that men will be saved by staying in their traditional role, rather than abdicating, as Adam supposedly did.

[70] Schreiner comments: "Egalitarian scholars have been busy remaking the background to the situation in 1 Timothy 2:11-15, but their reconstructions have been highly speculative and sometimes wildly implausible" (223).

[71] Catherine and Clark Kroeger suggest that Paul was combating some Gnostic heresies taught by women: 1) That Eve was created first, 2) That Eve enlightened Adam with her teaching, and 3) Sex and childbearing is bad. Verses 13-15 can thereby all be explained as refutations of specific erroneous teachings. Schreiner criticizes the Kroegers for using documents written after the New Testament (88). Admittedly, it cannot be proven that these ideas existed when Paul wrote, but since ideas often circulate before they are put into writing, it is plausible that such ideas existed in the first century. As Schreiner's own approach to verse 15 indicates, it is legitimate for scholars to try to understand difficulties in the text by speculating about an unusual need in that specific setting.

logic hard to understand, Gordon admits, but this is not a reason to reject what he says.[72] Moo concludes that "we are justified in requiring very good reasons *from the text itself* to limit the application of this text in any way. We find no such reasons. Therefore, we must conclude that the restrictions imposed by Paul in 1 Timothy 2:12 are valid for Christians in all places and all times."[73]

Questions remain

In the previous section, we presented the "traditional" view. However, as Proverbs 18:17 says, "The first to present his case seems right, till another comes forward and questions him." It would be foolish for us to decide the matter before we have heard the other side ask questions about the conclusions. We began this chapter with a number of observations, and the traditional interpretation addresses some of them better than others.

1. The text twice calls for women in particular to be quiet; it does not allow for *any* form of teaching.[74] However…

2. Women can prophesy in a worship service, saying things that instruct others (1 Cor. 11). Paul believed prophecy and teaching to be different activities, but it is difficult to prove any difference *in the results*. Men might learn something from either form of

---

Bruce Barron notes that "the internal examination of 1 Timothy points us toward Gnosticism and makes the connection between the two less 'tenuous'" ("Putting Women in Their Place: 1 Timothy 2 and Evangelical Views of Women in Church Leadership," *Journal of the Evangelical Theological Society* 33 [1990]: 454). This epistle addresses various ideas that were later called Gnostic.

[72] Gordon, 63.

[73] Moo, 193. By "the text itself," Moo apparently means the entire Bible, for he allows women to teach some subjects, and to be in authority in some situations, such as civil government, concepts not specifically allowed in 1 Tim. 2.

[74] Vicente Bejo, Jr. argues that the passage covers behavior not just in church, but "in every place" (verse 8). It would not be appropriate for men to pray with anger anywhere, and it would not be appropriate for women to wear ostentatious clothing anywhere. Paul's call for submission and quiet demeanor were not intended to apply only to church settings. "Exegesis of 1 Timothy 2:8-15," unpublished paper.

speech, and both types of speaking need to be evaluated. It is not clear why women should be allowed to speak spontaneously, for example, but not with advance preparation.

3. Females can *sometimes* have authority over males. Paul was dealing with teaching in the church setting; he was not addressing civil government, business, public schools, or evangelism. However, the rationale that complementarians sometimes use to support male authority based on Genesis 2 is not valid when it comes to civil authority, and this inconsistency suggests that the rationale itself may not be valid.

4. Was Paul stating his own policy, or a permanent rule for all churches? Traditional scholars may claim that everything in the letter is permanently applicable, but this is not true.[75]

Or they may say that Paul's restriction is permanently valid because Paul supports it from Genesis, but this ignores the fact that Paul used Genesis to argue for a cultural custom in 1 Cor. 11. Paul's policy *might* be appropriate in all churches at all ages, but the fact remains that it was inspired to be written as his *policy,* and his preferences are not always permanently valid (e.g., 1 Cor. 7:7).[76]

---

[75] "The pastoral epistles were not written to be manuals of church government. Rather they were written to combat false teaching and heresy. Approximately one-fifth of the 242 verses in the pastorals explicitly treat false teaching.... In 1 Timothy 1:3 the concern to prevent false teaching is expressed as the reason Timothy was left in Ephesus" (Evangelical Covenant Church, "Policy on Women in Ministry," 5). "The entire book of 1 Timothy seems to have been written...with six key problems in mind, each of which is referred to in the first eight verses and is elaborated throughout the epistle: false teaching, controversies, people leaving the faith, meaningless talk, antinomianism, and Judaizers.... Women were involved in each of the first five problems" (Payne, 185). Due to the situation the letter was written for, it should be no surprise that some aspects of the letter do not seem to fit the church today.

[76] Keener observes, "What is most significant about the wording of the passage, however, is that Paul does not assume that Timothy already knows this rule. Had this rule been established and universal, is it possible that Timothy, who had worked many years with Paul, would not have known it already?" (*Paul,*

5. A woman should learn in "with all submissiveness," but women do not have to submit to *all* men. In church, a woman's submission should be to God first, Scripture second, and the sermon third.[77] If the pastor says something that contradicts Scripture, a woman should not submit. It is doubtful that this type of submission can be described as "all." Since modern preaching may contain erroneous ideas and must be evaluated, it is *not* more authoritative than prophecy was. Perhaps the role of the pastor and the preacher's authority in the church is different today, significantly altered by the existence of the New Testament as *the* authoritative record of church teaching.[78] People in the pews now have an objective standard by which to judge what is taught, whereas before they did not.

6. 1 Tim. 2:12 uses the rare Greek verb *authenteō*. Although it is tempting to see a difference in meaning for a different word, there would be little point in Paul saying that he had a policy against

---

Women, and Wives, 112). Had the situation never arisen before that women wanted to teach? The situation in Corinth suggests that this is unlikely. As noted earlier, the reason that Paul felt it necessary to write this passage may have been because women were already speaking and seeking leadership.

[77] In the Septuagint, the Greek word for "permit" always "refers to permission for a specific situation, never for a universally applicable permission…. The vast majority of the NT occurrences…clearly refer to a specific time or to a short or limited time duration only" (Payne, 172). Vyhmeister writes:

The women are to "submit," but the text does not say to whom…. The text itself seems to be discussing attitudes in worship rather than the marriage relationship. The Bible does not elsewhere teach that all women are subject to all males. Submission to the teaching elder in 1 Tim. 3:2 does not fit the text. A natural understanding of the verse would be that the women are to submit to the gospel, to the teaching of Jesus, not to an unnamed person. Theirs is to be a receptive attitude. (342)

[78] 2 Tim. 2:2 suggests that "teaching" is the accurate transmission of apostolic sayings. However, most preaching today is not an attempt to transmit the apostolic teachings (members already have a copy), but is an attempt to explain them and encourage people to apply them in modern situations.

allowing one group of people to exercise a wrong kind of authority against another group; the verse more naturally says that Paul did not allow women to do something that was permissible for men.[79] It is not clear whether he prohibited teaching *and* authority, or teaching *with* authority, and it does not seem necessary to choose between these two—either way, the verse seems to contradict Paul's policy of allowing women to prophesy in the Corinthian church.[80]

7. In verses 13-15, Paul gives unusual *reasons* for what he says in verse 12.

    a. Adam was formed first, and that might give him authority—but there is nothing in Genesis to say why it would give him (and by implication all males) exclusive authority in doctrine but not in civil government. Traditional interpreters do not explain why one applies but the other does not; they base their belief on 1 Tim. 2:12 rather than Genesis 2, and it is erroneous to say that Genesis 2 gives males authority specifically in matters of worship.[81]

---

[79] However, a negative meaning is possible: Paul did say that males in particular should not pray with anger (2:8). We do not have the technical expertise to resolve the meaning of the word, and we cannot build our conclusions on what would surely be a debatable point.

[80] "It is...safe to say that Paul does not want women to teach at this time" (Vyhmeister, 346).

[81] "If there had been no doubt about whose creation came first, the assertion of verse 13 would not have been necessary" (ibid., 347). Vyhmeister reports Gnostic teachings that gave Eve priority: Adam addresses Eve: 'You are the one who has given me life.' Eve is said to have 'sent her breath into Adam, who had no soul.' Eve...declares herself the 'mother of my father and the sister of my husband,...to whom I gave birth'" (340, citing *Hypostasis of the Archons* 2.4.89.14-17, *On the Origin of the World* 115, and Thunder, *Perfect Mind* 6.2.13.30-32).
Douglas Moo, a complementarian, offers support:

    Some later gnostic texts interpret Eve's eating the fruit in the garden as a positive step—for by doing so, she gains access to knowledge (*gnosis*), the central feature of the gnostic system and the means of salvation....

b. Adam was a rebel. Traditional interpreters do not explain why this has any relevance to church authority, and it suggests that there was something going on behind the scenes in Ephesus that we do not know about.[82] The readers knew why this was relevant to Paul's prohibition because they had information that we do not. Otherwise, the structure of the verse implies that Eve's gullibility is relevant to contemporary women, but some complementarian scholars distance themselves from this traditional interpretation.

c. Verse 15 says that "women will be saved through childbearing." Interpreters agree that this is a difficult verse, and it again suggests that we are missing some crucial information. This increases the possibility that Paul is addressing a situation that is unusual.[83]

8. 1 Tim. 2 addresses several cultural matters. Traditional scholars say first, that we can see a universal principle behind verses 8-9, but verse 12 is a universal principle, and second, Paul supports verse 12 with evidence from Scripture, thereby indicating that it

---

Could it be that some of the Ephesian false teachers were arguing in a similar manner, stimulating Paul's categorical assertion: "Eve was deceived and became a sinner"?... It may be that this tradition was partially responsible for the statement. ("The Interpretation of 1 Timothy 2:11-15: A Rejoinder," *Trinity Journal* 2 (1981): 204)

[82] Ann Bowman summarizes: "Historical reconstructions generally fall into three categories. First, women may have been seeking to improperly assert authority over men in the worship assembly. Second, women may have been teaching heretical doctrine. Third, women generally were doctrinally untaught and thus in greater danger of falling into heresy" ("Women in Ministry," in *Two Views on Women in Ministry* [ed. James Beck and Craig Blomberg; Zondervan, 2001], 288).

[83] "While the sparseness of the information and the complex construction of the passage make it difficult for modern readers to know precisely what Paul had in mind, it is clear that he was addressing some current concern that Timothy and the Christians in Ephesus would have readily understood" (Vyhmeister, 350).

is a universal rule.[84] However, 1 Cor. 11 shows that Paul *can* use Scripture even when arguing for a cultural custom, and he could have cited a scripture to support verses 8-9, too, without making them universal. The principle behind verse 12 may be a general one, just as it is for 5:9 or 6:1.

9. Some of Paul's advice seems specific to Timothy's situation, without any specific "application" required today, so we cannot assume that every passage must be applied today—for example, 1 Tim. 5:9. Traditional scholars do not address the inconsistency very well.[85]

10. In 1 Tim. 6:1-2, Paul counsels slaves to submit to their masters for the sake of the gospel.[86] Paul's advice is not a permanent

---

[84] Schreiner writes, "The prohibition in 1 Timothy 2:12 is grounded by an appeal to creation, indicating that the command has universal validity" (109).

[85] Schreiner acknowledges the problem of inconsistency when he writes, "Perhaps we have not been serious enough about applying 1 Timothy 5:3-16 to our culture" (109). He offers a tentative application, but it still allows numerous exceptions. The Evangelical Covenant Church paper notes,

> Those who are quick to argue against women in ministry on the basis of texts like 1 Corinthians 14:34-36 and 1 Timothy 2:11,12 need to ask why they do not imitate the kind of church service described in 1 Corinthians 14:26-36 or why they do not institute widows' roles and care for widows according to the instructions of 1 Timothy 5. Using proof-texts out of context and using only the parts of the text that we like are not suitable practices for a church claiming to believe the Bible. (6)

[86] The evangelistic purpose of slave submission is explicit in 1 Tim. 6, but Eph. 6:5-9 shows that Paul can issue similar commands without any acknowledgement that they are given for expedience in a temporary cultural situation. Indeed, in this passage he seems to deal with slavery as if it were a legitimate social structure, like marriage and family. In Eph. 6:8, Paul gives a timeless reason for slave submission: because God will reward everyone for the good they do. The fact that the supporting reason is timeless does not change the fact that the initial command had a temporary application.

Some scholars argue that Paul taught female social conformity for the sake of the gospel. "Paul's missionary strategy provides the rationale for this approach. This is most succinctly described in 1 Cor 9:19-23, where Paul states that he conforms his behavior to those around him so that he can win as many as possible"

approval of slavery, and in the same way, his policy for women may be a temporary need, not a permanent approval of authority restricted to males. Paul did not directly command slavery, but his policy was that slaves should submit to their masters. By doing this, Paul "taught something less than God's ideal in order to advance the gospel"—which means that he *might* have done something similar for women.[87]

Hermeneutics

The question in this passage is not just one of exegesis (what *did* it mean?), but also one of hermeneutics (what does it mean *for us?*). We want to understand what Paul wrote, but we also want to understand whether and how we should *apply* it in churches today. That is a question of hermeneutics, the method of interpreting the text for modern application. Paul said that younger widows should get married (5:14), but does this advice apply to all younger widows today? Do cultural expectations make the situation of widows significantly different today? (In many cultures, they probably do, and in some, perhaps not.)

When Paul told slaves to submit to their masters, was he endorsing slavery? Christian slave-owners often said he was, but when other Christians perceived the injustice involved in owning a human being, they began to ask more questions of the texts. It is generally only when people see problems in the way that a text is applied, that they begin to ask more probing questions of it. People who are happy with the status quo don't see the need for questions, but when questions arise, we all need to look at the text more carefully. Sometimes the objections are valid; sometimes

(James G. Sigountos and Myron Shank, "Public Roles for Women in the Pauline Church: A Reappraisal of the Evidence," *Journal of the Evangelical Theological Society* 26 [1983]: 293). Sigountos and Shank show that Greek culture accepted women in priestly roles—prophesying and praying—but not teaching roles.

[87] Contra Grudem, 323. Paul made some comments that could be interpreted as criticisms of slavery, but none are clear denunciations. 1 Cor. 7:21 merely makes an allowance for specific situations; it could be claimed that Gal. 3:28 addresses salvation but not social roles, and Philemon 16 may apply only to Onesimus.

they are not.

Scholars on both sides of this controversy agree that 1 Tim. 2:12 puts certain restrictions on women: Paul did not allow women to teach or to have authority over men in the functioning of the church—he told them to be quiet.[88] The question is whether these restrictions were based on the situation in Ephesus, the culture in the Greco-Roman-Jewish world, or a principle rooted in the way that God wants men and women to interact with one another in worship.

Craig Keener presents an egalitarian view, but begins with this admission: "I believe that Paul probably prohibits not simply 'teaching authoritatively,' but both teaching Scripture at all and having (or usurping) authority at all." But he then asks, "Is this a universal rule? If so, it is a rule with some exceptions.... But it is also possible that this text is the exceptional one, which can be argued if it can be shown to address a particular situation. After all, if it were to be a universal rule, one might have expected... Timothy...to be aware of this rule already."[89]

Keener then gives evidence that there are exceptions, and he notes, "The one passage in the Bible that specifically prohibits women from teaching is addressed to the one church where we know that false teachers were effectively targeting women."[90]

---

[88] James Beck and Craig Blomberg note that some primarily American egalitarians have proposed "hermeneutical oddities" in an effort to show that these verses are not restrictive. Egalitarians in the British Commonwealth tend however "to argue that these texts did imply rather widespread prohibitions on women's leadership in the first-century world, but they were due to specific circumstances within that world that largely no longer obtain today" ("Reflections on Egalitarian Essays," 164).

[89] Craig Keener, "Women in Ministry," in *Two Views on Women in Ministry* (ed. James Beck and Craig Blomberg; Zondervan, 2001), 53. The choice is more complicated than Keener suggests, because a command can be local and temporary even if we cannot demonstrate the situation that prompted the command, and a command can be universal even if it was prompted by a local situation. For example, Paul says that men should pray without anger or disputing (1 Tim. 2:8). This admonition seems universally appropriate, yet prompted by some situation that we have no specifics on.

[90] Ibid., 53-54. He writes, "False teachers targeted women in the households

Many egalitarians do not argue about what 1 Tim 2:11-15 says—they disagree about its significance for the church today. Although there are a few disagreements about specific words in the text, much of the egalitarian case focuses instead on evidence that the text was not written "for all churches in all subsequent centuries." Much of this effort has been an attempt to show that Paul was addressing an unusual situation—they have tried to sketch a situation that motivated Paul to write these verses.[91]

These reconstructions are speculative, sometimes implausible, and sometimes contradictory. Since the original situation cannot be proven, we will not spend much effort along these lines. However, we will address some evidence that may suggest that Paul's policy is *not* intended for all time.

First, there is evidence that some commands in Scripture do not apply today. For example, as we saw in a previous chapter, women do not need to cover their heads when they pray in church today, nor do believers have to greet one another with a kiss. We do not have to pray for Paul to be rescued from the unbelievers in Judea, nor encourage virgins to avoid marriage. Some commands in Scripture *are* based in culture; the question here is whether Paul's policy on the conduct of women is one of them.[92]

(2 Tim. 3:6), who were proving incapable of learning correctly (2 Tim. 3:7; cf. 1 Tim. 4:7)." Nancy Vyhmeister writes, "Not only are women carried away by the false teachers, some of them 'learn to be idlers, gadding about from house to house, and not only idlers but gossips and busybodies, saying what they should not' (1 Tim 5:13), evidently spreading false teaching" (*Women in Ministry*, 337).

[91] Some suggest that the situation involved a culture that rejected female leadership, but this seems contradicted by archaeological evidence and by the role that Paul permitted women in 1 Cor. 11. Others suggest that Paul was concerned that women were generally poorly educated, and he told them to learn in silence—implying that they would not have to be silent after they had been taught. "If he prohibits women from teaching because they are unlearned, his demand that they learn constitutes a long-range solution to the problem" (Keener, *Paul*, 112).

[92] Grudem argues that governance is an essential aspect of the church, not a cultural matter (323). But this misses the point—egalitarians are not arguing against all governance, but saying that governance restricted to males is a cultural matter that is not essential to the church, just as greeting one another with a kiss is a cultural matter. We can have the core function without insisting on the specific

There is evidence within the Pastoral Epistles, too, that even though these letters give guidance on church matters, some commands are situation specific—even though the original readers might have assumed the commands to be universally true. When Paul says that older widows should be put on a list and younger widows should remarry, Timothy may well have thought the rule applicable for all time. When Paul commands Christian slaves to serve their Christian masters well, there is nothing in the text to indicate that Paul expects this situation to be a temporary one. Therefore, although we base our beliefs and practices on the Bible, this does not mean that we have to follow every instruction that the Bible contains; we have to see whether it applies to us. This does not prove that 1 Tim. 2:12 is a temporary admonition—it simply shows that it *may* be.

Summary

To put the matter in simple terms, we see in 1 Cor. 11 that Paul permitted women to speak in worship meetings, but in 1 Tim. 2:12 he said they should be silent—they cannot teach or have authority. There are two basic ways to address this difference:

1. Complementarian scholars try to resolve this contradiction by saying that 1 Cor. 11 permits a form of speaking that is not authoritative. Although they cannot prove that modern preaching is more authoritative than ancient prophecy, they believe that this distinction resolves the problem, and Paul's prohibition is still valid. In brief, "We know that women cannot have authority, so the speaking that Paul permitted in Corinth must not be authoritative."

2. Egalitarian scholars try to resolve the problem by saying that 1 Tim. 2:12 was a temporary restriction based on circumstances in Paul's churches at the time he wrote, a situation that apparently did not exist when he wrote to Corinth. Although they cannot prove what that situation was, it is not necessary to reconstruct it. The fact that Paul allowed women to prophesy in Corinth shows that the restriction was not a rule for all time. In brief, "We know

---

form found in the New Testament.

that Paul permitted women to speak, so the prohibition in 1 Tim. 2:12 (which includes speaking) must be temporary."

We believe that the second approach has more merit, for these reasons:

• Prophecy, by its very nature, seems to involve authority, for it means to speak words inspired by God. Prophecies must be "weighed" (1 Cor. 14:29),[93] but this is done not to disagree with God, but to ascertain *whether* the words are from God. If they are words of God, they should be heeded. Modern preaching does not have more authority than first-century prophecy, and it is odd to argue that women may be inspired by God to speak in church about everything *except* the Word of God.[94]

In Corinth, Paul allowed women to speak with authority in church,[95] which indicates that the prohibition in 1 Tim. 2:12 should not be taken as a universal or permanent rule. The inconsistent attempts by complementarians to draw lines between what women can do and what they cannot suggests that the task is impossible. [Beck and Blomberg note that conservative churches often allow female missionaries to have considerable authority in the mission field but not at home—this "often remains an embarrassing double standard that undermines some of the credibility of the hierarchicalist position" (310).]

---

[93] Complementarian scholars have suggested that churches had a designated time for evaluating prophecies. As discussed in the previous chapter, this is unlikely.

[94] Some scholars seem to focus on the question of authority, but leadership in the church depends more on personal example, and the truth of Scripture, than on bare assertion. "One is hard-pressed to find a biblical link between local church leadership and 'authority' (exousia). The New Testament writers simply do not make this connection.... It is the church that possesses authority and not particular individuals" (Linda Belleville, "Women in Ministry," in *Two Views on Women in Ministry* [ed. James Beck and Craig Blomberg; Zondervan, 2001], 104-6).

[95] Paul commended women as fellow workers in the gospel. Although he does not give them specific titles, the implication is that they had significant influence in his churches—and that probably involved some speaking, although we do not have enough details to be more precise.

- Paul was inspired to write this prohibition as his own policy, not as a command. True, his policies might sometimes be taken as a command, but we have also learned to discount the policies he describes in 1 Cor. 7, for example. When Paul wrote to Timothy, he had a policy against women in authority—but God does not seem to have that policy.[96] He gave Deborah authority as a prophetess and judge—and there is no logical reason why the creation priority of man gives males exclusive authority in the religious sphere but not in civil government. The Bible shows that although women rarely had civil authority, God does allow it, and the primary passage that would seem to limit female authority in the church is introduced as a policy rather than a command.
- Considering the nature of 1 Timothy, it is not surprising that Paul is describing a policy that was of temporary validity. It was written to help Timothy combat some heresies that were causing problems in Ephesus; its directives include cultural matters such as the posture of prayer and the way in which women might adorn themselves. Paul's advice concerning widows, despite being issued with commands, is not applicable to the church today. Although the letter is about church administration, it was written for a specific situation, and we should not assume in advance that its instructions are timeless truths.[97]

---

[96] Assuming that Paul was in agreement with God's policies, we conclude that his restrictive policy was necessitated by the situation his churches were in. As we saw in the previous chapter, that is the most likely explanation for the restriction that Paul gave in 1 Cor. 14:34.

[97] Gordon Fee and Douglas Stuart write,

That 1 Timothy 2:11-12 might be culturally relative can be supported first of all by exegesis of all three of the Pastoral Epistles. Certain women were troublesome in the church at Ephesus (1 Tim. 5:11-15; 2 Tim. 3:6-9) and they appear to have been a major part of the cause of the false teachers' making headway there. Since women are found teaching (Acts 18:26) and prophesying (Acts 21:8; 1 Cor. 11:5) elsewhere in the New Testament, it is altogether likely that 1 Timothy 2:11-12 speaks to a local problem. (*How to Read the Bible for All Its Worth* [Zondervan, 1982], 69)

Complementarians argue that Paul's policy must be universal, because he supports it from Scripture. However, we see in 1 Cor. 11 that Paul uses Scripture to support his command for women to wear head coverings, too. He can use Scripture to argue for a temporary policy. His use of Scripture is not an attempt to explain what Genesis means—it is simply a use of one part of Scripture to add support to one part of his argument.[98]

Moreover, the obscurity of 1 Tim. 2:13-15 suggests that Paul was dealing with an unusual situation, and that we do not understand the relevance of his arguments because we do not know the details of the situation. It is not clear why Adam being formed first would give all subsequent men authority in the church but not in civil government; it is even more obscure why men should have authority if Adam sinned deliberately.[99]

------

[98] Paul uses Scripture selectively (saying that men are in the image of God, not saying that women are, too). Paul's use of Scripture in support of this policy is no proof of permanence, just as his use of a timeless truth in Eph. 6:8 does not mean that his policy for slaves was permanent. Keener writes,

> In the polemical context of Galatians 3:16, where Paul may be responding to his opponents by using their own methods, he employs a standard interpretive technique of his contemporaries: Apply the text the way you need to in order to make your point. While some of us may not want to accept that Paul uses Scripture in an ad hoc way at times (it makes it more difficult for us to teach sound hermeneutics to our students), respect for Scripture requires us to revise our preconceptions in light of what we find in the text, rather than forcing the text to fit philosophical assumptions about what we think it should say" (61).

[99] Paul's policy would be appropriate under the following scenario: False teaching was sweeping the congregation, targeting women in particular, with the ideas that Eve was created first, that Adam was deceived, and that women should avoid marriage and giving birth. There is evidence for the first and fourth points in 1 Timothy itself; points two and three are speculative, but this scenario becomes more plausible when we see that these doctrines were later taught in this very area.

"It is now known that Ephesus was a major center for Mother Goddess worship...., major tenets being that a female goddess gave birth to the world, that Eve was created before Adam, and that to achieve highest exaltation woman must achieve independence from all males and from child-bearing" (JoAnn Davidson, "Women in Scripture," in *Women in Ministry* [ed. Nancy Vyhmeister; Andrews

In short, it is difficult to take this passage as a permanent command restricting all women from all leadership positions in all churches. It indicates that women should not speak in church, and yet Paul himself permitted women to speak authoritative words in church. His prohibition should therefore be seen as based on the situation at the time, not a rule that applies in all circumstances. It is not even written as a command, so it is preferable to take it as a policy of temporary validity, given because of a temporary need.

The early church had a different view.[100] We respect church history, but in this case we believe that Scripture, our standard for faith and practice, has been misunderstood—just as it was often misunderstood in the matter of slavery, and of salvation by grace. The culture of previous interpreters had blinded them to questions they should have asked but did not. Scholars of *all* persuasions today recognize errors in the historical interpretation of passages about women.

In our next chapter, we will conclude this series of studies with some policy recommendations for the diverse situations found within our denomination.

University Press, 1998], 178). Although the evidence comes from the second century, the teachings may have circulated before Paul wrote. Barron writes,

> 1 Tim 2:13-14 makes very good sense as a coherent counter-argument to a specific problem—namely, a false interpretation of Genesis by heretical women. Paul refutes the Gnostic arguments by reasserting that Adam was created first and that he was created perfect, not ignorant.... It is not simply that some women are teaching error. Rather, the placing of any woman, whether qualified or not, in authority, may be undesirably reinforcing pagan cultural baggage (Barron, 455-56).

[100] Dissenting voices may be found as early as the 17th century, but they became much more prominent in the 20th century. It was certainly not the modern feminist movement that caused Margaret Fell to write her book *Women's Speaking Justified, Proved and Allowed of by the Scriptures* (London, 1666). Beck and Blomberg note that "secular cultural forces have in part contributed to the ascendancy of hierarchicalism" as well as egalitarianism (168). All interpreters are influenced by their culture, often in ways they do not realize.

Appendix A: *Authenteō*

"A precise consensus as to the meaning of the word has not been achieved among well-known lexicographers."[101] The word sometimes had a negative meaning, sometimes a neutral meaning of exercising authority. The lexical question is what it meant when Paul wrote the Pastorals. Did it have a negative meaning—to use violence, to domineer, to usurp authority—or a neutral meaning, to exercise authority in general, in a way that might be either bad or good?

Baldwin analyzed 85 occurrences of *authenteō* and found only three uses before Paul. Philodemus used it in the sense of "to rule"; a private letter used it in the sense of "to compel," and Aristonicus used it to mean "instigate."[102] Some of the most negative meanings suggested have been based on the fact that the noun *authentēs* can mean murderer, but there is no evidence that the verb was used to mean "murder," and the noun may not necessarily be derived from this verb.

Two examples from Chrysostom (A.D. 390) are particularly interesting: "Eve exercised authority once wrongly." Baldwin comments: "The implication…is that Chrysostom could not make the negative force felt without the addition of *kakōs* ["wrongly"], and he therefore did not regard the verb *authenteō* as negative in itself."[103] However, in the second example Chrysostom uses *authenteō* with a negative meaning *without* adding any word: Do not try *to have your own way* with unbelievers, but redeem the time (he is commenting on Col. 4:5). Baldwin concludes that in this instance, the word means something like "domineer."[104]

---

[101] H. Scott Baldwin, "An Important Word: Αὐθεντέω in 1 Timothy 2:12," in *Women in the Church*, 2nd ed., 40.

[102] Ibid., 49-50.

[103] Ibid., 46.

[104] Ibid., 47, and see the first edition of Köstenberger et al., p. 286. Wayne Grudem is not as certain that the word has a negative meaning. "The sense could be, 'Don't just give orders all the time because your wife is subject to you.'… On the other hand, the parallel with telling the wife not to be puffed up (proud) argues for a more negative sense for the verb in this instance. In any case, it is still over three hundred years after the time of the New Testament" (308).

Baldwin concludes that the word *most often* has a neutral meaning, but as with any word, the final determination of meaning must be based on the context in which it is used.

Appendix B: Three key questions about 1 Timothy 2:12

This appendix provides a simpler approach to the problem. We identify three key questions that can help us clarify what this verse means.

1. Was this Paul's permanent policy, or was it a temporary policy?

Answer: It was apparently a temporary policy, needed for the situation that Timothy was in. This can be seen by looking at 1 Corinthians 11:3-16. In this passage, Paul said that women should have something covering their head whenever they prayed or prophesied. Scholars do not agree on precisely what this head covering was, and for our purposes it does not matter. What is important is that Paul was allowing women to speak.

Where were the women speaking? Paul would not need to give instructions about how women appeared when they were in private. This was some sort of public setting in which male and female believers gathered, prayed, and spoke to one another. This sounds like church.

What were the women speaking about? We know what prayer is, but what were the women doing when they prophesied? Paul tells us what prophecy is in 1 Cor. 14:3: a message spoken to strengthen, encourage, and comfort other people. It might concern the future, but need not. It might be like modern preaching, or might not. The important thing is simply that the women were speaking in a church meeting. Verse 5 says that these messages edify or build up the church.

So the women in Corinth were being inspired by God to give messages that helped men and women in the church. Paul allowed some sort of speaking in Corinth, but in 1 Timothy 2:12, he said that the women should be silent. So to avoid contradiction, at least one of these verses must be seen as temporary. If silence was a permanent policy, then Paul violated his own policy when he allowed women to speak in Corinth. But if permission was the normal policy, it would still be possible for Paul to issue a temporary restriction due to some need in Timothy's situation.

So this line of analysis tells us that 1 Timothy 2:12 should be seen as a temporary policy. Indeed, that is the way that Paul himself describes it: "I do not *permit…*" This was his policy at the time he wrote.

2. This was Paul's policy at the time; was it also God's policy?

In question 1, we focused on the *silence* that Paul commanded, and saw that Paul did not always require women to be silent in meetings of believers. Now we can look at the issue of *authority*. When Paul wrote 1 Timothy, he did not allow women to have authority over men. So we must ask, are we today supposed to have the same policy as Paul did? Or we can ask it another way: Does God have this policy? Does he ever allow women to have authority over men?

Yes, he does. Judges 4:4-6 gives a clear example. Deborah was a prophetess God used to lead the nation of Israel. She "held court under the Palm of Deborah," which was a public place that people could come to. God spoke to her, gave her commands, and she gave those commands to Barak, the military leader of Israel (verse 6). God gave her authority over Barak and the other Israelites.

This was not a worship service, but it is a clear case in which God allowed a woman to have authority over men. However, when Paul wrote 1 Timothy, he did not allow women to have authority over men—and he made no distinction about civil and religious authority (Deborah made no distinction in the two types of authority, either, since in her case they were combined). In question 1, we saw that Paul's policy about women speaking in church was apparently a temporary policy. Here, we see that his policy about authority is also temporary, since God does not make that sort of restriction permanently.

3. Is 1 Timothy a manual for how churches ought to operate today?

Sometimes people assume that if Paul had a particular policy, then we ought to, too, because he was inspired by God. But if we take a careful look at his letter, we will see that parts of it don't apply to us today. It was, after all, written to Timothy in first-century Ephesus, not directly to all of us. The letter has a lot of good material in it we *can* apply today, but is also has some things in it that we don't.

The best example is in chapter 5, verses 3-16. Paul is telling Timothy to put widows on some sort of list (apparently a list for financial support) only if they were over age 60. He says that younger widows are probably going to want to get married and will end up breaking "their first pledge" (apparently some sort of vow they took in order to be on the list for financial support).

Nowadays, we do not maintain this sort of list, and we do not put age restrictions on which widows we will help. Our social and economic circumstances are quite different, and almost all church leaders and biblical scholars recognize this. Nevertheless, Paul gives several commands in this passage that we ignore—even *commands* can be limited to the culture they were given in. How much more so the *policy* that Paul states in 1 Timothy 2:12?

Paul also commands in verse 8 that men should lift their hands when they pray. We do not enforce this as a command today, nor do we greet one another with a holy kiss, as several letters command (for example, 1 Thessalonians 5:26). The principle of friendly greeting is good in today's church, but Paul went beyond generalities and commanded a specific *form* of greeting that is not appropriate in our culture today.

Clearly, there are some things in Paul's epistles that do not apply in our culture. The question that we should ask is, Is 1 Timothy 2:12 one of those temporary instructions? From our analysis above, apparently so. This does not mean that it is less inspired, or that we are choosing to ignore the Word of God—no more so than when we decide not to command kissing in church, or commanding women to wear head coverings, or when we decide that men do *not* have to raise their hands when they pray. We are not ignoring the Word of God when we recognize that some of it was written for ancient Israel, or for the ancient church, and it does not necessarily apply today in all its details.

Not all Christians agree on this matter. Some people believe that the church should restrict women from having leadership roles in the church. We believed that for a long time, but we believe that we have now come to a better understanding of the scriptures—more like what Paul really meant, and what God really meant, and what the epistle really is. We believe that when God gives pastoral gifts to women—the ability to teach, to encourage, and to inspire people to follow Christ—then those women may be recognized as elders or leaders within the church.

WOMEN IN CHURCH LEADERSHIP, CONCLUSION

Many people can probably agree with Thomas Schreiner when he writes, "The role of women in the church is probably the most emotionally charged issue in American evangelicalism today."[1] It is being debated among Roman Catholics and the Eastern Orthodox as well as among Evangelical Protestants. It is a difficult subject, sometimes filled with bitter accusations, sometimes with claims about the Bible that are not biblically substantiated or justified, and sometimes with fears about what might happen if a change is made, or fears about what might happen if one isn't.

For nearly three years, we studied this issue cautiously, with prayer, with a desire to understand what the Bible teaches us to do. At each stage of our work, we shared the preliminary results with pastoral supervisors and then pastors, seeking comments and feedback. After revising the study papers based on their input, we published them in print or on our website. We did not want to ignore any evidence, nor any important question. Sometimes we had to acknowledge that there is not sufficient information available to be completely certain about a few issues, but this does not, in the final analysis, prevent a conclusion about the overall question.

In this final chapter, we summarize what we have found, and then tackle some questions about how we will apply these findings in the church today. It is our prayer that we all approach this subject with the love, joy, peace, patience, kindness, goodness, faithfulness, gentleness and self-control of God's Spirit.

Biblical teaching and modern application

In the previous ten chapters, we surveyed the teaching of Scripture as it pertains to women in leadership. Here is a summary of each chapter:

Chapter 1: "Women in Church Leadership: An Introduction." The question is complex, and scholars with equal allegiance to the Scriptures

---

[1] Thomas Schreiner, "An Interpretation of 1 Timothy 2:9-15," in *Women in the Church* (2nd ed.; edited by Andreas Köstenberger and Thomas Schreiner; Baker, 2005), 85.

come to different conclusions on the matter. It is not a question over which Christians should condemn one another, nor a question about which we need to break fellowship with people who come to different conclusions.

Chapter 2: "The Nature of Leadership in the Church." Leadership in the church entails service—it is not a right, nor a personal privilege. People should not be seeking positions of leadership (or defending them) in order to get respect or any other personal benefit. People do not have to become leaders in order to be fully human, fully Christian, or equal to others. People can have leadership gifts without necessarily being leaders *in the church.*

A leader in the church must set a good example, have a good reputation, and be able to teach. The effectiveness of a person's leadership in the church is largely dependent on whether members actually look to that person for spiritual leadership. With authority comes responsibility, and authority must be used to serve others.

Chapter 3: "Men and Women in Genesis 1–3." In the beginning, God created male and female in the image of God, as persons who could be equal heirs of eternal life as his children. God gave both male and female authority over Earth and its creatures (Gen. 1:26-27). Genesis 2 tells us that God created the man before the woman, but it does not draw any conclusion about authority from this. The point being emphasized in Genesis 2 is that it is not good for a man to be alone.

The apostle Paul uses Genesis in a selective way. He notes that men are made in the image of God without mentioning that women also are (1 Cor. 11:7); he notes that men were created first when he argues that women should wear head coverings when they prophesy in church (verses 8-10). Paul is not commenting on the meaning of Genesis itself, and the fact that he uses Scripture in his argument does not automatically mean that his conclusions about head coverings apply in all cultures.

The first biblical mention of the rule of men over women comes in Gen. 3:16, in which God describes the consequences of sin. The verse indicates a *change* in the relationship between men and women—that man's rule over woman is a result of sin. This suggests (but does not prove) that when men and women are in the Lord, authority is not based on gender.

Chapter 4: "Men and Women in the Books of Moses." Old Testament laws sometimes mentioned women specifically, but they were normally written as if only men were involved. Both in custom and in law, men had advantages over women. As Jesus noted, the laws of Moses did not prescribe an ideal society, but those laws were often concessions to an imperfect society (Matt. 19:8). The fact that only men were priests (only from one tribe, we should note), therefore, carries no weight in the question we have regarding leadership in the church. It was a rule for a different culture and a different covenant.

Chapter 5: "Women in Ancient Israel, From the Conquest to the Exile." Although Israelite culture gave advantages to men, there are examples of women who had important roles. God chose Deborah to be a prophetess and a judge; the people "came to her to have their disputes decided" (Judges 4:5). She was a civil leader, and as a prophetess, she gave orders from God to the male leader of Israel's army. God gave this woman authority over men—an authority that was both religious and civil.

God used Huldah the prophetess to give authoritative words to Hilkiah the priest and other men (2 Kings 22:14-20). She had spiritual authority. Later, God gave Esther civil authority over Jews in the Persian Empire. These examples show that, even in a patriarchal society, God permitted certain women to have significant civil and/or spiritual authority.

Chapter 6: "Women in the Ministry and Teachings of Jesus." Jesus treated women with more respect than was common in that culture, and women had important roles in his ministry, traveling with him and providing for him. Jesus did not try to correct every social wrong. It would have been nearly impossible for women to function as apostles in that society, and the fact that all twelve apostles were men may also be due to the fact that they corresponded to the twelve sons of Jacob. Further, the twelve did not set a pattern for future church leaders—not in ethnicity, not in number, and therefore possibly not in gender.

Chapter 7: "Women in the Early Church." Women had important roles in the early church—influential enough that when Saul persecuted the church, he imprisoned women as well as men. After Saul's conversion, women were some of his most-praised co-workers. Paul mentioned women who worked "at my side in the cause of the gospel" (Phil. 4:3). This indicates that women had a significant role in evangelism. Gal. 3:28 mentions three prominent social divisions in the first-century world, and proclaims that these disparate social groups become one in Christ. This equality should affect relationships among believers, although it may not require identical roles.

Chapter 8: "Women Who Pray or Prophesy: 1 Cor. 11:3-16." In 1 Cor. 11, Paul argues that women who pray or prophesy in the church should wear a head covering. Although we cannot be sure what this covering was, or its role in Greco-Roman society, we conclude that Paul was telling the believers to conform to certain cultural customs. He uses several supporting arguments, some of which do not apply in our culture, and others that are not clear today because he was arguing for a custom of his own culture.

Although the custom was based in culture, Paul uses Genesis as one of his supporting arguments (verses 7-12), showing that an argument from Scripture does not necessarily indicate a normative or permanent conclusion. Paul's instructions were appropriate for his society, but the specific details are not necessary today. However, this passage clearly shows that women may prophesy in church, and Paul later describes this type of speaking as something that strengthens, encourages, comforts and edifies the church (1 Cor. 14:3-4).

Chapter 9: "'Women Should Remain Silent': 1 Cor. 14:34-35." In 1 Cor. 14, Paul calls for orderliness in the worship service. He says that people should speak in turn, and then be quiet. He says that women were not allowed to talk, but should be quiet and ask their questions later. In 1 Corinthians 11, Paul has already acknowledged that women were speaking in church; he does not mean here that they cannot speak at all. Since we assume that chapter 14 does not contradict chapter 11, we conclude that Paul prohibits some other form of talking. He calls for women to be quiet not as a universal rule, but apparently because they were causing problems with disruptive questions in Corinth.

Chapter 10: "Questions About 1 Timothy 2:11-15." When Paul wrote 1 Tim. 2:12, he again wrote that women should be quiet; he did not permit them to teach or to have authority over men. The reasons he gave for this policy are less than clear, since it is not self-evident that males should have exclusive authority in church simply because the man was created before the woman.[2] The obscurity of verses 14-15 suggests that Paul was addressing erroneous ideas that were being taught in Ephesus at the time.

Paul clearly permitted women to speak edifying messages in the

---

[2] Scripture allows women to have authority over men in civil government, and it is not self-evident why this would be allowed in civil matters but not in religious matters. It is not self-evident that temporal priority should be connected to authority in one sphere but not the other.

Corinthian church; his prohibition here should be seen not as revoking that permission, but as a policy needed for the situation that Timothy faced.[3] We believe it is not a universal rule that must govern all churches for all time. It was, just as Paul stated, a *policy,* not a permanent restriction based on gender.

Just as Paul counseled slaves to be obedient without endorsing slavery itself, he counseled women to be submissive in Ephesus without intending to make that social situation permanent. Just as we accept his policies about widows (1 Tim. 5:3-16) as temporary, so we accept his policies about women in church leadership as temporary.

An elder must be a husband?

We will add here a further comment on 1 Tim. 3:2—"The overseer must be...the husband of but one wife." There are a number of questions about this verse, but we will focus on one: Does this mean that elders must be husbands, and therefore male? No. There are five responses.

1. Paul wrote to the situation that Timothy was in, and that situation did not then allow female elders, so Paul did not cover possibilities that were not viable options at the time, just as he did not discuss what pastors should do with widows after social situations had changed.

2. We do not believe that elders must be married only once. Single men, and widowers who remarry, may also be elders. The focus of the passage is that *if* the elder is a husband, he should be faithful to his wife. The verse covers the most common situation, and Paul assumed that Timothy could figure out the other situations.

3. Paul did not intend his list to be interpreted in a legalistic way— his recommendation that new Christians not be appointed as elders

---

[3] In the Old Testament, the office of prophet was open to women as well as men. It had more spiritual authority than the office of priest, which was restricted to men. Priests had authority only to carry out rituals and teach previous laws, but prophets could give new information and new directives with divine authority. In the New Testament, too, prophecy can involve information newly revealed by God; teaching requires that old material be repeated accurately. This again suggests that prophecy requires a greater authority than teaching does, and since women can have the authority to prophesy, they can also have the lesser authority, to teach; the prohibition in 1 Tim. 2 is best seen as a temporary prohibition.

(1 Tim. 3:6) would not apply in new churches (and consequently Paul does not include this requirement in Titus 1:6-9).

4. Biblical laws are often phrased in the masculine even when they apply to women as well. (Paul's frequent use of "brothers" includes female believers, too.) Throughout 1 Tim. 3, Paul stresses that an elder should be a good example; verse 2 simply gives details about what this means for a husband: *If* the elder is a husband, he should be a good one. It does not address all other possible situations.

5. Even though Paul told Timothy that "a deacon must be the husband of but one wife" (verse 12), it is still possible to have a female deacon (verse 11; Rom. 16:1)—this rule was written in the masculine even though a similar rule would apply to women. In the same way, verse 2 may apply to women even though it is written in the masculine.

Difficulties in application

In our detailed examination of the Bible, we did not find any scripture that forbids women from being recognized as spiritual leaders in the church; there is no verse that makes a permanent restriction on women. Our understanding is that the question of whether women may serve as elders and pastors is a cultural question on which the Bible doesn't set forth a permanent restriction. The scriptures concerning this question are cultural and social in character, concerning the leadership of the church in the first century. In most parts of the world, today's cultural context is not the same as it was in the first century. For example, in the first century the church allowed slavery, something we would not allow today. And the role of women in the public sphere was different in the first century than it is today.

Selection of elders and pastors should be based on seeking out the best person to fill the responsibility, according to the principles in the Scriptures, the needs of the congregation, how the congregation sees these issues, the cultural environment, and whom God can be seen using, without regard to whether the candidate is male or female.

Just as we consider the holy kiss, footwashing, the widows' roster, and headcoverings to be rooted in culture and not required today, we conclude that Paul's restrictions on women in leadership were rooted in culture or based on specific circumstances in his churches, and it is not necessary for the church to consider that restriction permanent. Since we do not want to forbid something that the Bible does not forbid, we will no longer forbid women from being ordained as elders and appointed as pastors. We want churches to be led by the best personnel available, without making unnecessary restrictions on who that might be.

However, we recognize that there are a number of practical considerations involved in applying this change in policy.

First, not all members will agree with our conclusion. Reasonable, well-trained scholars sometimes come to a different conclusion—perhaps by concluding that 1 Tim. 2:12 is the "clear" scripture and 1 Cor. 11 is the unclear one.[4] We respect honest differences of opinion, and do not want to impose leaders on congregations in which most of the members will resist their leadership.[5]

Second, not all women are suited for leadership, just as not all men are. Only people who have the spiritual gifts needed for leadership should be appointed as leaders. We expect that if spiritual gifts are present and the need exists within the congregation, they will be recognized by the congregation.

Ordination of elders emerges out of the local congregational situation where a person's recognized spiritual gifts and heart for ministry, regardless of gender, determine aptness for ordination.

Third, there are local situations (just as there was in Ephesus) in which it would be counterproductive to have female leaders. Some cultures and subcultures around the world view female leadership as offensive. Although cultures sometimes surprise us in allowing exceptions to

---

[4] They may be influenced by their culture, or their fears of cultural change, in ways they do not realize, just as we may be influenced by our culture in ways we do not realize. Despite the inability of anyone to achieve complete objectivity, we all have to make conclusions as best we can, without condemning those who come to different conclusions. Evangelical churches began ordaining women in the 19th century, long before the modern push for women's rights.

[5] Conservative Thomas Schreiner writes, "Some women unquestionably have the spiritual gift of teaching. Men should be open to receiving biblical and doctrinal instruction from women.... Moreover, women should be encouraged to share what they have learned from the Scriptures when the church gathers. The mutual teaching recommended in Colossians 3:16 and 1 Corinthians 14:26 is not limited to men" ("Women in Ministry," in Beck and Blomberg, *Two Views on Women in Ministry* [Zondervan, 2001], 191).

tradition, it is still necessary to assess which leaders will have "a good reputation with outsiders" (1 Tim. 3:7).

In short, our position is that women may be ordained as elders and appointed as pastors. This is a permission, not a requirement. We do not plan to seek female candidates for the office of elder or pastor merely on the basis of their being female, but elders and pastors may from henceforth be chosen from among males and females alike. Elders and pastors, whether male or female, should be ordained and/or appointed based on 1) whether the person has the appropriate leadership gifts, 2) whether members of the congregation affirm these gifts by looking to that person for spiritual leadership, and whether the congregation needs another elder or a pastor.

Questions and concerns

What happens when a woman ordained as an elder in a given congregation moves to a different congregation within our denomination? When an elder, male or female, moves to a different congregation, the person is not automatically licensed as an elder in the new congregation.[6] Leadership in our congregations depends on congregational need and the approval of denominational supervisors. A candidate for ordination, male or female, is thus affirmed through recognition of that person's ministry and leadership capabilities. If the person has leadership gifts, those gifts will presumably be apparent as they are used in other roles, although it may take some time.[7]

Functional titles for ordained personnel vary locally. Some elders function as ministry leaders, some as assistant pastors, etc. Some pastoral spouses may function informally in a sort of "co-pastor" role; others may not, according to their own spiritual gifts. To avoid a conflict of interest, elders should not initiate the ordination of their own spouses, nor be on the committees that make such recommendations. A pastor's spouse who

---

[6] In the same way, someone who leads worship in one congregation should not assume that the same ministry position should be available in another congregation.

[7] Since the style of leadership can differ considerably from one culture to another, subtle in one and blunt in another, it is possible that the spiritual gifts that helped a person lead in one congregation are simply not useful in the other.

wishes to be a candidate for ordination as an elder will be subject to the same selection process as any other potential candidate.

Some members, even if they have a male pastor in their own congregation, may be troubled that a congregation in some other part of the world has a female pastor. If they are troubled by this, we believe that they are looking for conformity in the wrong place. Just as we can have differing opinions about what the Bible says about soul-sleep, the millennium, or the rapture, we can also have different opinions about what the Bible says about women in leadership.

Often the matter boils down to how a person prefers to resolve Paul's statements: in one place Paul permits women to speak, and in another he prohibits it. Which policy is more likely to be the permanent one? Is the prohibition temporary in the same way as his policy on widows is?[8] We believe that there is room in our denomination for people of either viewpoint regarding female ordination, and that this is not a matter on which people should accuse, condemn, or break fellowship.

Some people are worried that if churches allow women as well as men to be leaders in church, then they are unwittingly contributing to the gender confusion found in Western society. This is a "fear of the consequences" argument that touches deep emotional concerns, but is not logically or biblically valid.[9] The fact that God called women to leadership roles in ancient Israel is evidence against this argument. People could just as easily claim that female civil leaders create gender confusion, but we have to acknowledge that God raised up a female civil leader for ancient Israel.[10]

---

[8] As another example of a temporary policy, Paul tolerated slavery, even though it was less than ideal, due to its prevalence in the first century.

[9] A few people have expressed concern that the principles used in reaching our conclusions about the ordination of women might also lead us to revise our teaching about the ordination of practicing homosexuals. In our view, arguments in favor of the ordination of homosexuals, while perhaps overlapping in a few ways with arguments about ordaining women, are nonetheless substantially different from the arguments about ordaining women, and it is our position that the former cannot be argued to from the latter.

[10] Some say that God raised up Deborah only because of exceptional circumstances. We could also note that there are exceptional circumstances in some of our churches today.

We believe that Scripture allows society to have females as schoolteachers, doctors, and political leaders without causing gender confusion; the church can also have female leaders without causing confusion.[11] The church teaches that we are all made in God's image and are equal heirs of salvation. The gender confusion found in society today is regrettable, but it cannot be solved by the church making restrictions that are not supported by Scripture.

We dedicated several years to an in-depth study of the role of women in church leadership—specifically focusing on the question of the ordination of women as elders and the related topic of women serving as church pastors. All along the way, input was sought, received and carefully considered from our members, our pastors, our pastoral supervisors, our doctrinal review team and other church staff. We based our study on the Bible, not contemporary culture or experience.

While we have read and weighed the writings of many authors on this topic, we have done so with the purpose of gaining a clearer understanding of the Scriptures, surrendered to the guidance of the Holy Spirit. Not wanting to forbid what the Bible does not forbid, and desiring to allow all our members to use their God-given gifts to their fullest potential for the benefit of the church, our position is that, based on local circumstances and an individual's characteristics, women may be ordained as elders and appointed as pastors.

We conclude with a statement from a complementarian scholar:

> God did not assemble that body [the church] and give gifts to its members so that we may quarrel or pass our time contemplating who shall be greatest in the kingdom. He has done these things so that both men and women, joint heirs of the gracious gift of life, may use all their talents and gifts in his service to spread his kingdom and to call humans of all sorts from death to new life in Jesus Christ.[12]

---

[11] The presence of female leaders does not—and cannot—do away with the obvious biological and reproductive differences between males and females. Our study has not addressed the question of the role of men and women in families.

[12] James Hurley, *Man and Woman in Biblical Perspective* (Zondervan, 1981), 253.

ABOUT THE AUTHORS

Sheila Graham wrote the chapters on Miriam, Bathsheba, Proverbs 31, and Jesus, and conducted the interview in chapter 8. She worked for Grace Communion International for many years as a writer and editor. She has a master's degree in theology from Azusa Pacific University and another from Claremont Graduate University.

The chapters on Deborah, Ruth and Esther are a corporate product, originally written for our series *Exploring the Word of God,* edited by Jim Herst and Tim Finlay.

Michael Morrison wrote chapters 10-13, and edited this book. He is also the primary author for part 2: he wrote the initial draft (in 2004-2006), and as explained in the preface, this was edited by a committee of GCI leaders based on input from members, pastors, and pastoral supervisors. He received a PhD from Fuller Theological Seminary in 2006 and is Dean of Faculty and Instructor in New Testament for Grace Communion Seminary. He is the author of several books, including:

- *Christians and Old Testament Laws*
- *Exploring the Word of God: The Letters of Paul*
- *Sabbath, Circumcision and Tithing: Which Old Testament Laws Apply to Christians?*
- *Who Needs a New Covenant? The Rhetorical Function of the Covenant Motif in the Argument of Hebrews*
- *Theology of the Apostle Paul*

ABOUT THE PUBLISHER...

Grace Communion International is a Christian denomination with about 50,000 members, worshiping in about 750 congregations in almost 100 nations and territories. We began in 1934 and our main office is in North Carolina. In the United States, we are members of the National Association of Evangelicals and similar organizations in other nations. We welcome you to visit our website at www.gci.org.

If you want to know more about the gospel of Jesus Christ, we offer help. First, we offer weekly worship services in hundreds of congregations worldwide. Perhaps you'd like to visit us. A typical worship service includes songs of praise, a message based on the Bible, and opportunity to meet people who have found Jesus Christ to be the answer to their spiritual quest. We try to be friendly, but without putting you on the spot.

To find a congregation, write to one of our offices, phone us or visit our website. If we do not have a congregation near you, we encourage you to find another Christian church that teaches the gospel of grace.

We also offer personal counsel. If you have questions about the Bible, salvation or Christian living, we are happy to talk. If you want to discuss faith, baptism or other matters, a pastor near you can discuss these on the phone or set up an appointment for a longer discussion. We are convinced that Jesus offers what people need most, and we are happy to share the good news of what he has done for all humanity. We like to help people find new life in Christ, and to grow in that life. Come and see why we believe it's the best news there could be!

Our work is funded by members of the church who donate part of their income to support the gospel. Jesus told his disciples to share the good news, and that is what we strive to do in our literature, in our worship services, and in our day-to-day lives.

If this book has helped you and you want to pay some expenses, all donations are gratefully welcomed, and in several nations, are tax-deductible. If you can't afford to give anything, don't worry about it. It is our gift to you. To donate online, go to www.gci.org/online-giving.

Thank you for letting us share what we value most – Jesus Christ. The good news is too good to keep it to ourselves.

See our website for hundreds of articles, locations of our churches, addresses in various nations, audio and video messages, and much more.

www.gci.org
Grace Communion International
3120 Whitehall Park Dr.
Charlotte, NC 28273
800-423-4444

You're Included...

We interview Trinitarian theologians about the good news that God loves you, wants you, and includes you in Jesus Christ. Most programs are about 28 minutes long. We have interviewed more than 35 theologians. They have included:

Ray Anderson, Fuller Theological Seminary
Douglas A. Campbell, Duke Divinity School
Cathy Deddo, Trinity Study Center
Gordon Fee, Regent College
Jeannine Graham, George Fox University
George Hunsinger, Princeton Theological Seminary
C. Baxter Kruger, Perichoresis
Paul Louis Metzger, Multnomah University
Paul Molnar, St. John's University
Cherith Fee Nordling, Northern Seminary
Andrew Root, Luther Seminary
Alan Torrance, University of St. Andrews
Robert T. Walker, Edinburgh University
N.T. Wright, University of St. Andrews
William P. Young, author of *The Shack*

Programs are available free for viewing and downloading at https://www.gcs.edu/course/view.php?id=58.

GRACE COMMUNION
SEMINARY

GRACE COMMUNION SEMINARY

Ministry based on the life and love of the Father, Son, and Spirit

Grace Communion Seminary serves the needs of people engaged in Christian service who want to grow deeper in relationship with our Triune God and to be able to more effectively serve in the church. We offer three degrees: Master of Pastoral Studies, Master of Theological Studies, and Master of Divinity.

Why study at Grace Communion Seminary?

- Worship: to love God with all your mind.
- Service: to help others apply truth to life.
- Practical: a balanced range of useful topics for ministry.
- Trinitarian theology: a survey of theology with the merits of a Trinitarian perspective. We begin with the question, "Who is God?" Then, "Who are we in relationship to God?" In this context, "How then do we serve?"
- Part-time study: designed to help people who are already serving in local congregations. There is no need to leave your current ministry. Full-time students are also welcome.
- Flexibility: your choice of master's level courses or pursuit of a degree.
- Affordable, accredited study: Everything can be done online.

For more information, go to www.gcs.edu.

Grace Communion Seminary is accredited by the Distance Education Accrediting Commission, www.deac.org. The Accrediting Commission is listed by the U.S. Department of Education as a nationally recognized accrediting agency.

Made in the USA
Columbia, SC
14 March 2021

34471180R00143